POWER AND IDEOLOGY IN AMERICAN SPORT

A CRITICAL PERSPECTIVE

George H. Sage, EdD
University of Northern Colorado

Human Kinetics Books
Champaign, Illinois

For Tyler and Garrett—
a new generation from which
I draw hope and inspiration

Library of Congress Cataloging-in-Publication Data

Sage, George Harvey.
  Power and ideology in American sport : a critical perspective /
George H. Sage.
    p.   cm.
  Includes bibliographical references.
  ISBN 0-87322-286-5
  1. Sports--Social aspects--United States.   I. Title.
  GV706.5.S228 1990
  306.4'83--dc20   89-48740
                                                                              CIP

ISBN: 0-87322-286-5

Photo on page 1 by John Zich, courtesy of *Daily Illini* (Champaign, IL); photo
on page 13 by Hal Brown; photo on page 31 by Robert King; photo on page 63
courtesy of UPI and Bettmann Archive; photo on page 87 courtesy of Coors Brewing Company; photo on page 115 by Kimberlie Henris; photo on page 137 courtesy
of Dallas Mavericks; photo on page 167 by Scott Vesecky, courtesy of *Daily Illini*
(Champaign, IL); photo on page 189 courtesy of American Coaching Effectiveness
Program; photo on page 207 by Brett Amole, courtesy of *Tribune* (Greeley, CO).

Developmental Editor: Christine Drews
Copyeditor: Molly Bentsen
Assistant Editors: Valerie Hall,
    Julia Anderson, and Robert King
Proofreader: Pam Johnson
Production Director: Ernie Noa

Typesetter: Sandra Meier
Text Design: Keith Blomberg
Text Layout: Tara Welsch
Cover Design: Hunter Graphics
Illustrations: Jerry Thompson
Printer: Braun-Brumfield

Printed in the United States of America

10 9 8 7 6 5 4 3 2 1

Human Kinetics Books
A Division of Human Kinetics Publishers, Inc.
Box 5076, Champaign, IL 61825-5076
1-800-747-4HKP

Contents

Preface

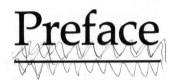

Sport is one of the most popular cultural practices in American society. Indeed, involvement in sport, as either a participant or a spectator, is considered almost a public duty. Furthermore, sport is woven into the patterns of all the major social institutions—politics, economics, education, mass media. James Reston (1971), columnist for *The New York Times*, has claimed that sport in America plays a role in our lives that is probably more important than even the social scientists believe.

Reston may be right, but social scientists do believe that sport is an important and pervasive social practice that deserves serious study. The 1970s and 1980s have produced a substantial body of scholarly literature on the social aspects of sport, and several journals regularly publish theoretical and empirical research about the subject. Two professional societies serve as outlets for scholars to share their work—the North American Society for the Sociology of Sport (NASSS) and the International Committee for the Sociology of Sport (ICSS).

I intend this book to be an introduction to the sociology of sport, presented in a particular theoretical framework. I have also chosen to pursue a critical theme (thus the subtitle *A Critical Perspective*). I discuss in chapter 1 what this means along with the role of critique and criticism. I see critical analysis as the first step in improving existing conditions in sport. When social reality is defined by one group and alternative interpretations are suppressed, distortion may be the result. It is the role of the critic to flesh out inconsistencies and inaccuracies promulgated by a one-sided view of social reality, exposing them for what they are, communicating alternative perspectives, and hoping that truth will prevail and the human condition will be improved.

To gain an accurate understanding of sport, I believe it must be situated historically and culturally within the larger social entity. The traditional tendency to separate sport from the rest of society, treating it and its participants as isolated from the rest of the social world and as existing in a value-free and ideologically pristine environment is erroneous—it presumes that there are no links between sport and our other social institutions and cultural practices. Such a view disguises the real connections between sport and society and opens the door to serious social dangers, for sport can be used to conceal material and cultural exploitation and oppression.

I want with this book to provoke you into thinking more critically and carefully about both American society and American sport. You will need an open mind and a willingness to consider views that may challenge your ideas about both to achieve this end. I hope that you will become more aware of the problems, issues, and controversies facing the world of contemporary sport—especially highly organized and commercialized sport—and that you will arrive at some conclusions and potential collective solutions. My vision for what American sport can be entails egalitarian cooperation, solidarity of people with one another, respect for individual and group differences, and guarantees of individual rights. It involves an ongoing process of change in social and cultural consciousness that may generate a revolution in social relations among people in sport. Perhaps together we can effect that change.

Acknowledgments

A book like this represents the work of not one but a community of scholars. What is valuable here I have learned from others.

Many colleagues throughout the world have contributed to this book. I give thanks to all of them for the ideas and insights I have gained in hearing them speak at conventions of NASSS and reading their work. It is impossible for me to acknowledge my indebtedness to them individually. I have attempted through citations and references to indicate the sources of original information and ideas, and I hope I have met the demands of that task. I want to extend special thanks to Janet C. Harris and Michael A. Messner, whose reviews and critiques of an earlier draft of this work were invaluable in my final revision.

To my students, I owe a special debt of gratitude for their continuing challenges to my lectures and comments in class discussions. I wish especially to thank Sandy Cottle, who made pertinent suggestions on several chapters, and Becky Crumpton, whose work on the citations and references was invaluable.

Finally, I express my heartfelt gratitude to my wife, Liz, for her steadfast encouragement and support. Without that the lonely and arduous task of writing this book would have been impossible.

CHAPTER 1

A Sociological Perspective of Sport

Sports are not simply . . . surface rituals for us. . . . Sport has entered the fabric and structure of our whole way of life. Sport is a constant, a model, a value system. It is our strength and our weakness, our redeemer and destroyer. . . . Intellectually and

philosophically, emotionally and psychologically,
sexually and physically, sport governs our lives.
Neil D. Isaacs, professor of English

Myriad evidence attests to the fact that Americans love sport. Today the average person is inundated by it. In the 1970s and 1980s sport emerged as an active domain of study and research in the social sciences. This has been due, in part, to the enormous increase in youth, high school, and intercollegiate athletics, enlarged physical recreation programs, and the massive growth of professional sports; it has also resulted from the expanded mass media coverage of sport events, especially on television. Sport has also aroused increasing interest as a social phenomenon as its meanings and practices have changed in the transformation from casual, informal play forms to commodity-governed spectacles shaped by marketplace rationality.

A number of good books describe the current conditions and demographics of sport involvement, but few place sport and physical recreation in the context of history and the general power structure of modern society. Most make no attempt to pursue relationships between sport and the political economy and ideological power and domination. (There are numerous variations of the definition of *ideology*, but the concept generally implies a system of interdependent ideas that explain and justify particular political, economic, moral, and social conditions and interests. If something is *ideological*, then, it relates to or is concerned with this system of ideas.)

A Different Approach

My approach to studying sport assumes that a full sociological analysis of sport must be rooted in an understanding of its societal moorings; thus, I take a specific theoretical orientation toward social institutions, cultural practices, and sport in American society. This orientation centers on what is called *hegemony* ('hej-ə-,mō-nē or hi-'jem-ə-nē), which refers to dominance and influence. This approach provides insights into the historical construction of societal dominance and the roles of political, economic, and cultural patterns in capitalist societies. Although hegemony embodies varying interpretations and unresolved issues, it nonetheless forces us to think more critically about the operative and underlying roots of modern society, a perspective not generally fostered by mainstream analysts of American culture.

I will use selected aspects of the theory of hegemony to sensitize you to how the dominant power interests of our government, economic system, mass media, and education influence sport and the role of sport in maintaining the cultural status quo. I will emphasize relationships between power, domination, and ideology and social class, gender, and race as they relate to sport. I expect in the process to challenge the views you hold, perhaps even rather unknowingly, about sport vis-à-vis American society and culture.

I want to hasten to make two points: Please don't fear this book as one of those tomes devoted to the dreary weighing of pros and cons about ideas promulgated by social theorists long since dead. My description of social theory is brief and targeted to readers with little background in the subject. (Professional scholars of sport studies and others whose interest is piqued can turn to other books for more in-depth theoretical analyses.)

Critical Analysis

The subtitle of this book proclaims that it is a critical perspective. Anthony Giddens (1987) has argued that "sociology cannot be a neutral intellectual endeavor, indifferent to the practical consequences of its analyses for those whose conduct forms its object of study" (p. vii), it must attempt to enhance social justice and improve conditions for the general welfare. I feel the same about a social analysis of sport. So this volume is "critical" in two ways. First, it is critical of the ideas that form the conventional wisdom about sport in American society. In the realm of sport, as in many others, dominant groups use political, economic, and cultural resources to define societal norms and values and to sustain their influence. Their interests are legitimated by compatible ideologies disseminated by schools, mass media, and various agencies of social control, and the processes they use tend to suppress alternative versions. Second, this book is inherently critical through my use of the orientation of hegemony, which is directly linked to social criticism of modern capitalist society. One consequence of employing this perspective is that I unmask myths and distortions that have crept into the social discourse about sport.

Because there may be times when you think I am overly critical, I want to assure you that I am sensitive to and supportive of the many strengths of American society and its forms of sport. My critical assessment of contemporary sport should not be mistaken for an objection to sport per se or as criticism of those involved in sports. Indeed, I continue to experience the joy and excitement of sports. But the inspiration that sport gives us through our own accomplishments and through the achievements of outstanding athletes should not deter us from taking a critical stance when we think it is called for. Criticism is actually a form of commitment, a way of saying, There are problems here and unwarranted abuses; let's identify them and work to make things better for everyone.

The Framework of a Sociological Perspective

Sociology is dedicated to the study of human society, to observing and analyzing human social activities wherever and whenever they occur. Such study can take both global and personal forms; at one extreme you can find sociologists investigating international relations among governments and at the other sociologists studying divorce patterns of couples belonging to different churches. There is fertile ground for sociological analysis wherever you find social organizations and people interacting with each other. Moreover, there is no precise dividing line between sociology and the other social sciences (economics, political science, etc.); indeed, there is a great deal of interdependence among all of them.

Sociology, then, is first and foremost a study of social organization and behavior, based on social theory and empirical research as opposed to hunch, tradition, or blind faith. A sociological perspective requires taking a particular orientation toward human social organization and actions, which has been expressed in various metaphors. One suggests a "recalibration" of one's way of thinking about social life, another proposes using "a different lens for viewing," another advises that one must assume a "social consciousness," and finally there is the notion that one must take on what sociologist C. Wright Mills (1959) called a "sociological imagination." The assumption of all these is that a sociological perspective requires a unique framework, or special mind-set, for trying to understand society. Several of the most important foundations of this perspective are described in the remainder of this section.

The Social Construction of Reality

All ideas arise from human existence; it cannot be otherwise. There are no ideas that exist independent of human existence. It follows, then, that all meanings about human social life are *socially constructed*. Meanings are interpretations about situations, ideas, objects, or events with reference to how one should respond. Thus, meanings are rooted in the collective responses—in behaviors—that become mobilized around situations, ideas, objects, or events. People are the bearers of all meaning, either in the isolation of personal use or as the product of complex social processes of group interaction.

Social reality, then, is socially constructed; that is, humans actively contribute to the creation of meaning. As sociologist Max Weber (1938) said, human beings live in webs of meaning they themselves have spun. So we cannot approach the study of human society as we do the study of objects or events in the natural world. Natural laws can be defined precisely, and they hold true without variation throughout the world; they do not change with time or by human negotiation. But such is not the case for human social behavior. It varies from group to group (e.g., poor and wealthy), from country to country (e.g., language, customs, attitudes, and values), and across time (e.g., colonial and contemporary lifestyles). Societies exist only in so far as they are created and re-created in human actions. This being the case, definitions, explanations, and meanings of social reality are open to reinterpretation and change.

For an example of how meanings are socially constructed, we can take a slogan familiar to most: Winning isn't everything, it's the only thing. Is this a universal truth, a law of nature? Of course not. It is a socially constructed piece of lore around which some very specific meanings about the quest for victory in sport have been formed. But take another example: It's not whether you win or lose, but how you play the game. This, too, is a socially constructed description about sport competition that implies particular social attitudes and behaviors toward sport activities. These slogans convey two very different views about the meaning of winning in sport. At different times and in different places each has been the leading view of one group or another. And yet which is the "correct" view?

Meanings have limited importance in themselves; their real significance is that they shape how people behave. That is, they are real in their consequences. If someone walked by you holding a pole with a sheet of white cloth attached, you probably would not move, but if the cloth was colored with the stars and stripes, you would probably stand up. Why the different behavior? Because of the *meaning* of the American flag to Americans. The meanings in the two sport slogans I cited suggest a number of social attitudes, perceptions, and behaviors toward winning in sport. In the context of this discussion, the "correctness" of one or the other is moot. What the slogans demonstrate is that meanings (in this case, of winning in sport) are socially constructed, and certain norms, values, and behaviors will be mobilized around the meaning that an idea, object, or event has come to have.

Another sport example of the social construction of meaning is the word *excellence*. For the ancient Greeks—the civilization that gave us the original Olympic Games—sporting excellence meant to be an all-around athlete, good in a variety of events. The truly excellent athlete was the pentathlete. From the time organized sports became a part of popular culture in the United States in the latter 19th century until about 25 years ago, the athlete considered the epitome of excellence was the three-sport, all-around athlete. It is only in the past quarter of a century that specialization has become the basis for excellence. Only quite recently has the specialist, with a single-minded devotion to being good at one sport, been viewed as the athlete truly pursuing excellence. The changed meaning of the word *excellence* has resulted in an increased number of athletes specializing in one sport. Thus is demonstrated again the social construction of meaning in sport, how it can change over time, and how it can shape attitudes and behaviors.

The Influence of Social Structure

At the heart of the sociological perspective is the notion that *structural forces* beyond an individual's conscious control have a profound effect on human behavior. In other words, social structure shapes conduct, independent of the characteristics of individuals. For example, social class status is related to variations in occupation, educational achievement, criminal behavior, and the presence of mental disorders. This contrasts sharply with the dominant American opinion about the chief determinants of human actions; in this perspective, the individual is held accountable for all of his or her behaviors, which are considered to emanate from individual internal motivations.

This tradition of attributing human actions solely to the individual derives from several sources central to our culture. First, the rugged individualism of the colonial and frontier periods in American history has been glorified through folklore and legend. Second, capitalism, the economic foundation of American society, has as its basic constituents private initiative and private enterprise, both passionately individualistic. The influence of this perspective is so potent that it is difficult to displace in the American mind. Indeed, because of powerful societal forces nurturing and promoting this perspective, there tends to be little realization that there is an alternative vision—a sociological perspective—of human social action.

Sociologist C. Wright Mills (1959) provides a good description of the differences between the individual, or psychological, and sociological perspectives. According to Mills, problems that at first glance seem to require solutions at the personal level are actually the consequence of broader political, economic, or social forces. Divorce, for instance, is a very personal matter. Yet the fact that divorce rates vary with social class, ethnic and religious affiliation, level of industrial development, and other demographic variables suggests that divorce, despite its personal nature, is greatly affected by social structure. Mills supplies us with another example in unemployment.

When in a city of 100,000 only one man is unemployed, that is his personal trouble, and for its relief we properly look to the character of the man, his skills, and his immediate opportunities. But when in a nation of 100 million employees, 12 million are unemployed, that is a public issue, and we may not hope to find its solution within

the range of opportunities open to any one individual. The very structure of opportunities has collapsed. Both the correct statement of the
problem and the range of possible solutions require us to consider
the economic and political institutions of the society, and not merely
the personal situation and character of a scatter of individuals. (p. 9)

Certainly, the psychological perspective makes important contributions to our understanding of humans and their patterns of organization
and behavior. The sociological perspective moves the focus beyond the
individual, examining the ways the individual is shaped by the social
environment. Both perspectives contribute to a more wholistic understanding of humans.

The Sociological Imagination

A sociological perspective necessitates what Mills (1959) calls a "sociological imagination." Having a sociological imagination means standing
apart mentally from our place in society and seeing (imagining) the linkage between personal and social events—tracing the connections between
patterns and events in our own lives and those in our society. A sociological imagination involves three kinds of sensitivity: historical, comparative, and critical.

Historical Sensitivity.   Mills (1959) claims that "all sociology worthy of
the name is 'historical sociology' " (p. 146). In support of Mills, sociologist Irving Zeitlin (1973) has said that "the social scientist who studies
a social structure without studying its history will never truly understand
any given state of that structure or the forces operating to change it"
(p. 14). I could readily apply that statement to the present discussion:
The person who studies sport without studying its history will never truly
understand any given state of sport or the forces operating to change it.
Finally, E.G. Boring (1963), eminent historian of psychology, supplied
additional sanction to Mills's notion about the importance of developing
a historical sensitivity in forming a sociological imagination. According
to Boring, one studies history not to predict the future, but to understand
the present better. A historical perspective in the study of sport, then,
is a good defense against imagining that particular sport forms are either
unique to a specific period or common to all times.

Comparative Sensitivity.   Mills's call for comparative sensitivity refers to
the necessity for learning about and understanding other cultures and
societies. Only by doing so do we come to appreciate the diversity of
human societies and of the social constructions of the meanings of social
organization and behavior. It also allows us to break free of ethnocentrism,
or our tendency to believe that the modes of social organization and behavior in our society are somehow superior to those of all other cultures.

And there is no doubt that such an attitude is firmly entrenched in American society. We have a strong tendency to universalize our own cultural norms and practices. A comparative sensitivity in the study of sport can help us understand that the popularity and meanings of different sports vary across cultures; for example, the game we know as football is rarely played elsewhere, but soccer—what other countries call football—is immensely popular throughout the world.

Critical Sensitivity.   Mills notes that the sociological imagination combines with the task of sociology in contributing to the critique of societal forms. In other words, sociology necessarily has a critical quality; it cannot be a disinterested and remote scholarly pursuit. Indeed, an underlying assumption of the sociological perspective is that things are *not* as they seem. Peter Berger (1963), a prominent sociologist, wrote that "the sociological perspective involves a process of 'seeing through' the facades of social structures" (p. 31). The sociological imagination looks beyond commonly accepted descriptions of social structures and social processes to demystify and demythologize. Thus, a critical examination of conventional wisdom and inconsistencies in society is central to the sociological perspective.

The Legacy of Karl Marx

Study in sociology, even the sociology of sport, invariably brings references to Karl Marx and "Marxism" because Marx is one of history's most noted social theorists. There are several dimensions to Marx's work: his own social theoretical writing, numerous interpreters and revisers of his ideas, and nation-states that purport to follow them. It is only that last dimension that most people are familiar with, and discourse about so-called "Marxist" states tends to be highly politicized. Many Americans have come to think of Marx and Marxism as synonymous with evil because of the link to communism and the socialist states, such as the Soviet Union, that are viewed as our opponents. But it is essential to distinguish between Marxism as a body of knowledge providing insights into society, politics, and economics and Marxism as ideology guiding contemporary socialist states.

Karl Marx died in 1883, long before the Russian Revolution in 1917. So he had nothing to do with the creation of the Soviet Union as a socialist country. Moreover, Marx would never have expected that Russia might experiment with his political-economic ideas, because it was the industrial, economically advanced countries that Marx wrote about, and Russia during Marx's lifetime was feudalistic and industrially underdeveloped. Finally, the most prominent figure—after Friedrich Engels—in the enlargement and elaboration of Marx's ideas was Lenin, and he greatly distorted much of Marx's work and ideas.

Marx cannot really be held responsible for contemporary socialism; much of what has gone on in socialist countries in his name would have horrified him. Marx was a critic of oppression, discrimination, and domination. He was the leading social scientist to place power and class relations at the center of an interpretation of the social structure of capitalist societies, but he was a critic of the corrupting quality of power and class society, not the corrupt quality of some human beings. Fundamentally, he supported the promotion of human liberty, dignity, and equality. Perhaps the most distinctive heritage of Marx's ideas is their ecumenical character of internationalism and the insistence that all people throughout the world are dependent on one another. His vision was a profoundly moral and ethical one, and perhaps this is one reason for its enduring strength.

The best-known socialist countries—the Soviet Union, East Germany, Cuba—are not necessarily the best representatives of Marxism. Indeed, many Marxists are as critical of these socialist countries as they are of capitalist countries because they are antithetical to the socialist ideals of a democratic, classless economy and society. Workers there have not been "freed from their chains." In fact, wage labor has not been abolished, strikes and industrial conflict still exist, gender and racial domination have not been eliminated, and little advancement to the free and full development of all individuals has occurred.

There are many forms of Marxism; indeed, the two largest countries where Marxism is the state ideology, the Soviet Union and the People's Republic of China, are in direct opposition. In America, Marxist ideas have never posed a revolutionary threat to the established order, though they have taken root as the major theoretical critique of capitalist society.

In his recent book *Sociology: A Brief But Critical Introduction*, Anthony Giddens (1987) wrote, "To declare sympathy with certain of Marx's conceptions does not imply accepting his views, or those of his self-professed followers, in their entirety. . . . But neither do I reject Marx. Marx's writings are of continuing significance to sociology. . . . At the same time, there are conspicuous weaknesses in Marx's work" (pp. 24-25). A similar point was made by C. Wright Mills (1962): "No one who does not come to grips with Marxism can be an adequate social scientist; no one who believes that Marxism contains the last word can be one either" (p. 34). These insights inform and guide my references to Karl Marx and his social theories.

My Sociological Perspective

Value judgments necessarily permeate almost all aspects of the social sciences, and I make no claim to neutrality here. In his now-classic work on what he called the sociological imagination, Mills (1959) made a point that I want to affirm: "I am hopeful of course that all my biases will show. . . . Let those who do not care for [my biases] use their rejections of them to make their own as explicit and as acknowledged as I am going to try to make mine!" (p. 21). One of the strengths of a social science perspective lies in its rich diversity and in the vigor of the debate between different analysts trying to make sense of the social world.

Benefits of a Sociological Analysis of Sport

Americans are not encouraged to critically examine the prevalent attitudes, values, myths, and folklore about sports. This is unfortunate in any social arena, because those who do not examine cultural practices cannot see the extent to which these activities are socially conditioned. They will have difficulties not just in separating facts from values but also in recognizing how their viewpoints are influenced by the surrounding political and economic context. One of the leading social scientists of the first half of this century said that as long as one unquestioningly holds one's own points of view as absolute while interpreting opponents as misguided, the most important step has not been taken; one must have the courage to subject all points of view, including one's own, to critical analysis (Mannheim, 1936).

Sport needs to be studied as part of a larger political, economic, and ideological configuration. Relevant issues involve how sport is related to social class, race, and gender and the control, production, and distribution of economic and cultural power. I strive here to probe beyond the sport establishment propaganda and examine sport and physical activity in American society as they really are practiced. At the same time, I recognize that we are all products of an ideological system that has socialized us into what might be called the American sport creed—which is essentially the Protestant ethic with a strong dose of industrial corporate ethics, all applied to sport.

For some readers my approach will appear to tear down sport. This is an understandable reaction, one that has been conditioned, to some extent, by what we have been told about sport and by our own sport experiences: "We've got to pull together to win"; "Be a team player." These sport slogans, and the hierarchical arrangements pervading sport organizations, condition people against independent thought. Moreover, a powerful cheerleader/boosterism mentality is promoted by all sport organizations. Their message to fans and players is to give uncritical support; if you don't, you're not being loyal or you're not a team player, and that is un-American. That most of us fail to consider alternatives to contemporary sport practices is testimony to the effectiveness of our socialization.

Is criticism of contemporary sport un-American? I would reply by substituting "sport" for "country" in the following quote from John Fulbright, a distinguished senator from Arkansas:

To criticize one's country is to do it a service and pay it a compliment. It is a service because it may spur the country to do better than it is doing, it is a compliment because it evidences a belief that a country can do better than it is doing. Criticism, in short, is an act of patriotism, a higher form of patriotism, I believe, than the familiar rituals of national adulation. (Holt, 1984, p. 33)

Former slave, social reformer, and foremost black American of the 19th century, Frederick Douglass, was fond of saying that if there is no struggle, there is no progress. "Those who profess to favor freedom, and yet depreciate agitation, are persons who want crops without plowing up the ground, they want rain without thunder and lightning. They want the ocean without the awful roar of its many waters" (Foner, 1950, p. 437). Sometimes those who employ critical analysis are confronted with the question, You're good at criticizing, but what is your plan for reform? The clear implication is that unless the critic has a strategy for social change, merely identifying existing injustices, corruption, and exploitation is worthless. But critical analysis implies a concern for identifying, scrutinizing, and clarifying, and in this way helping overcome the obstacles to a complete understanding of the object of study. The purpose is to understand what is, and not present a detailed plan for what ought to be (Parenti, 1988).

Obstacles to a Sociological Analysis of Sport

Social analysis of sport is confronted by several obstacles. First, throughout American society there tends to be a blissful ignorance about the social relations that control sport and other forms of physical activity, a frightening naiveté about the social context and material conditions underlying physical culture. Although sport practices embody specific and identifiable purposes, values, and meanings, they are typically viewed by both participants and spectators as ahistorical and apolitical in nature. This is true largely because most of our written and broadcast information does not confront people with questions about the larger social issues and political and economic consequences of modern sport and physical activity. Instead, we are fed a diet of traditional slogans, clichés, and ritualized trivia about sport. These may all be very comforting but they do not come to grips with reality.

Another obstacle to a serious analysis of American sport is that people typically receive little encouragement to become aware of the sociocultural forces and institutions that shape the world of sport. Moreover, sport leaders tend to view themselves as impartial facilitators operating in a value-free and ideologically neutral setting. Few have thought through their own basic premises, but instead proceed on unexamined assertions, mottoes, and slogans. The assumed unproblematic nature of current sport forms is reflected in a recent statement extolling a school "sport education" program, whose purpose was said to be to socialize students "to participate and behave toward sport that serves to preserve, protect, and enhance the sport culture" (Siedentop, 1987, p. 79). Contemporary sport culture is not presented as even potentially problematic; instead, it is something to be blindly learned and followed.

A final obstacle to an analysis of American sport is that sport and society have traditionally been seen as discrete social institutions, with sport being a realm where character is built and virtue pursued. Americans tend to cherish an illusion that coaches and athletes are paragons of nobility. The sports world itself has encouraged the belief that sports are "fun and games" and has vigorously fought any attempt to change this image. This separating of sport from anything serious in American life has been one of the most persistent barriers to meaningful study of the relationship of sport to society. Sport cannot be examined as isolated from the social, economic, political, and cultural context in which it is situated. Sport is a set of social practices and relations that are structured by the culture in which they exist, and any adequate account of sport must be rooted in an understanding of its location within society. The essence of sport is to be found within the nature of its relationship to the broader stream of societal forces of which it is a part.

Summary and Preview

Sport and physical recreation are extremely popular in American life, and there is a growing interest among social scientists in the organization and behavior of people involved in sport and in sport's larger social meanings. Connections between sport and political, economic, and cultural systems are of particular interest. One of my major purposes in this book is to apply a sociological perspective to sport so as to better understand its important sociocultural role. In this chapter, I have discussed the characteristics of a sociological perspective and described some of the ramifications for studying sport with a "sociological imagination."

In chapter 2 I explain the theoretical orientation of this book by identifying two social images that have been constructed for examining questions about who governs and what role those who govern play in the social and cultural life of society. I then draw various links between these social images and their relationship to sport.

CHAPTER 2

Social Images and Sport

We cannot *approach society . . . as we do objects or events in the natural world, because societies only exist in so far as they are created and re-created in our own actions as human beings.*

Anthony Giddens, sociologist

Many people begin the sociological study of sport with little knowledge about social theories, the explanations formulated by social scientists about how societies work. They also typically understand little about the nature of social institutions, corporate organizations, and cultural practices and their compelling role in the making of social and cultural life. Finally, there is often no awareness of the links between social theory, social life, and cultural practices like sport and other physical activities. I will begin to articulate these relationships by describing two social theories—which I call *images*—and examining them in light of American culture and social institutions.

Two Images of American Society

Most social theories, or explanations of how societies work, constitute verbal images of society rather than thoroughly elaborated sets of theoretical statements organized into logically coherent formats. Consequently, much of what is called social theory is really a general perspective or orientation for analyzing various features of the social world (Turner, 1982). This is how the theories, or images, discussed in this chapter should be understood. No attempt is made in this book to fully articulate the subtleties and complexities of any social theory; instead, only the basic outlines of two social images are described in an effort to acquaint readers to different ways of perceiving the social realities of American society.

The average person has usually internalized a particular view of American social life as though it were the single legitimate image of social reality, not realizing that there are several conceptualizations of modern society that are portrayed through various social images. This chapter introduces two prominent but contrasting social models, with an emphasis on their applications to American society and their relationships to sport.

We can begin with two general questions about society:

- Who governs?
- What role do those who govern play in social and cultural life?

By *govern* I mean more than just who is elected to political office; instead, who are the major controlling influences over the attitudes, values, beliefs, norms, and worldviews of American society? The question, Who governs? seeks to understand "whose interests and whose agenda are served by who governs, who benefits, and who does not" (Parenti, 1988, p. 198). Power, control, and influence in our society are not restricted to government, although much of each does reside there; instead, they are distributed in a variety of organizations and social groupings that make up civil society. The term *civil society* encompasses the " 'so-called private organizations' like political parties, trade unions, schools, churches, voluntary and cultural associations, and the family, as opposed to the public character of the state" (Simon, 1977, p. 83).

I frame my approach to the questions regarding who governs our society in the context of social images that have been formulated for characterizing democratic, capitalist societies, for the United States is one of those. The importance of trying to understand the locus of power and control (identifying who governs) is that those who have these resources can set the social agenda for a society. Those with power and control mold societal attitudes, values, and beliefs and influence all our cultural practices, including sport.

The two social-political images of society that I describe are the *pluralistic image* and the *hegemonic image*. Let us examine how each addresses our two questions: Who governs? and What role do those who govern play in society and culture?

The Pluralistic Image

The orthodox view fostered by major American social institutions (e.g., business, schools, mass media, the government) and cultural groups is called *pluralism*. A pluralistic image contends that a broad and diverse set of social institutions, organizations, and interest groups embodies the beliefs, values, and worldviews of society's citizens. This model asserts that power is exerted by a multitude of interests whose countervailing centers of power check each other to prevent abusive power and agenda-setting by any one group. Thus, according to pluralism, although groups are not necessarily equal in terms of power, no particular groups are able to dominate the decision-making process.

According to this view, the major business, government, and cultural organizations are unable to achieve a collective unity because of the unorganized mass of people who exercise some power over interest groups; no one private or public sector is capable of acting with unity and power on the range of issues. With respect to the corporate business community, Maitland (1983) said, "In view of the extreme heterogeneity of the business community, it may be questioned whether business has any collective interests at all" (p. 3). Berg and Zald (1978) agreed: "Business [owners] are decreasingly a coherent and self-sufficient autonomous elite; increasingly, business leaders are differentiated by their heterogeneous interests and find it difficult to weld themselves into a solidified group" (p. 137).

Social and cultural influence within society are seen as broadly distributed among a variety of groups and organizations. Through public policy, cultural tendencies are seen to be set by a rough equilibrium of group influences, and there is therefore a reasonable approximation of society's preferences—a sort of equality of cultural production. According to this view of society, although most citizens may not participate directly in social-cultural decision making, norm setting, and value creation, they can make their influence felt through participation in organized groups; there is, then, an underlying ideology of equality.

It may be seen, then, that the pluralistic model of American society as an amalgam of the general population's ideals, values, and worldviews includes implicit assumptions about power and its distribution. The most obvious of these is that commercial, government, and civil organizations are personifications of everyone's collective attitudes, interests, and values and that no group or class is favored significantly over others. All citizens have roughly the same interests in society, and all have basically equal shares of power; thus, social order is based upon a consensus of their cultural values. A pluralistic image represents society as though there are few serious economic or cultural problems, minimal pressing conflicts of interests between social classes and various groups.

That the interests of the people form the policies of business and government is a pervasive theme broadcast by many American public forums. They suggest that civil and governmental goals correspond with and are indistinguishable from those of society itself. Moreover, in this role they are seen to harmonize and accommodate conflicting interests and values, thereby preserving the consensus and social accord.

The Hegemonic Image

A second and very different vision of the nature of capitalist societies—and the one for which I argue—is the hegemonic (ˌhej-ə-'män-ik) image. Hegemony literally means dominance, but more broadly it describes a sociopolitical situation in which one way of thought and life is dominant and is diffused throughout various social institutions and cultural practices. But hegemony is not static; it also refers to the *processes* of social relations that tend to exist in modern capitalist (e.g., American) society (Gramsci, 1971; Williams, 1960).

The writings of Italian social theorist Antonio Gramsci (1971), completed while he was in a fascist prison (where he was put by Mussolini) between 1926 and his death in 1937, have popularized the word *hegemony,* and when it is used it is almost always associated with him. But the concept is not unique to Gramsci, and it has been used by a number of social scientists both before him and after his death (Hoffman, 1984). Although the strains of hegemonic social thought vary considerably, the theme of dominance is common throughout. I do not attempt to be fully faithful to Gramsci's hegemony theory—even his own use of the term varied

(Anderson, 1976/7), and one of Gramsci's interpreters calls his concept of hegemony "elusive" and "disjointed" (Femia, 1975, p. 29)—but I embrace the concept and its interpretations as a focal and organizing concept, a vision of social reality that is quite different than pluralism.

A hegemonic image of society provides a compelling reinterpretation and expansion of Karl Marx's theories and a powerful framework for analyzing social organization and social processes within contemporary societies. It complements Marx's emphasis on the economic institution but goes beyond Marx to analyze the ways that political, cultural, and ideological institutions and practices are integrated with the economy to form the whole. Gramsci's work (1971) unravels the complex web of political, economic, cultural, and ideological practices that cement a society into a relative unity. Nevertheless he, as well as others writing in this tradition, makes the underlying assumption that capitalist societies are first and foremost *class societies*. He saw the character of capitalist societies in terms of class relations and disharmony between classes, so the pertinent social institutions, organizations, and processes are exactly those through which the various classes are constituted and through which they are associated with each other. Gramsci noted that "though hegemony is ethico-political, it must also be economic, must necessarily be based on the decisive function exercised by the leading group in the decisive nucleus of economic activity" (p. 161).

Societal Power

For Gramsci, the process of hegemony is one in which a dominant class, which controls the critically important economic and political institutions of a society, also has principal access to the fundamental ideological institutions—education, mass media, religion, cultural practices. The dominant class uses its access to promote and reproduce the norms and values that tend to reinforce its structural advantage.

In the hegemonic image of society, sociocultural values and beliefs are viewed as embodying the values, ideals, and interests of an elite, or dominant, class more than any sort of pluralistic, generalized interests. To be specific, the hegemonic image sees political-economic domination and intellectual and moral leadership carried out not by a single, unified "ruling class," but by a complex coalition of dominant-group factions through which the common sense and everyday practices of subordinate groups are managed by the elaboration and penetration of ideology. It is a systematic engineering of mass consent to the established order. It refers to a complex set of processes by which an alliance of powerful and wealthy groups—who own most of the capital, land, and technology, and employ most of the country's labor force—extends its influence to manipulate and fashion its conceptualizations and its ways of life, and its versions of culture and civilization in a direction that, while perhaps not yielding immediate profit for narrow dominant class interests, persuades the masses to embrace a consensus that supports the status quo.

In describing power relations, Gramsci identified two ways in which the dominant class exercises power and preserves social control: force and consent. Gramsci (1971) said that the dominant social group "dominates antagonistic groups, which it tends to 'liquidate,' or to subjugate perhaps even by armed force; it leads kindred and allied groups" (p. 57). Concerning antagonists, the powerful groups utilize their control over the resources of government, the legal system, the police, the military, and other services to establish their view of the world as legitimate, all-inclusive, and universal. Concerning kindred and allied groups, they exercise control through a moral and intellectual leadership whereby their interpretations and meanings become widely understood and shared and beliefs and actions become accompanied by a common definition of the situation. Bates (1975) refers to this as a "leadership based on the consent of the led, a consent which is secured by the diffusion and popularization of the world view of the [dominant class]" (p. 352).

To a large extent, hegemony is a silent domination, not overtly experienced because there is an orchestration of consent and a forcing (or coercion) of subordinate groups into harmony with the established order. Hard-and-fast lines cannot be drawn between the mechanisms of consent and the mechanisms of coercion, but in any society they are interwoven. According to Gramsci, consent is normally in the lead, but operating behind "the armour of coercion" (1971, p. 263).

Means of Domination

The specific actions pursued by dominant groups to maintain their power and status vary according to the precipitating conditions and the historical moment. They may range from various forms of persuasion, negotiation, concession, and compromise to manipulation and repressive action. Regardless of the tactics, the preferable means of domination is to domesticate opposition, absorbing it into patterns of thought that are congruent with the ideological inclinations of the dominant group. Thus, domination is contoured primarily based on an "active consent" of subordinate groups, but a consent that has been engineered through intellectual, political, and moral leadership and that ultimately rests on the monopolistic, repressive apparatus of the state (i.e., government, the military, the legal system). Hargreaves (1982) explains the point another way:

> Most of the time dominant groups manage to incorporate potential opposition by negotiation, concessions, threats and pressure before opposition can reach serious proportions, which would bring their legitimacy into question, and at times, particularly when consent breaks down and opposition results in a crisis situation, the balance

between the use of force and persuasion may shift in favor of the former. But exclusive reliance upon force in the long run will render hegemony unstable. (pp. 114-115)

The point to be emphasized is that hegemony is not simply forcing beliefs and thought patterns of the dominant class into the heads of subordinates. Instead, an important way in which it is produced and disseminated is through "popular beliefs" that Gramsci (1971) described as "themselves material forces" (p. 165), because they help to organize human actions and are a way in which social consciousness itself is molded. How popular beliefs become part of the dominant group milieu is a complex process, involving the school system, mass media, religion, patriotic rituals and ceremonies, and a political system that creates a facade of popular consensus. But the specific medium through which various ideas and assumptions become dominant material forces in society is ideology (Femia, 1975).

Ideological Domination

Gramsci stressed what he called *rule by consent* or *ideological domination.* He argued that

hegemony works through ideology but it does not consist of false ideas, perceptions, definitions. It works *primarily* by inserting the subordinate class into the key institutions and structures which support the power and social authority of the dominant order. It is, above all, in these structures and relations that a subordinate class *lives its subordination.* (1971, p. 164)

In other words, working-class people, whose labor is crucial in industries that enable a society to function smoothly, tend to internalize and endorse dominant visions and definitions. In this way, a hegemonic class can penetrate all levels of the society with its version of social reality.

Ideology, according to the hegemonic model, persuades the general public to consider their society and its norms and values to be natural, good, and just, concealing the inherent system of domination. Kellner (1978) elaborated:

Hegemonic ideology assumes an attempt to legitimate the existing society, its institutions and ways of life. Ideology becomes hegemonic when it is widely accepted as describing "the way things are," inducing people to consent to their society and its way of life. . . . In this way hegemonic ideology is translated into everyday consciousness and serves as a means of "indirect rule" that is a powerful force for social cohesion and stability. (pp. 49-50)

In the hegemonic view the fundamental consequence of ideology is to consolidate the present social conditions with rationalizations stemming from the status quo, thus protecting and shielding particularized interests—mainly those of the dominant class—and the existing society against alternatives (Wilson, 1987). Struggles against the dominant ideology are made to seem disruptive and counterproductive to the social order. Labor union activities and environmental protests are two contemporary examples of unwanted disruptions. So hegemonic ideology is a smokescreen behind which the relevant structures and forces of domination exist, and it provides the cement in a social formation that tends to promote and preserve the ideological unity of the entire society.

Hegemonic ideology of dominant beliefs, values, and social practices is produced and disseminated through social institutions, including the family, schools, mass media, the workplace, and mass cultural practices. The services of intellectuals and other cultural workers (e.g., scientists, teachers, writers, artists), whom Gramsci called the "functionaries" of hegemony, are especially valuable for fostering cohesion and promulgating ideologies that describe and prescribe conformist acceptance of existing social arrangements because they have the know-how and creativity to organize and run cultural organizations like the schools and the mass media.

Maintaining Hegemony

It is a continual and formidable task for dominant groups to initiate and sustain their hegemony. Williams (1977) points out that hegemony "does not just passively exist as a form of dominance. It has continually to be renewed, recreated, defended, and modified. It is also continually resisted, limited, altered, challenged by pressures not at all its own" (p. 112). The task of sustaining power and dominance is always specific to its immediate context; consequently, patterns of hegemony vary among societies according to their history, structure, and current circumstances.

Hegemony, then, is never guaranteed to a dominant group; indeed, the group must work hard for it by anticipating challenges to its vision and by assessing accurately what combination of coercion and persuasion to use (Hargreaves, 1982). Thus, it is an ongoing process of accommodation and compromise. Because there is never a single, unified ruling class, but instead there are coalitions of powerful groups pursuing an enduring foundation for legitimate authority, the characteristic hegemonic ideology is not simple. Indeed, Gitlin (1987) argued that

> ideological domination . . . requires an *alliance* between powerful economic and political groups on the one hand, and cultural elites on the other. . . . It is best understood as a collaborative process rather

than an imposed, definitively structured order; in general, hegemony is a condition of the social system as a whole rather than a cunning project of the ruling group. (p. 241)

The study of social power and dominance is not restricted to social class; scholars of feminist theory and racial ideology have begun to incorporate hegemonic themes into their work. They examine gender and racial domination as relatively autonomous yet related systems of power, inequality, and domination. They see a close link between economic inequality and other forms of social inequality between different racial groups and between men and women. Their perspectives are particularly useful in the study of sport and are illustrated in various places in this book—especially chapter 3.

Dominant Groups

In any discussion of hegemony, the question arises, Who are the dominant groups? From the hegemonic perspective, there is no single dominant group, but an alliance of factions of the most powerful, wealthy, and influential persons and groups in business, commerce, government, education, and mass media (and in some societies religion). In every society it is these dominant groups that have the most opportunities for intervening in and manipulating cultural values, beliefs, and practices in their own interests. A class is hegemonic when it has managed to articulate its version of social reality to a majority of the population of a given social formation, thus allowing it to become the class expressing the "national interest."

Consider the following facts in reflecting on whether such a concentration of power, wealth, and influence could be said to represent dominant group interests—and thus the national interest in the United States.

† The *richest 20%* of America's families and individuals possess 76% of the country's personal wealth. At the other extreme, the *poorest 40%* hold *less than 3%* of private wealth; in other words, the bottom half of American families have only about a nickel of every dollar's worth of all our personal and family wealth (see Figure 2.1).

† Of that top 20%, the super-rich—the top 1/2%—now own 35% of the nation's wealth, a greater share than at any time since the 1920s. Meanwhile, the *bottom 90%* of the population owns just 28% of the wealth, a drop of 20% in as many years.

† Of all families who own financial assets like savings and government bonds, 2% hold over half of such assets; the top 10% hold 86%.

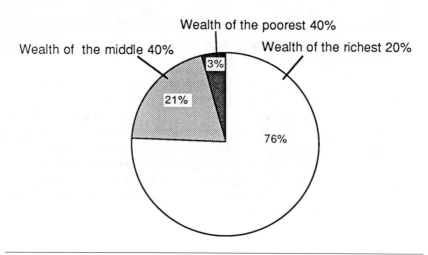

Figure 2.1   A small percentage of America's population controls a large percentage of the country's personal wealth.

† About half of all top corporate and governmental leaders are alumni of just 12 well-known private universities, most notably Ivy League colleges.

† The top echelons of American corporate life are occupied primarily by people of upper-middle and upper-class social origin, most of whom attended Ivy League colleges and universities.

† Of the 500 largest industrial corporations, 150 are controlled by one or more members of a single family.

† It is estimated that about 6,000 Americans—*less than .003%!*— exercise formal authority over institutions that control roughly half of the nation's resources in industry, finance, utilities, insurance, mass media, foundations, education, law, and civic and cultural affairs.

† Most politicians in America are lawyers. Many past and present top politicians (such as the Roosevelts, Rockefellers, Kennedys, and Bushes) have inherited great wealth.

† There are about 200,000 industrial corporations in the United States with total assets of about $2 trillion. The *100* largest corporations control *60%* of all industrial assets. And this concentration of resources among a tiny proportion has increased from 40% in 1954.

† The concentration of assets is even greater in the financial world; of 14,763 banks serving our nation, the 50 largest control *64%* of all banking assets. Three (Bank America, Citicorp, and Chase Manhattan) control 18% of all banking assets.

† In the insurance field, *50* companies out of 2,048 control *over 80%* of all insurance assets.

† The people who control the flow of information in America are among the most powerful. American television is dominated by three private corporations—the American Broadcasting Company (ABC), the Columbia Broadcasting System (CBS), and the National Broadcasting Company (NBC). Two of these, ABC and NBC, are only subsidiaries of even larger corporations. ABC is owned by Capital Cities Communications and NBC by General Electric.

† Newspaper ownership is concentrated as well; of the nation's 1,748 daily newspapers, *9* newspaper chains account for *33%* of total newspaper circulation.

† About 32% of some 7,000 top corporate positions are interlocked with other top positions, resulting in linkages between corporations where some individuals serve on the boards of directors of two or more companies.

† Governmental power is even more concentrated than corporate power. All governmental expenditures account for *one third* of the gross national product of the United States.

† Very few top corporate or governmental leaders are female or black. In the 1989 special issue of *Business Week* entitled "The Corporate Elite: Chief Executives of the *Business Week* Top 1000" no blacks and only four women were included.

These facts about our society of course are not themselves sufficient evidence that the rich and powerful exercise dominance directly or uniformly. But as Domhoff (1983) has explained, although wealth and income are not equated with power, "the possession of great wealth or income is one visible sign that a class has power in relation to other classes" (p. 11). In other words, wealth can be translated into economic and political power. Thus, while no social grouping does hegemonic work only, nor is any devoid of hegemonic functions, dominant interests within politics and business as well as in the cultural industry as a whole (writers, artists, the mass media, the educational system) certainly have the resources of material wealth, status, and power to specialize in producing, relaying, and sustaining hegemonic ideology. However, their primary hegemonic influence is exercised through the organizations they control and the social networks to which they belong (Allen, 1987).

A Conspiracy of Power?

The actual degree of coordination and implementation of ideology by dominant interests in America is hotly debated by social analysts.

Pluralists typically argue against any significant accord among powerful private and public organizations (Berg & Zald, 1978; Maitland, 1983). But their argument is belied by considerable evidence that capitalists and the top managerial class have sufficiently mutual class interests to evolve a collective class strategy (Domhoff, 1978, 1983; Dye, 1986; Mintz & Schwartz, 1985; Neustadtl & Clawson, 1988) and, furthermore, that there is a symbiosis between top governmental officials and the capitalist class (witness the 1980s Pentagon weapons procurement scandal). So the hegemonic analytical framework sees much more unity within the dominant group community than does the pluralistic one, as shared material interests and a set of formal and informal organizations engineer consent, and, if necessary, coerce behavior in the interests of the dominant class as a whole and in the system of power and privilege.

Which Image Is Accurate?

What we have, then, are two views of how American society is governed and what the role of those who govern is in our society—the pluralistic image and the hegemonic image. The first assumes the existence of equality of opportunity, that everyone plays a somewhat equal role in affecting society. The pluralistic perspective maintains that where power and influence do exist, they are the collective result of all citizens' attitudes, interests, and values. This view is propagated by the major social institutions and cultural agencies on the forefront of image impression and manufacturing consent in America. They advance this view of social reality because it is in their interests; after all, they are the major beneficiaries of the present system. As long as people can be convinced that they live in an egalitarian system, they will not see the inequalities; as long as they do not see inequality, they will support the status quo.

The hegemonic image identifies the existence of dominant groups—those who control power, wealth, and influence, who set the social agenda. In this view, dominant groups in American society do not govern by force, intimidation, or violence; they do it more subtly, by controlling the major social institutions and agencies. There is an orchestration of social life by an alliance of factions; they promote pluralism while practicing hegemony.

The question of whether the pluralistic or hegemonic image more accurately represents American society cannot be settled with ease or with certainty. Both models are subject to differing interpretations. They should be seen as sensitizing perspectives, each providing a different interpretation of social reality, each having plausible elements.

The most important result of exploring the pluralistic and hegemonic images is realizing that there *is* more than one view of the social reality in the United States and other modern, capitalist societies. And likewise there is more than one way of understanding the relationship of sport and leisure activities to the larger society—which returns us to the specific thesis of this book.

By and large, the pluralistic view is the "official" model of social reality conveyed by the dominant groups through private and public organizations and social groups that they control, or at least exert a great deal of influence over. The image of pluralism so thoroughly permeates the major organizations that shape American attitudes and beliefs that it is considered to be "common sense" and is taken for granted by the average person—which is not surprising, because alternative visions of social reality are marginalized or discredited as un-American. Pluralistic ideology leads us to believe that federal and state lawmakers watch out for the interests of *all* their constituents in an equitable way. It also causes us to believe that the mass media present unbiased accounts of events and actions. The hegemonic image would have us believe otherwise. I feel there is sufficient empirical evidence to demonstrate that the hegemonic model is more consonant with American historical experience and corresponds more closely to the realities of contemporary American life than the pluralistic one.

Applying the Images to Sport

Having learned how the pluralistic and hegemonic images view society at large, we are now in a position to turn to an examination of how they relate to sport and physical recreation. Their perspectives of how society is structured and controlled have necessary implications for the structure and control of sport as a cultural practice.

Pluralism and Sport

In the pluralistic model, sports and physical recreational activities are seen primarily as innocent, voluntary social practices that let people release tension and enjoy themselves. Accompanying these assumptions is the notion that sport's main organizational structures, systems of rules, and collective meanings are shared by most of society. Baseball, for example, is said to be "the national pastime."

For the pluralist, sport is a realm of social life set off from the "realities" of economic and political life—a benign sphere free from material and historical constraints. Although sport and society are seen as discrete, separate social domains, sport is often touted as an arena where "appropriate" sociocultural attitudes, values, and beliefs are nurtured and an activity where society's collective interests are promoted and sustained. Beyond that, sport and physical activities are viewed as apolitical. Therefore, government involvement in sport is expected to be minimal, limited to formulating the ways and means by which sport activities can support laws pertaining to public order and morality, support public sport and leisure facilities, and generate taxable revenues. By and large, though, political intervention into sport is seen as an intrusion. Thus, many amateur and professional sport leaders publicly condemn the expansion of government involvement into sport and the "politicization" of sport that seems to have accompanied this expansion (Gruneau, 1982a).

Hegemony and Sport

Applying the insights of hegemony to sport and leisure activities produces a number of implications. One of the most foundational is that, in order to grasp the significance of these social practices, we must see them as a part of a larger political-economic and ideological configuration. From the view of hegemony, any notion that sport is an autonomous province of cultural practice segregated from the social processes of society at large is naive and misguided. In fact, sport in all of its forms is seen as fully integrated into the power structure and social relations of society, relations substantially maintained by the dominant ideology.

Sport is considered to be an important site upon which dominant ideology is constructed and maintained because sport's institutional and ideological features have evolved in a way that corresponds with, and helps to reproduce, the conditions upon which dominant interests are based (Gruneau, 1982a). In other words, the changing practices and ideas surrounding sport continually create a setting where the interests of the dominant groups can best be served. In fact, one of the most compelling functions of sport is to promote initiatives and activities that help shape the structure of the economic, political, and cultural hegemony of the dominant class. Sport's importance, then, is rooted in its power to promote and structure relations in accordance with the proclivities of the dominant interests who own and control it.

As a type of cultural practice and as a direct reflection of the power-holders' interests, sport is viewed as promoting and supporting the social inequality endemic to capitalism. This is seen in class, gender, and race social relations and the control, production, and distribution of economic, political, and cultural power in sport. In class relations, for example, sport reproduces the class structure by socializing participants and spectators into the dominant culture, which legitimates the capitalist system of allocating rewards and reconciling the working class to a subordinate societal role. In this role, wrote Whitson (1986), youth sport "prepares young men [and increasingly young women] to take for granted the norms of the capitalist workplace; and central among these is that every aspect of the process is necessarily geared to the 'natural' goal of increasing productivity" within the sport arena (p. 101). Young athletes, then, may be viewed as engaged in a form of "anticipatory productive labour" (Ingham & Hardy, 1984); that is, they are already working in a workplace and are being taught how to fit into capitalist workplaces. A slogan such as "sport builds character" must be seen in light of its ideological message, which is that sport experiences encourage character traits that perpetuate the status quo.

The pervasive commodification in contemporary society is increasingly turning sport and leisure activities into commercial pursuits. (A commodity is something whose value is defined in monetary terms; commodity production is one in which goods and services are produced to be sold. *Commodification* means the buying and selling of goods and services, including labor power [such as hiring people for wages and salaries], to make a profit; something that has been *commodified* has become subject to this process.) Braverman (1974) contends that corporate organizations have transformed all types of spontaneously initiated and often creative leisure activities, including sport, into productive, capitalistic enterprises. So aggressive is the capitalist system, says Braverman, that any informal, anonymous, unorganized sport form is rapidly incorporated into the market as far as possible.

The running boom provides a good example. It began with the desire of individuals who had been excluded from high-performance, elitist sport to enjoy a simple form of exercise on their own terms. Within a few years a massive commercial "running industry," with multinational firms merchandising running shoes and other accessories, had grown up. Moreover, running for fun became overshadowed by marathon races, triathlons, and "ironman" competitions, many sponsored by large corporations and whose winners were paid for their labor (Whitson, 1984). Thus, individual leisure and group fun runs became incorporated into dominant sport structures and meanings.

Aerobic exercise is on the same trajectory. What began as a movement to improve the cardiovascular condition of people who were overweight, underexercised, and high coronary risks and who initially worked out in simple shorts and T-shirts has spawned industries in aerobic centers, aerobic shoes, and aerobic clothing. It is now even possible to compete for a national aerobic championship (Rogoznica, 1988)!

The characteristics of spectator sports make it easy for them to penetrate everyday life and to represent and reproduce the dominant ideology. Their popularity among subordinate groups may be seen as one manifestation of their incorporation into the reigning ideological system. From this perspective, sport serves as one means of winning the hearts and minds of subordinate classes and of instilling their respect and conformity to society's powerholders. Meanwhile it actually inhibits the development of a critical social consciousness. This does not mean, however, that there is only passive compliance to hegemonic domination; resistance to, evasion of, and challenges to the oppressive measures of hegemony are constantly taking place.

Analysts of hegemony contend that modern sport reflects and promotes capitalist ideology through its emphasis on success based on skill, its glorification of commercialism, and its presentation of a false view of social progress through the continued assault on the record books. Gruneau (1982a) has made a point that deserves to be quoted at length:

> One cannot help but be struck by the degree to which so much of the organization and culture of modern sport seems to have been influenced by capitalist productive forces and relations. For example, "amateur" sports at their highest levels have almost become monuments to such new sciences as biomechanics, exercise physiology, and sport psychology where a market rationality is expressed in a mechanical quest for efficiency in human performance that is indentured to state and commercial sponsorship. Professional sports, meanwhile, have gone a great distance toward reducing the meaning of athletic contests to a simple dramatization of commodity relations. (p. 24)

To illustrate, elite amateur athletes now train year-round in special Olympic training centers where resident sport scientists use the latest technology to enhance performance for the sole purpose of producing medal winners. In addition, professional athletes are bought (drafted) and traded in much the same way as Wall Street tycoons buy, sell, and trade securities.

Rojek (1985) argues that leisure relations are increasingly shaped by emphasis on impersonality, standardization, and observance of routine and claims that they are increasingly private (e.g., TV viewing), individual, and commercial. Leisure relations have become part of the modern rationalization process.

A significant component in sustaining dominant interests involves control by the state, and sport serves as a vehicle for advancing the dominant groups' values and meanings, particularly through ritual and ceremony. The state depends on both for transmitting the symbolic codes of the dominant culture and its own worldview. Hargreaves (1986) observes that sporting events are a focal point for formal ritual and ceremony centering around state symbols. He notes that sport rituals and ceremonies

> articulate on the structure of hegemony in particular when they are staged around the great national festive sporting occasions and/or occasions when the prestige of the nation is symbolically at stake. . . . On such occasions the national symbols and the pageantry are vividly brought into play by weaving them into the sportive occasion. . . .

Members of the political elite and other national leading figures are usually in prominent attendance and/or participate in the ceremonial. Emblems such as flags, colours, uniforms, opening and closing ceremonies, parades, national anthem, hymns, martial music, victory accolades and presentation ceremonies, all form a constituent part of a political ritual whose ideological work celebrates, above all, national unity and the legitimacy of the existing social order. . . . The subtle interpenetration of political culture and sports culture can be seen in the way sports discourse forms an integral part of political discourse. (p. 199)

One of the institutional mechanisms by which citizens are politically socialized is through the use of sport as a means of social control, in that those who are the gatekeepers of sport events (coaches, athletic directors, broadcasters, etc.) restrict the exposition of ideological perspectives to those supportive of the prevailing political-economic system.

The whole domain of popular culture is a critical area for constructing forms of consent and conformity. The system of popular culture, including organized sport and physical recreation of all kinds, has a prominent place alongside other social practices like language, formal and informal education, the media, art, the theater, and habits and customs for helping to fashion hegemony and through which it is affirmed and negotiated (Gitlin, 1982). The system of social domination functions through symbols and rituals embedded in various aspects of sport culture—literature, customs, media sport presentations, and "official" sport mythology—that closely reflect the culture of the dominant social classes. Dominant classes and groups use sport effectively to reproduce their views and interests through its rituals and ceremonies and through the opportunities it provides large masses of people to be part of the "action."

Sport practice—indeed, all leisure activity—is seen as helping to continually reinforce the hegemonic structure of power and privilege in capitalist society. Spectator sports in particular, because they are commercialized, play a significant role in high school and colleges, are mediated by the press and broadcasting, and are subject to government intervention, provide many opportunities for dominant groups to associate themselves with them in various ways and to intervene in and use them to advance their own interests (Hargreaves, 1982).

By learning to see sport through a perspective of hegemony, one can be more aware of its societal role for producing and reproducing the present power and dominance relationships. One will also likely become more skeptical of suggestions about the "naturalness" of contemporary practices and events, and more willing to seriously consider alternatives for the promotion of personal development and social justice through sport.

Summary and Preview

The reality of American society is not perceived by everyone in the same way. As a consequence, there are various social images about how our society works—how power, control, and influence are distributed in the major social institutions and cultural practices—and who the major beneficiaries of this system are. Whoever has power, control, and influence can set the social agenda; the powerful are the dominant forces over societal attitudes, values, beliefs, norms, and worldviews.

I have identified and described two social images—the pluralist and the hegemonic—in terms of two foundational questions: Who governs? and What role do those who govern play in the social and cultural life of society? I believe that the hegemonic image more accurately reflects the realities of contemporary American society.

One of the most pervasive characteristics of human social organization is that people with certain characteristics come to be treated unequally. Sociologists call this structured inequality *social stratification*; it exists when entire categories of people have unequal access to various societal rewards. Despite popular beliefs that in America there is equality of opportunity and we are all treated equally, the fact is that widespread social inequality exists. Much of this inequality is based on social class, sex, and race. In chapter 3 I describe these three prominent forms of social stratification and their links to sport.

CHAPTER 3

Class, Gender, and Racial Stratification and Sport

Difficulty in establishing one's authority can have serious limiting consequences for a coach trying to do a job. Consider the [female] . . . coach [of a men's

*basketball team] who related that when she stood
in the coaches box an official said, "Lady, sit down
and shut up." When she approached the official at
half time, he indicated he wasn't aware of who she
was. . . . Who else would have been standing in the
coaches box and why couldn't the official figure that
out?*

Staurowsky, sport sociologist

Having a sociological perspective requires coming to grips with the concept of *social stratification*, the process by which certain categories of a population come to possess more or less of the valued rewards—such as money, power, and prestige—that a society has to distribute among them. Social stratification may be thought of as a human layering or ranking, with people in different layers having different proportions of the rewards and resources of society. It is also an institutionalization of social power arrangements—of domination and subordination—because those who possess the disproportionate share of social rewards and resources have the power to control and shape the lives of those who lack them. Social stratification is said to be institutionalized because its patterns are sustained and reproduced by the main institutions of society—the family, the economy, and the religious, educational, and political systems.

Stratification is inherently a constant source of injustice and oppression, and often even conflict and violence, in the lives of those subject to it. As VanFossen (1979) has pointed out,

Without our awareness, inequality affects health and wealth, training and occupation, experience and happiness. It influences whom we marry, where we live and how well, with whom we eat and relax, what kind of illnesses we will get and how often, and what we read and think. (p. 2)

A fundamental feature of all modern societies—and most pre-modern societies as well—is that they are stratified along a variety of categorical lines. Because stratification is so pervasive throughout the world, it is one of the most profound topics in the social sciences. Documenting, interpreting, and explaining structured inequality has been a central focus for sociologists since sociology became a separate field of study. Because the consequences of social stratification cut across all of the topics in this book, I will lay the foundations of American stratification and its major forms in this chapter. In the chapters that follow, stratification and its concomitant social inequality will be a continuing background theme.

The three most prominent and pervasive interrelated categories of stratification in American society are class, gender, and race. In each, and collectively, inequalities exist that shape the patterns of social life of many people, severely limiting the extent of social justice, social health, and opportunities for self-development that they experience. American society can only be understood in light of the class, gender, and racial stratification systems that underlie its social institutional and cultural life; furthermore, these systems are central and fundamental for understanding sport in American society. Integrating and analyzing the complex intersections and cross-currents of these stratification systems is a formidable task, and I hope that I make some contribution to it here.

Class Stratification

There is no universally accepted definition of the concept of class in the social sciences, and indeed one of the continuing debates among sociologists is waged over its definition; a hybrid of several viewpoints will serve our purposes here. A social class can be defined as a group of people whose members are characterized by relative similarities—of wealth, income, prestige, power, lifestyle, education, and culture. Members of a social class tend to be conscious of their class position and to focus their social interaction within their class.

Just as there is no single definition of class, there is no universal set of class designations. Class as an economic concept was first articulated by Karl Marx, who analyzed the structure of industrial capitalist societies in terms of two great classes: the capitalists (those who own the means of production) and the proletariat (the workers, who do not own the means of production). Marx considered such social factors as prestige, lifestyle, and social interaction patterns as being derived solely from economic class conditions. Subsequent social theorists have broadened the concept of class to apply to categories of people who share resources of economic, prestige, and political power. With this definition, social class divisions have come to be labeled upper, middle, and lower, with subcategories within each (upper-middle, lower-middle, etc.).

The terminology I use relative to American class stratification is based on the concept of a capitalist class, a middle class, and a working class. The capitalist class is elite in terms of wealth, ownership, privilege, and power; it holds extensive control over the economic system because it owns most of the nation's capital. *Capital* refers to goods or other forms of wealth that are not needed for immediate consumption but can be used to produce further capital or other goods or services. Although numerically it is very small, the capitalist class wields great influence because it has the wherewithal to control important societal resources;

consequently, it can routinely shape the beliefs and thought patterns that legitimate and perpetuate the existing social class system (Allen, 1987; Domhoff, 1983). The capitalist class is the dominant group that was described in chapter 2.

At the other end of the spectrum is the working class, the many people who own no productive property, who do not supervise others, and who do not help plan the work or private lives of others. The proportion of the population classified as working class varies between 55% and 70%, depending on the criteria used for class assignment (Ehrenreich & Ehrenreich, 1979; Szymanski, 1983; Vanneman & Cannon, 1987).

The middle class, as its name suggests, is a bridge between the other two classes. Members of this class comprise the approximately 90% of income earners who do not own sufficient means of production to otherwise support themselves; they share this characteristic with the working class. On the other hand, the middle class does share some of the power that capital exercises over workers through ownership of small productive property, exercising supervisory authority over workers, or designing and planning the work of others. In recognizing this power, the middle class typically aligns itself with the capitalist elite, and constitutes ''a genuine class with interests *in opposition to the working class*'' (Vanneman & Cannon, 1987, p. 55). Ehrenreich and Ehrenreich (1979) elaborated on this point:

> The relationship between the [middle class] and the working class is objectively antagonistic. The functions and interests of the two classes are not merely different; they are mutually contradictory. True, both groups are forced to sell their labor power to the capitalist class; both are necessary to the productive process under capitalism; and they share an antagonistic relation to the capitalist class. . . . But these commonalities should not distract us from the fact that the professional-managerial workers exist, as a mass grouping in monopoly capitalist society, only by virtue of the expropriation of the skills and culture once indigenous to the working class. (p. 17)

The middle class dominates labor but is itself subordinate to capital; this simultaneous dominance and subordination is what puts it in the middle (Vanneman & Cannon, 1987).

Wherever stratification occurs, institutional barriers are created by those in power to insure that unequal access to resources and rewards is maintained. For example, not only do members of the elite class have more property, income, and wealth than lower-class groups, this inequality is reproduced from one generation to the next through such means as inheritance and education. Class stratification is also perpetuated through a widespread legitimation of inequality asserting that it is basically appropriate and reasonable, based on justifications that come to be believed even by those who are oppressed. One such justification is that persons who possess wealth and power deserve their privileged status because they have a wide range of positive characteristics and talents, whereas those lower on the totem pole must be there because they possess inferior traits. The consequence is, as Fave (1980) has wryly observed, that "an ideology which justifies stratification comes to be commonly accepted by all strata—even the poor, in apparent contradiction to their self-interest" (p. 966).

Capitalism and Stratification

American society is driven by a particular form of economic enterprise—capitalism—that is inextricably related to our other social institutions as well as our cultural practices. Some people avoid using the word *capitalism* or referring to the United States's economy as capitalistic. For example, many business leaders, politicians, and journalists and even some social scientists use euphemisms such as *free enterprise* or *free market system* in place of *capitalism*. But *capitalism* is the more precise term to use when referring to the American economic system.

There seem to be two basic reasons why other terms are used in place of *capitalism* in private and public discourse. The first appears to be an effort to take public focus off of criticisms of the American capitalist system by worker-oriented scholars and organizations who have emphasized the fundamental inequalities endemic to capitalism. A second reason relates to the debate over capitalism versus communism that is a chronic part of private and public discussions. Using either term seems inevitably to contour the discussion along contentious lines (e.g., the United States, a capitalist country, versus the Soviet Union, a communist country), even when the focus of the discussion may have originally been a general economic issue rather than any such comparisons. To sidestep this problem, many writers and speakers simply avoid the word capitalism.

In its basic meaning, capitalism is nothing more than an economic system based on the accumulation and investment of capital by private individuals, who then become the owners of the means of production and distributors of goods and services—an accurate characterization of the American economy. No purpose is served, then, by not using *capitalism* to refer to the American economic system and similar economies in other countries. Moreover, capitalism is merely one means of producing and distributing goods and services—there is nothing inherently American about it.

Capitalist organization presupposes a system stratified into social classes based on the relations between capital and wage labor, especially power relations whereby those who own and control the means of production—capitalists—hold power over those who produce the goods and services—workers. Furthermore, in its control of the means of production, the capitalist class has much greater resources and power than workers without productive ownership. Thus, although capitalists (and their agents, such as managers and supervisors) and the working class depend on one another, the dependence is fundamentally unbalanced. This imbalance means that the capitalist view of the world becomes the dominant view.

Because the United States has a capitalist economy, it is intrinsically a class society, and class relationships directly link the economic organization of capitalism to the social relations and institutions making up the rest of the society. Indeed, social class is one of the most pervasive variables determining social behavior; daily experiences, lifestyle, and life chances (probabilities of suffering societal disadvantages or benefiting from societal opportunities) are structured to a great extent by individual class position and the class position of one's parents. Patterns of social interaction, including family life, friendships, neighborhoods, patterns of sport involvement, political attitudes, and even religious involvement are heavily influenced by class position (Szymanski, 1983). Capitalism, then, is not only an economic system, it is a complete social system. It functions not only to produce cars and television sets that make a profit for industry owners, "it also produces a whole communication universe, a symbolic field, a culture, a control over various social institutions" (Barsamian, 1989, p. 101).

For many Americans the notion that we live in a system of social classes is quite foreign, even terribly disturbing. The source of this attitude is rooted in the everyday socialization most of us experienced. Americans are typically told, and come to firmly believe, ideas about equality and opportunity derived from our most important national documents, including the Declaration of Independence and the U.S. Constitution: America is the land of opportunity. All men [sic] are created equal. We all enjoy equality of opportunity. These slogans, and others like them, are embedded in the hegemonic ideology to such an extent that, as Paul Fussell (1983) said in his book *Class*,

> Although most Americans sense that they live within an extremely complicated system of social classes and suspect that much of what is thought and done here is prompted by considerations of [class], the subject has remained murky. And always touchy. You can outrage people today simply by mentioning social class. (p. 1)

In *Inequality in an Age of Decline*, sociologist Paul Blumberg (1980) calls class "America's forbidden thought."

Reasons for this seeming lack of class consciousness by Americans have been the subject of much speculation and research. After their massive study of the perception of class in the U.S., Vanneman and Cannon (1987) convincingly argued that it is not that Americans, especially working-class Americans, actually lack a class consciousness, but that during the past 150 years every display of militancy or struggle by workers has consistently been crushed by the power of the capitalist class and the enormous resources it commands. As they note, "in the face of this overwhelming power, the U.S. working class has had a . . . difficult time constructing political and class organizations to defend its interests" (p. 167). Workers believe that class exists, but have been unable to unite with sufficient power to improve their existence.

The awesome power of capital has also been accompanied by a systematic and consistent ideological discourse designed to convince Americans that considerations of class are irrelevant. Corporate advertising continually suggests that owners, managers, and workers are all part of one big team with no social distinctions; witness the Ford Motor Company commercials showing assembly-line workers, engineers, and managers seemingly working together and its slogan: "Quality is job 1." The effectiveness of this combination of power and persuasion in stifling class consciousness in the general population is seen in the absence of a viable political party that stands for working-class interests, the absence of any major newspapers and magazines representing working-class interests, a general hostility toward union organization, and a relatively small, disunited union movement (in 1989 only 17% of employed Americans were union members).

In spite of popular slogans and a societal mythology touting the absence of class in America, even a cursory analysis convincingly shows that American society is a class society. To make any headway toward understanding our society—its social institutions, organizations, and the behaviors of its people—it is essential to come to terms with this fact about American life. A social analysis of any aspect of American culture that marginalizes the importance of social class differences is simply incomplete and unsatisfactory.

Class Stratification and Sport

In sport, class stratification is particularly manifested in terms of patronage, access, control, and social mobility. The socioeconomic elite have always been prominent figures in sport. Styles in sport, like in fashion, have generally trickled down from the upper to the lower classes. Indeed, patronage of the upper class was responsible for the creation and promotion of a number of American sports. For example, America's national pastime, baseball, when its rules were first codified around the mid-19th century, was played primarily in "gentlemen's clubs" made up of men of wealth or professional status. According to historian Harold Seymour

(1960), the first of these baseball clubs, the Knickerbockers of New York, was

> primarily a social club with a distinctly exclusive flavor—somewhat similar to what country clubs represented in the 1920s and 1930s, before they became popular with the middle class in general. . . . To the Knickerbockers a ball game was a vehicle for genteel amateur recreation and polite social intercourse rather than a hard-fought contest for victory. (p. 15)

American football got its early start and achieved its initial popularity in the elite private colleges of the Northeast. Students of these colleges were overwhelmingly from wealthy families. There are exceptions to this pattern of patronage, of course, but most modern sports have a social-class link with the upper classes of the past.

Economic Access to Sport.   Class barriers to equal access in sport are evident in the time and material resources needed to engage in many sports and in various formal and informal restrictions to participation. Persons in the upper class tend to play sports more often because they have the leisure time and the money to engage in such "nonproductive" activities. Thorstein Veblen (1899), a social theorist influential at the turn of this century, advanced the idea that those in what he referred to as the "leisure class" engaged in sport as a means of conspicuously displaying their wealth and status; in other words, social elites could flaunt themselves by lavishing time and money on sport.

At the other extreme, historically, working-class people devoted so much time to their labor that little time or energy was left for leisure activities. And lack of money limited their sport involvement as well. This situation has improved somewhat over time—today's working class has more "non-work" time and more discretionary money than workers in any previous generations—but these developments for the employed working class have certainly not eliminated the inequities in access to sport. Although sport may no longer be an exclusive privilege of the affluent, it is far from being a democratized, universal activity. Involvement in various sports is not distributed evenly among the social classes. Moreover, in 1988 over 34 million Americans (about 14% of the population) were living below the poverty line ("Many Who Work," 1988). For both the poor and the homeless—a growing segment of the population—lack of resources and the unavailability of teams, equipment, or facilities make access to organized sport almost nonexistent. Class stratification in sport is acute for these groups.

Barriers to Sport Participation.   Wealthy and powerful groups have traditionally restricted access to "their" sports. A common mechanism of control has been sport and country clubs with steep fees and rules requiring that new members be approved by election, thus creating both economic and social barriers to access. Historian Donald Mrozek (1983) noted that this pattern was set in place over 100 years ago:

> The first American country club, Brookline, opened in 1882 as a center for Boston's elite in polo, [horse] racing, and the hunt. Soon it added golf links, making available to its aristocratic membership yet another sport whose expense barred it from the common citizen. (p. 109)

Restricted access and class inequalities are inevitable in many professional and elite amateur sports because of the enormous amounts of money needed for quality coaching and competitive experiences. It is almost impossible to become a professional athlete in golf or tennis without years of private instruction and access to country clubs and national tournaments. Working-class families simply cannot provide the financial support for their children to excel in such sports. Elite national and international level gymnasts, swimmers, figure skaters, and skiers (to name a few sports) must have years of private instruction—in fact, many athletes move far from home to get the best coaching—in order to acquire the skills and experience necessary to achieve elite standing. Here again, low social class status excludes many.

Contemporary sport is highly commercialized and, like all commercial enterprises, it depends on consumers to purchase its product. In the case of sport, consumers are called spectators, who fall into two categories: those who attend a contest and those who see or hear it broadcast. Seeing games live can be expensive, given the cost of tickets and related expenses; consequently, there is a strong relationship between sport attendance and social class, with those with higher incomes being much more likely to attend (Yergin, 1986). Network television is ostensibly free, but advertising costs are passed on to consumers in higher prices for products that comprise a greater proportion of expenditures of lower-class than upper-class people.

Not all sports require connections with wealth and power. Certain sports—like boxing, wrestling, and stock car racing—have working-class cultural origins and have maintained their links with the lower social class. Basketball, though it originated in an American college and received its early promotion in higher education, has become a "city game." The inner city has become a training ground, especially for poor black youth, for the upper reaches of basketball competition—colleges and the NBA. So some opportunities and resources do exist for working-class achievement at the highest levels in a few popular sports.

Control of sport is unequally distributed among the social classes, and it is, in fact, almost totally vested in the wealthy and powerful social

Owners of professional sport teams are among the wealthiest ꞁn the United States. (The topic of class stratification in profes-˲˛˰˛˲˲ ˴ports is examined in detail in chapter 7.)

Amateur athletics was controlled and dominated by the Amateur Athletic Union (AAU) from the latter 19th century until the 1960s, when the U.S. Olympic Committee and its sport federations began to seize the control of amateur sports from the AAU. Both organizations have been and continue to be overwhelmingly associated with American wealth and power. The system of amateur athletics was another means of discouraging working-class participation in sport, for amateurism (participation without financial remuneration and for social, emotional, or personal satisfaction) is a product of the 19th-century aristocratic class that established rules and social arrangements that were exclusionary and based on social class; in effect it created sport segregation, with white, upper-class males firmly in control. Although contemporary sport appears to be more democratized than in previous generations, several studies have demonstrated a continued relationship between high socioeconomic status and authority and control of amateur sport organizations.

Despite some apparent improvements, there has been no significant reduction of control over sport organizations and policies on the part of the upper echelon; class inequities remain large. Furthermore, when the level of class stratification is narrowed to an analysis within sport itself, inequalities of control are glaring. Athletes, the equivalent of the working class in sport, have very little significant control over any aspects of the sport they play (discussed in detail in chapter 7).

Social Mobility Through Sport. An important issue in class stratification is the extent to which, and how, social mobility—movement from one social class to another—occurs. How does sport affect social mobility? The substantial body of literature on the topic is of two types. The first is largely polemical and impressionistic and claims that sport pulls many young people upward in social standing. One form of evidence consists of testimonials from former athletes that sport taught them skills that also brought success in the occupational world, resulting in achievements that would not otherwise have occurred. Other accounts describe former athletes from lower-class social backgrounds who are now successful and wealthy, the implication being that sport is responsible for their social mobility.

The second type of argument for sport's ability to bring upward mobility takes a more skeptical, empirical view, focusing on the extent to which sport career opportunities are actually available and a given person's likelihood of securing one of these positions (these questions are taken up in detail in chapter 7). The likelihood of a male high school athlete becoming a professional athlete is about 1 in 10,000; for a black male the odds rise to 1 in 3,500. The chance is even smaller for a female athlete because there are so few women's professional sports. Fewer than 3,600 jobs exist in professional sports, so the potential for sport to directly provide social mobility for significant numbers of people is largely imaginary.

Despite the limited extent of actual social mobility through sport, sport nonetheless serves to promote and sustain the hegemonic ideology about widespread social climbing in the larger American social structure. One of the most deep-seated beliefs among Americans is that this country is dedicated to the ideal of an egalitarian, socially mobile society in which everyone can reach the top. One of our basic cultural creeds is equality of opportunity, which is reinforced by rags-to-riches stories about Americans born into poverty who applied themselves to their work, saved their money, and rose through sheer initiative and effort to positions of social, economic, and occupational importance.

The dominant American ideology, functioning through slogans and symbols and notions about equality of opportunity and rags to riches, has been incorporated into the so-called work ethic orientation toward social mobility. The essence of this orientation is that individuals are responsible for their own fates and that each person who wants to get ahead can do so—all that is necessary is hard work. Accordingly, those who do work hard, so the message goes, become successful in material terms while those who do not try do not succeed, but they have only themselves to blame for their lack of dedication and hard work.

Sport is a powerful contributor to the ideology that legitimizes the social inequalities of class stratification in American society and promotes the notion of social mobility based on effort. Because sport is by nature meritocratic—that is, superior performance brings status and rewards—it provides convincing symbolic support for hegemonic ideology—that ambitious, dedicated, hard-working individuals, regardless of social origin, can achieve success and ascend in the social hierarchy, obtaining high status and material rewards, while those who don't move upward simply didn't work hard enough. Because the few rags-to-riches athletes are made so visible, the social mobility theme is maintained. This reflects the opportunity structure of society in general—the success of a few reproduces the belief in social mobility among the many.

Gender Stratification

Stratification that ranks males and females unequally and in which there is differential distribution between women and men of privileges, prestige, and power is called *gender stratification*. It is a system that combines biologically based sex roles with socially constructed gender roles. As Zinn and Eitzen (1987) have explained,

Sex roles refer to behaviors determined by an individual's biological sex, such as menstruation, pregnancy, lactation, erection, orgasm, and seminal ejaculation. Gender roles are social constructions; they contain self-concepts, psychological traits, as well as family, occupational, and political roles assigned dichotomously to each sex. (p. 176)

All humans are immersed in a complex network of sex and gender roles throughout life, and all societies have attitudes, values, beliefs, and expectations based on one's sex.

As expectations about sex and gender roles are communicated by various means, they produce and reproduce people who tend to conform to their socialized concepts of masculinity and femininity. In American society, traditional expectations for females have emphasized passive, nurturing, and dependent behaviors, whereas traditional expectations for males have accentuated individual achievement, aggressiveness, and independence. Women as mothers, nurses, and teachers and men as soldiers, physicians, and politicians are social manifestations of these gender images (Lipman-Blumen, 1984).

Our images of "appropriate" gender roles and behaviors have had far-reaching consequences for both males and females as well as society at large; the differentiation has valued the sexes in a way that has historically made females unequal in wealth, power, prestige, and presumed worth in relation to men. Furthermore, men have had more dominant positions in the control of both their personal lives and their social activities. This process of male hegemony that ranks and rewards males over females is known as *patriarchy*; it is "a set of personal, social, and economic relationships that enable men to have power over women and the services they provide" (Strober, 1984, p. 147). It is a structured and ideological system of power in which males possess superior power and privilege, and it is a social and economic arrangement whose material basis is men's control over the major social institutions and over women's labor power, fertility, and sexuality; as such, it is the core of women's oppression. Finally, a patriarchal society is driven by a male-centered ideology rooted in a male worldview; mainstream thought is male-stream thought, and biased as a result (Chafetz, 1984; Crompton & Mann, 1986).

All societies that have been studied by social scientists have some elements of patriarchy in their private and public forms of social organization, although the degree and nature of male superiority and dominance have varied considerably (Rogers, 1980). As Michelle Rosaldo (1974) noted, "Everywhere men have some *authority* over women [and] they have a culturally legitimated right to her subordination and compliance" (p. 21). Private patriarchy is found in male domination and female oppression in interpersonal relations of men and women—especially within the family—and public patriarchy exists in the male domination and exploitation of females in social institutions of the larger society, such as the economy, education, and politics.

Gender stratification is obvious in the labor market. With some exceptions, at the beginning of the 1990s, women fill the lower ranks while men occupy the prestigious and decision-making positions. Indeed, over one third of all employed women work in clerical jobs. Of the 400 to 500 job categories in the United States, men are distributed throughout most of the occupational hierarchy, whereas women are concentrated in about 30 categories. Women are greatly underrepresented at all levels of government, and most religious organizations reflect male supremacy in their hierarchical structures. Women hold only 10% of the seats on boards of directors in the country's top 1,000 companies. Women are 71% of the nation's classroom teachers, but fewer than 2% of the school superintendents; 96% of elementary school teachers are women yet only 32% of the elementary and secondary school administrators are women. Thus, children learn the differential status of men and women simply by attending school (Rix, 1987; Shakeshaft, 1986).

Women earn less than men for comparable jobs. In 1989 the average earnings for women working full-time, year-round were 68% of men's earnings. Women college graduates working full-time had earnings approximately equal to those of male high school dropouts. The consequence of these various occupational conditions is male control over the production and distribution of goods and services, assuring them control over economic wealth and power, whereas females' career and occupational outlets typically rank low in income, power, and prestige.

Gender relationships in the public sector are tied to gender roles in the private sector, especially in the family. As wives and mothers, women earn no money for their domestic labor of caring for the needs of their children, husbands, or homes. These roles also carry low societal power and prestige because domestic labor does not produce exchangeable commodities, which are the foundation of wealth, power, and prestige in capitalist societies. Furthermore, women in the work force still bear most of the responsibility for housework. The shift to paid employment has not meant a corresponding decline in the number of hours most married women spend in the household economy (Barrett, 1987; Bielby & Bielby, 1988). Hartmann (1981) has noted that patriarchy's material base is in men's control over women's labor; both in the household and in the labor market, the division of labor benefits men.

Patriarchy is a web of structured social practices that systematically fosters the development of men while constraining the development of women. It encompasses a general set of norms and values that reinforce the needs of status quo relations and attitudes toward women that explain and legitimize their relative subordinate position. In effect, it is an important means by which males control the social relations from which they benefit (Connell, 1987; Epstein, 1988).

Eisenstein (1979) argued that the combination in the United States of capitalism and patriarchy makes gender stratification pervasive to American society. In support of this position, Hall (1985) noted that

> gender relations, like class relations, are in essence power relations whereby men, as a social group, have more power over women than women have over men. These relations are characterized by male dominance and female subordination in both a sexual and economic sense. (p. 27)

Gender Stratification and Sport

Patriarchal ideology and resultant gender differentiations are produced and reproduced in family life, places of work, and various cultural practices. Organized sport is one of the most powerful cultural arenas for perpetuating the ideology and actuality of male superiority and dominance; it presents symbols and values that preserve patriarchy and women's subordinate position in society (Birrell, 1988; Hall, 1988; Theberge, 1985). Sport celebrates gender differences; recently one writer even argued that

> women should . . . be prohibited from sport: they are the true defenders of the humanist values that emanate from the household, the values of tenderness, nurture and compassion, and this most important role must not be confused by the military and political values inherent in sport. Likewise sport should not be muzzled by humanist values: it is the living arena for the great virtue of manliness. (Carroll, 1986, p. 98)

Bruce Kidd (1987) has articulately enumerated sport's role in advancing male hegemony:

> [Sports] perpetuate patriarchy by reinforcing the sexual division of labor. By giving males exciting opportunities, preaching that the qualities they learn from them are ''masculine,'' and preventing girls and women from learning in the same situations, sports confirm the prejudice that males are a breed apart. By encouraging us to spend our most creative and engrossing moments as children and our favorite forms of recreation as adults in the company of other males, they condition us to trust each other more than women. By publicly celebrating the dramatic achievements of the best males, while marginalizing females as cheerleaders and spectators, they validate the male claim to the important positions in society. . . . Sports con-

tribute to the underdevelopment of the female majority of the population and the undervaluing of those traditionally "feminine" skills of nurturing and emotional maintenance essential to human survival and growth. (p. 255)

Although patriarchy is an ancient phenomenon, its links with the rise of sport in the latter 19th century can be seen through two major social movements that coincided with the rise of organized sport: the American industrial revolution and the cult of masculinity. Conditions for industrialized labor were typically physically harsh and psychologically unpleasant, alienating workers from their work and creating a need in workers for recreational outlets. At the same time, lifestyles outside the workplace in industrialized society were transforming traditional means of male expression and identity through tasks that were less independent, assertive, and physically demanding, while women's increasing encroachment into the work force and public life was weakening the traditional basis of male dominance in the family and public sector. One consequence of these trends was a growing concern about male effeminacy. Sport was an activity that served two purposes for men: It met their recreational needs, and it was a perfect antidote for their anxieties about effeminacy. Sport's demands for strength, aggressiveness, and displays of courage were congruent with perceptions of masculinity and incongruent with those of femininity. Thus, sport became a popular means for men to reaffirm their masculinity and, hence, a powerful tool for maintaining patriarchal relations (Lenskyj, 1986; Messner, 1988).

The final piece in this social matrix was the Victorian values and attitudes embodied in the "cult of manliness" that had widespread social appeal in the latter 19th and early 20th centuries. As Mangan and Walvin (1987) said,

Male dominance owes much to the ideal of manliness . . . [that] became a widely pervasive and inescapable feature of middle class existence in Britain and America. . . . It captured that excessive commitment to physical activity which was an unquestionable feature of . . . male society in Britain and the United States in the second half of the nineteenth century. (pp. 2-3)

It was through sport activities that manliness as then defined was developed, reaffirmed, and reproduced (Armstrong, 1984; Kimmel, 1987; I will elaborate on this in chapter 5).

These social conditions made being both a woman and an athlete an anomaly in American life until the early 1970s. Women who participated in competitive sports faced social isolation and censure. By choosing the physically active life, a female was renouncing traditional female gender-role expectations. Female athletes did not suit society's ideal of femininity, and those who persisted in sport suffered various aversive sanctions, especially derogation and public ridicule.

Shaping Gender Roles.   One's gender-role ideology is shaped by a range of social forces—parents, peers, teachers, ministers, mass media, and others—but the earliest and most persistent influence comes from parents, who typically behave differently toward sons and daughters from birth throughout life. The traditional American parental message has been boys should be aggressive, independent, and achievement-oriented, whereas girls should be passive, sociable, nurturing, and dependent.

It is under parental aegis that boys are encouraged—even forced—into competitive sports. Parents overwhelmingly believe that sports are good training for making men out of boys and for preparing boys for working life. At the same time, parents have traditionally discouraged their daughters from organized sports, especially after the girls reach adolescence. Parents have been the organizers and promoters of Little League baseball, Biddie basketball, Pop Warner football, and other youth sport programs, all for boys until recent years (Sage, 1980). It is from experiences like these that children learn that sport is a male preserve.

Schools reinforce and reproduce gender-differentiated identities, perceptions, and cultural visions that begin in the home. Traditional inter-school sport programs are testimony to the importance of boys and men and the subordinance of girls and women. Because athletic events are the most popular social events of secondary schools, male athletes enjoy high visibility and prestige. Also, through athletics boys are socialized to be competitive, aggressive, and achievement-oriented. Traditionally, high-status roles for females in high school have been cheerleader and pom-pom girl, through which girls are admonished about the significance of their support for male achievements and the importance of their personal appearance.

Hegemony is rooted in the symbols, rituals, and ceremonial practices that structure daily life and legitimate dominant interests. School athletics support the status quo by reproducing images of masculinity and femininity that sustain asymmetrical gender relations in the larger society (Eder & Parker, 1987). And social contexts and descriptions of women in the mass media's sport coverage contribute additional support to the social construction of gender stereotyping and the perpetuation of patriarchy (to be discussed in chapter 6).

Socialization is clearly a powerful force in shaping beliefs about appropriate male and female attitudes, values, and behaviors, and once established, these are resistant to change. Through sport, along with other social practices, male hegemony has become part of our commonsense understanding of the world, legitimating not only inequities in sports but patriarchal relations generally.

Females' Access to Sport.   Wherever social stratification is found, there are typically discrimination practices designed to deny particular groups equal access to and control over the rewards and resources of the system. Since the latter 19th century, when sport began its rise to public prominence, one of the most persistent and widespread forms of discrimination in American society has been in women's lack of access to sport opportunities. Historically, females have been denied equal opportunity to sport in numerous ways. Not only have their opportunities and rewards been unequal, but their facilities and sport organizations—where they have existed—have been segregated from and inferior to men's. Even today, males have access to more sport opportunities and public resources, and though opportunities for female sport participants have improved tremendously in the past 20 years and more females are involved in sport than ever before, there is little evidence that the men who control sport are truly committed to redressing the continuing inequities.

The major international sporting event of the 20th century has been the Olympic Games. To participate in the Olympics is the dream of almost everyone who has ever considered himself or herself an athlete. But until 1932 women were all but excluded from taking part in the Games, primarily because the founder of the modern Olympic Games, Baron de Coubertin, opposed what he called the "indecency, ugliness and impropriety of women in . . . sports [because] women engaging in strenuous activities were destroying their feminine charm and leading to the downfall and degradation of . . . sport" (Mitchell, 1977, p. 213). De Coubertin, and sport leaders throughout the world, fought fiercely against female inroads into the Games. Although the major barriers have gradually been torn down, the remnants of this heritage remain, and there are still far fewer events for women than for men in the Olympic Games. Of the American athletes who participated in the 1988 Summer Olympics in Seoul, 74% were male while only 26% were female (Cravens, 1988).

Sport inequities for females in high schools and colleges were conspicuous and widespread prior to the mid-1970s. Several states actually had legislation prohibiting interscholastic sports for girls, and numerous colleges had minimal intercollegiate programs for women. Where female sports were played, schools commonly sponsored 8 to 12 sports for males but only a couple for females. Playing seasons for male sports were typically 3 to 4 months long, with numerous contests; seasons for female sports usually lasted only 3 to 4 weeks, with only 5 to 8 contests.

A veritable revolution in girls' and women's sport participation was unleashed with passage of the Educational Amendments Act of 1972. A key provision of this Act—Title IX—required, or at least it was widely interpreted as requiring, that educational institutions receiving federal funds must provide equivalent programs for males and females. Title IX constituted a considerable weapon against sex discrimination in high school and intercollegiate athletics, because some 16,000 school districts and over 2,500 colleges and universities are recipients of federal funds. Within 10 years, the number of female high school athletes jumped from 294,000 to almost 2 million (see Table 3.1 for statistics on female and male participants). By 1988, 35% of all high school participants were female, and the number of sports available to them had more than doubled.

Table 3.1 Sports Participation Survey Totals

Year	Boy participants	Girl participants
1971	3,666,917	294,015
1972-73	3,770,621	817,073
1973-74	4,070,125	1,300,169
1975-76	4,109,021	1,645,039
1977-78	4,367,442	2,083,040
1978-79	3,709,512	1,854,400
1979-80	3,517,829	1,750,264
1980-81	3,503,124	1,853,789
1981-82	3,409,081	1,810,671
1982-83	3,355,558	1,779,972
1983-84	3,303,599	1,747,346
1984-85	3,354,284	1,757,884
1985-86	3,344,275	1,807,121
1986-87	3,364,082	1,836,356

Note. From National Federation Handbook 1987-88 by National Federation of State High School Associations. Reprinted by permission.

Before the passage of Title IX, only about 15% of college athletes were women, and women's sport programs received only 2% of the money colleges spent on athletics. Facilities for female programs were customarily second-rate. The newer and larger gym routinely went to the men and the older gym to the women; where men and women used the same facilities, the women were expected to use them in the off-hours—during mealtimes, early in the morning, late at night. Finally, the women got cheaper equipment than the men and they were expected to keep it longer.

Conditions for women athletes improved greatly in the 1970s. By 1981, more than 120,000 college women were taking part in intercollegiate sports. The Association for Intercollegiate Athletics for Women (AIAW), a counterpart to the National Collegiate Athletic Association (NCAA), was founded in 1971 with 278 member institutions; by 1981 it had over 950 members. Forty-one national championships were contested in 19 sports under AIAW's aegis in 1980-81 (Grant, 1989).

Male-controlled sport organizations only begrudgingly complied with Title IX, many contending that only those programs specifically receiving federal funds were bound by the law. Because no athletic programs received federal aid directly, proponents of this narrow definition argued that no athletic program was subject to Title IX regulations. The U.S. Supreme Court ruled in the case of *Grove City College v. Bell* (1984) that the Title IX language applied only to specific programs or departments that receive federal funds, not to entire institutions. Although the Grove City case was not directly about sport, the effect of the Court's decision was to say that women could be denied equality in sports. Within a year of the Court's decision, the Office of Civil Rights suspended 64 investigations, more than half involving college athletics. As one lawyer said, "The discrimination is so apparent, so blatant. Without the support and nourishment of the law, we see how fragile the support to maintain women's athletics really is" (Becker, 1986a, p. 2C).

Immediately after the Grove City decision, various women's groups began to lobby Congress to pass legislation restoring civil rights weakened by the ruling. On March 22, 1988, both houses of Congress overrode President Reagan's veto, and the Civil Rights Restoration Act became law. One of its implications is the restoration of the original broad interpretation of Title IX (Krupa, 1988a; Neff, 1988).

Historically, professional sport opportunities for women have been severely restricted and differential rewards the norm, with professional female athletes earning less public recognition and money than men for their performances. But progress has been made since the 1970s. In 1978 there were fewer than 90 professional women tennis players; in 1989 there were over 300, and 30 of them earned over $100,000 each. Attendance and national television exposure has increased significantly for the top women's tennis events. The top 5 women pros in tennis and golf now earn almost as much as the top 5 men (Clement, 1987; Lehr & Washington, 1987). However, overall, women professionals in both sports earn less than men for comparable performance.

The most popular professional sports for women have been individual ones, particularly golf and tennis, that have been socially approved for women, especially among the upper social classes, for several generations. But professional opportunities for women in sport are beginning to diversify. Professional ice skating has provided a chance for a few skaters to make very high incomes, over 100 women are doing well as jockeys in thoroughbred horse racing, and Susan Butcher is the first person—man or woman—to win the Iditarod Trail Sled Dog Race in Alaska three times in a row. Professional women's team sports have been less successful in their struggle for public support and acceptance. In basketball, there are opportunities outside the U.S. About 100 American women were playing on teams overseas in 1988, earning salaries up to $100,000 (Moore, 1988).

One additional dimension of American sport works as a subtle but potent contributor to male hegemony and thus acts as an indirect access constraint. Because our most popular sports facilitate achievement based on strength, power, height, and weight—and thus are biased toward biological male traits—they favor superior performance by males. Women are inherently disadvantaged. Although there is considerable overlap in physical characteristics in the entire male and female populations, at the extremes of the distributions—from which come record-setting, idolized athletes—men are stronger, taller, and heavier. Thus, women's performance statistics tend to remain below men's. Willis (1982) argues that sports favoring male biological advantages provide insidious reinforcement for male "natural" superiority because it is hard to deny the validity of an ideology that is supported by such compelling "natural" evidence.

Various sport modifications for women—smaller basketballs, softball instead of baseball, and three sets in tennis championships instead of the men's five—also subtly promote and reproduce male hegemony. An unfortunate dilemma of increasing female participation in our most popular sports and of making rule and equipment accommodations for females in these sports is the potential continued institutional reinforcement of the idea of natural female inferiority and of unequal gender relations.

Male Control of Sport.   Men control sport. Almost every major professional, amateur, and educational sport organization in the U.S. is under the management and control of males. In spite of federal law requiring that secondary schools and colleges treat the sexes equally in their athletic programs, those who direct high school and intercollegiate sports have moved to consolidate and entrench male control. Two examples illustrate this point: First, in the mid-1970s, fearing a loss of control and power through the growth of sports for girls, the National Federation of State High School Associations (NFSHSA) extended its jurisdiction over the growing girls' programs by publishing rule books for girls in several sports. This action usurped the control of the National Association for Girls and Women in Sport (NAGWS), a professional physical education organization that had provided leadership for girls' sports for years. In effect, then, the NFSHSA action transferred the leadership of girls' high school sport programs from an organization controlled by women to one dominated by men.

Second, throughout the 1970s the National Collegiate Athletic Association (NCAA), a bastion of male hegemony, fought the application of Title IX to collegiate athletics with every resource at its command, including litigation. But in 1980 the NCAA switched tactics and moved to bring women's collegiate sport under its control. It voted to begin sponsoring women's championships in five sports in its medium-sized and small schools (Divisions II and III). AIAW leadership denounced the decision as an attempt by the men's organization to seize control of all women's sports and as a direct threat to the AIAW.

One year later, despite protests by the AIAW, the NCAA established women's championships in 12 sports for Division I (the major universities)—an action clearly designed to destroy the AIAW and bring women's athletics into the NCAA. Disclaiming its obvious motive of subsuming women's sports to male control, the NCAA said that it merely wanted to bestow visibility, money, and the NCAA name on women's sports. Beset by loss of income, championships, and members (35% of AIAW's member institutions switched allegiance to the NCAA for the 1981-82 school year), the AIAW ceased operations in 1982.

The NCAA and the much smaller National Association of Intercollegiate Athletics (NAIA) now govern college sport for women. Leadership opportunities for women in these associations have been token at best. They have been relegated to less than 20% representation on the NCAA Council and about 25% on other important NCAA structures. Of those casting institutional votes (each NCAA member institution has a single vote on convention issues) at NCAA conventions, about 95% have been male.

While participation opportunities for female athletes have greatly increased, women have lost ground in coaching and athletic administration. In high school, for example, in 1973-74 about 90% of high school girls' sports were coached by women; in 1988-89 women coached less than 50% of the teams in the most popular girls' sports. Tables 3.2 and 3.3 show this pattern in two states, which are representative of the nation.

A common explanation for the increasing percentages of men coaching high school girls' teams is that males are hired because they are better qualified, with more extensive background in the sports they coach. Although this is sometimes true, it is not always the case. Comparing the characteristics of male and female coaches of girls' high school basketball in Iowa, Anderson and Gill (1983) found that the female coaches were actually more qualified than the males.

When Title IX was enacted in 1972, 90% to 100% of women's intercollegiate athletic teams were coached by females. But between 1974 and 1979 the number of male head coaches and assistants in AIAW institutions increased by 182%, while the number of women coaches increased by only 3%. Of 768 new coaching jobs with women's collegiate teams in 335 colleges and universities from 1974 to 1979, 724 (95%!) went to men. By 1988 less than half of the coaches of women's intercollegiate teams were women (see Figure 3.1).

Female athletic administrators have been losing out, too. Women's intercollegiate athletic programs in the early 1970s were administered

**Table 3.2   Women and Men Head High School Coaches
of Interscholastic Girls' Sports in Colorado, 1973-1988**

Scholastic year	Total girls' head coaches	Women (n)	Women (%)	Men (n)	Men (%)	Sex unknown (n)	Sex unknown (%)
1973-74	434	388	89	40	9	6	2
1978-79	1130	538	48	505	45	87	7
1980-81	1190	478	40	620	52	92	8
1983-84	1226	465	38	672	55	89	7
1984-85	1226	475	39	731	60	20	1
1985-86	1242	508	41	721	58	13	1
1986-87	1356	556	41	787	58	13	1
1987-88	1376	571	41	805	58	0	0

Note. From Susan P. Schafer, state equity consultant, Colorado Department of
Education, Denver. Used with permission.

**Table 3.3   Fifteen-Year Comparison of Female Coaches
of High School Girls' Sports in Virginia**

	% (n)		
Sport	1971-72	1986-87	% Change[a]
Basketball	80.0 (132)	37.4 (102)	−42.6
Cross country	NA	8.8 (136)	NA
Field hockey	81.8 (36)	74.0 (48)	−7.8
Gymnastics	76.6 (62)	68.5 (63)	−8.1
Indoor track	100 (1)	13.6 (8)	−86.4
Outdoor track	86.2 (56)	40.3 (94)	−45.9
Soccer	NA	53.3 (16)	NA
Softball	84.6 (82)	45.2 (94)	−39.4
Swimming	NA	34.3 (11)	NA
Tennis	70.2 (33)	53.4 (95)	−16.8
Volleyball	82.8 (24)	67.2 (88)	−15.6

Note. From "The Decline of Women Leaders (Coaches and Athletic Directors) in
Girls Interscholastic Sports Programs in Virginia From 1971 to 1987" by Mary
Frances Heishman and Roland W. Tutwiler, *Research Quarterly for Exercise and Sport,*
in press. Reprinted by permission.

[a]The percentage of female coaches in 1971-72 minus the percentage of female
coaches in 1986-87.

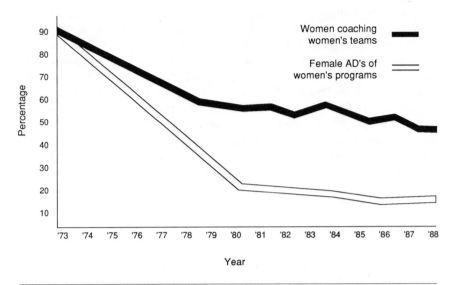

Figure 3.1   The declining percentage of women's intercollegiate teams and athletic programs that are directed by women.

almost exclusively by women with the title of athletic director. Then, as women's programs grew, many colleges combined their men's and women's athletic departments into one. Most such mergers followed a pattern: After the merger, there was a male athletic director and several assistant directors, one usually a woman in charge of women's athletics or the less visible sports. In a survey of colleges and universities, Acosta and Carpenter (1988) found that by 1988 84.8% had placed women's athletic programs under male administrators. Some 32% of all intercollegiate programs for women had no female involved in the administrative structure (McManus, 1988a). Figure 3.1 illustrates the decline in the percentage of women running women's athletic programs.

It is evident that the proportion of women in leadership and decision-making positions—those with power and influence—in American sport is quite small; far smaller, certainly, than would be expected based on the number of female sport participants.

Sport opportunities for girls and women have increased tremendously in recent years—mainly because of court decisions and federal laws—and sport for females is a fast-growing, fast-changing element in American society. But simply furnishing opportunities for equal participation is not enough to produce meaningful social changes. Fundamental social relations are not altered by courts and legislation, and culturally conditioned responses to gender ideology are ubiquitous and resistant to sudden changes. Therefore, although laws may force compliance in equality of opportunity for females in the world of sport, stratification continues, albeit in more subtle and insidious forms, as has been the case with racism (discussed next). Organized sport—from its beginnings in the late 19th century—has been one of the most powerful cultural practices for perpetuating the ideology of male superiority and dominance. It has been an important vehicle by which symbols and values that are institutionalized in patriarchy have been preserved and women's subordinate position in society has been maintained. In spite of enormous changes since the mid-1970s, the world of sport still promotes and preserves traditional gender differences, and patriarchal ideology is still firmly entrenched in American institutions and social practices. More females playing sports does not signify that a revolution has been won for women, not so long as the organization of sport promotes and sustains the dominance of men in social relations.

Racial Stratification

The United States is characterized by the presence of multiple stratification systems, each having its own qualities, contours, and consequences. Race is another of the traditional stratifying categories of American society; racial discrimination excludes people of color—blacks, particularly, as well as Hispanics and other non-Caucasians—from equal access to socially valued rewards and resources. People of color tend to have less wealth, power, and social prestige than white Americans. Moreover, racial stratification has brought about policies and practices that systematically discriminate in employment, housing, politics, education, health care, and many other areas. Such discrimination results in fewer resources and diminished life chances for racial minorities.

Although there are many racial and ethnic minorities in the U.S., my focus is on blacks, for several reasons: First, blacks are the largest minority population (currently about 30 million, or 12% of our population); second, they are the only racial group to have been subjected to an extended period of slavery; third, they are the only racial group to have segregation laws passed against them, which were supported and fully sanctioned by the Supreme Court; finally, they are the only group to have had to struggle against unbelievable odds for basic civil rights (e.g., personal freedom, the right to live where you want to, etc.) that others enjoy (Watson, 1987).

American racial stratification is rooted deeply in our early history. Black slaves were first brought to colonial America in 1619. By the end of the 17th century enslaved black Africans became a major source of labor and were fundamental to colonial agricultural and commercial interests. Slave-owners of the preindustrial agricultural South, together with Northern trading and shipping firms, created a racist social structure with blacks at the bottom.

This stratification was incorporated into the basic documents of the newly formed United States: The Declaration of Independence and the U.S. Constitution condoned racial subordination of and discrimination against blacks. In spite of their enlightened stance toward freedom and liberty, the framers of these documents did not apply them to blacks— indeed, slavery was sanctioned, and blacks were denied the right to vote.

Slavery was abolished in 1863, but Jim Crow laws—segregation laws that legalized white domination and thus left racism essentially intact— and the "separate but equal" doctrine became even more efficient instruments of domination and subordination than slavery had been. It has been only since the 1960s that the civil rights of black citizens have been protected by law. But even though such laws are now in place and social norms have improved conditions in some private and public spheres, the domination and subordination of blacks is still a basic attribute of American society, and race is a primary determinant of position in the social structure. People of color are still defined as racially different by white groups and are singled out for a broad range of discrimination, including individual, institutionalized, and systemic (Williams, 1987; Wilson, 1987).

A national poll conducted in 1988 by Media General and the Associated Press revealed that 55% of Americans think our society is racist and 42% do not think minorities have the same opportunities as whites ("Poll," 1988). More surprising perhaps is the documentation of racial incidents on 130 college campuses in 18 months of 1987 and 1988 (H. Johnson, 1988) by the National Institute Against Prejudice and Violence, a group that monitors racist acts. (And college students are supposed to be the most enlightened sector of the population!)

The economic gap between whites and blacks continues to widen. The poverty rate among the nation's blacks in 1989 was 33%, compared with 10.5% for whites. Blacks' family income was only 56% of whites', and it declined during the 1980s. The jobless rate for blacks has consistently been over twice that of whites. Not only are blacks twice as likely to be unemployed, but those who are employed are overrepresented in jobs whose pay, power, and prestige are low. Only a smattering of black managers have moved beyond middle levels of authority and control. Less than 3% of the nation's physicians, dentists, and pharmacists are black.

In spite of some economic, political, and social gains in the 1970s and 1980s, this period has been a time of increasing black hardship, with inner-city communities devastated by crime and drugs, and national policies of retreat from efforts to increase opportunities for blacks (Dewart, 1989). Although there is less overt bigotry now, institutional racism persists, and Martin Luther King's dream that "one day racism would end in America" still awaits fulfillment.

During the 1980s the New Right and the Moral Majority, both influential groups in contemporary American life, and other conservatives sought to reverse the progressive social and political initiatives of the previous two decades. Camouflaging their dominant ideological rhetoric with arguments about the "declining significance of race," they attempted to explain racial inequalities as primarily attributable to social class rather than color. Some insisted that racial stratification, if it ever existed in American society, had disappeared because of increased opportunities available to blacks.

Although such arguments have achieved some credibility, they have come under intense attack by several analysts who, while acknowledging that racism is intertwined with class, see racial stratification as being created and maintained by institutionalized discrimination in the larger society and aggravated by callous attitudes toward minorities (Boston, 1988; Staples, 1986). From this perspective, racist ideology, zealously cultivated to legitimate the relations of domination in plantation society, has continued to define the status of blacks. Although American blacks have made gains economically, politically, and educationally, many barriers to social equality remain, rooted in institutional patterns and practices of discrimination that are deeply ingrained in the structure of our society (Wilson, 1987).

Where racial stratification coexists with class stratification, as in the U.S., there is compelling evidence that the racial stratification is more basic to social structure and therefore the ultimate determinant of inequality between racial minorities and the dominant class (Ogbu, 1988). The basic fact is that much inequality and discrimination against blacks continues, whether one measures income, employment rates, educational attainment, or political office-holding. Blacks remain among the most disadvantaged people in American society, and it is *racial barriers* that block their achievement, not merely economic or class barriers.

Racial Stratification and Sport

Unlike the patriarchal ideology that has barred most women from sport, the ideology underlying racism is not incompatible with black sport participation, but it has dictated that black athletes be subordinate and in certain times and places totally segregated from playing with whites. A growing literature describes a wide variety of games and sports that black slaves played among themselves (Wiggins, 1977, 1980a, 1980b). Many plantation owners actually encouraged such use of leisure time because it was seen as preferable to other options such as drinking, fighting, and general mischief.

Social Relations and Access to Sport. Social relations between whites and blacks during the slavery era (1619 to 1863) involving sport centered around two activities: boxing and horse racing. Holidays and special occasions in the colonial (1607-1789) and Antebellum (1790-1861) periods were often enlivened with sports and games, especially those on which people could wager. Many plantation owners selected—and even trained—one or more male slaves to enter in boxing matches held in conjunction with festive occasions. The black boxers under such conditions were merely used to entertain their white "masters" and their friends.

Horse racing was another popular sporting event that allowed spectators to bet on the outcome. Horses were, of course, owned by whites, and when training was done it was usually by whites, but blacks were used as jockeys. There was little status and no significant material reward for jockeying, because slave labor of any kind was unpaid; jockeying was viewed as basically mechanical, so blacks were trusted with a task that whites did not care to do anyway. Social relations, then, were seen as distant, with whites in control and blacks in subordinate roles, pleasing the dominant white groups (Davis, 1966).

Black emancipation had little effect on the social relations between blacks and whites in sports. Although a number of blacks played on professional baseball teams in the early years of the National League, Jim Crowism gradually raised its ugly head. White players threatened to quit rather than share the diamond with black men. White opponents tried to spike black players at every opportunity; pitchers aimed at their heads. In 1888 major league club owners made a gentleman's agreement not to sign any more black players. This unwritten law against hiring black players was not violated until 1945 when Branch Rickey, general manager of the Brooklyn Dodgers, signed Jackie Robinson to a contract (Tygiel, 1983). As other professional sports developed, they too barred blacks from participation. One of the many consequences of excluding blacks from professional sports was to perpetuate privileges for white athletes, who did not have to compete with an entire segment of the population for sport jobs.

Although blacks had been active in boxing throughout the time of slavery, they found their aspirations for top prizes blocked when they tried to compete as free men. For example, when John L. Sullivan became the first American heavyweight boxing champion in 1882, he announced that he would fight any—or almost any—contender: "In this challenge, I include all fighters—first come, first served—who are white. I will not fight a negro. I never have, and never shall" (Betts, 1974). And he never did. One of the greatest heavyweight boxing champions of all time, Jack Dempsey, in his first public statement after he beat Jess Willard for the championship in 1919, said that he would not under any circumstances "pay any attention to negro challengers" ("Dempsey Will Meet," 1919, p. 17).

Times in sport have changed, however—during the past 30 years blacks have gradually assumed a remarkably prominent role in several professional sports. In 1956, only 14% of professional football players were black; by 1989 55% of NFL players were black. In baseball's major leagues, about 25% of 1989 players were black, up from less than 10% in the mid-1950s. The most striking increase is in basketball; in the early 1960s only about 20% of NBA players were black, but in 1989 black athletes comprised over 80% of NBA teams.

But these changes have not taken place purely from humanitarian concerns. Sport opportunities for blacks in professional sport grew only as discrimination became incompatible with good capitalist financial policy. It was in those team sports where spectator appeal was strong and growing, and in which the profit motive was foremost, that blacks were given a chance, and the valuable contributions of outstanding black athletes in winning championships opened up further opportunities. Those sports most closely linked to upper-class patronage and with less spectator interest have been slow to provide access to blacks.

Intercollegiate sports were dominated by white, upper-class, Protestant males in the late 19th and early 20th centuries. In fact, collegiate sports remained segregated, with isolated exceptions, until after World War II. At the University of Michigan, for example, from 1882 to 1945 there were only four black lettermen in football and none in basketball. In 1948 only 10% of college basketball teams had one or more blacks on their rosters. This proportion increased to 45% of the teams in 1962 and 92% by 1975. The transition from segregated to integrated programs is perhaps best illustrated by the University of Alabama: In 1968 there were no blacks on any of its teams, but its 1975 basketball team had an all-black starting lineup (Eitzen & Sage, 1989).

For the most part, though, black college athletes historically have played at black colleges in black leagues (known as Negro colleges and Negro leagues), which existed because of institutionalized racial prejudice and discrimination. Black colleges fielded teams in all of the popular sports and have played a leading role in women's sports, especially in track and field—Tuskegee Institute and Tennessee State are prominent examples. Although the educational system was segregated, black colleges have provided an avenue to prominence for many athletes and have developed more outstanding black athletes than any other agency of higher education, though many never became known outside the black community.

The impact of World War II in opening up social and economic opportunities for blacks, the 1954 Supreme Court decision forbidding racially separate educational facilities, and the growing commercialization of collegiate sports led more and more formerly white schools to recruit talented blacks to bolster their teams; consequently, black colleges lost their monopoly on black athletic talent. The best athletes found it advantageous to play at predominantly white schools because of greater visibility, especially on television, which boosted their chances for signing professional contracts at the conclusion of their eligibility. Athletic programs at black colleges were rapidly depleted, forcing several schools to drastically modify their athletic programs and some black leagues to disband.

Despite the many opportunities now available in sport for blacks that did not exist a generation ago, racial stratification in sport has not been eliminated. Many professional and college sports still have very few black participants. These sports tend to be linked to upper-class patronage, but that is not the entire explanation. Dominant classes have the wherewithal to insulate themselves against those with whom they do not wish to associate. Laws that prevent blacks from being kept out do not assure that they will get in. Ample evidence exists that those who control certain sports have created barriers to black participation, thus reproducing some of the more odious features of racial stratification.

Social Mobility Through Sport for Blacks.   Even though racial inequalities are widespread in sports, it is often contended that sport has been one of the most responsive social practices for serving as an avenue of upward social mobility for blacks; indeed, it has been argued that sport has done more in this regard than any other social practice or institution. Though it is certainly true that sport has provided some black athletes with opportunities for mobility denied them in other sectors of American life, and a few have become prominent figures in American sport—Joe Louis, Willie Mays, Wilma Rudolph, Julius "Doctor J" Erving, "Magic" Johnson, Jackie Joyner-Kersee, and others—sport has not moved large numbers of blacks into higher social-class standing. The powerful rags-to-riches stories of individual blacks actually disguise the extent of immobility and thus contribute to the legitimization of racial inequality.

In the late 1980s there were fewer than 1,200 professional black athletes. Given about 3 million black males between 20 and 30 (the age of most professional athletes), that makes the odds of a black man becoming a professional athlete about 1 in 3,500 (Stanton, 1987). As sociologist Harry Edwards once remarked about a black's chances of becoming a professional athlete, "You have a better chance of getting hit by a meteorite in the next 10 years than getting work as an athlete" (Oates, 1979, p. 32A). Beyond professional athletes, very few blacks have found high-paying, high-status jobs in sport; there are fewer than 400 black coaches and athletic administrators in professional and college sport (I will pursue this issue further in the next section).

Blacks have received athletic scholarships at predominantly white schools since the early 1970s, and this has been a mixed blessing. On one hand, a few athletically talented blacks have been enabled to attend and graduate from colleges otherwise inaccessible to them, and this has allowed some to achieve social mobility and financial success. But on the other hand, the evidence is clear and abundant that many black college athletes have been exploited by their schools. They have been recruited lacking the academic background to succeed in higher education, and they have been advised into courses that keep them eligible but are dead-end choices for acquiring a college diploma (Adler & Adler, 1985; Leach & Conners, 1984; Purdy, Eitzen, & Hufnagel, 1982). When their eligibility is used up or they become academically ineligible to compete for the team, they are discarded and ignored by the coaches who recruited them. Lapchick (1988) reported that an estimated 80% of black NCAA Division I football and basketball players do not graduate.

Leadership and Management Opportunities.   The stratification pattern for blacks has been similar to that for women with regard to sport leadership and management. Access for black athletes has expanded greatly in recent years, but very few blacks have been hired for positions high in the sport hierarchy. The immediate results of legislative and judicial efforts to eliminate discrimination are always most noticeable at the lower levels of the social formation. The higher levels, with the greatest power, prestige, and material rewards, are more insulated from direct scrutiny, so those who control access to those higher levels can subtly continue discriminatory practices. Thus, members of the oppressed group typically have difficulty securing the higher-paying and prestigious positions.

In both professional and intercollegiate athletics, coaching and management jobs are under the control of those who presently have the power for determining who gets selected for the upper-level positions. As of 1989 there had been only one black head coach and no black general managers in the NFL; only 14% of the assistant coaches were black, and only two were offensive or defensive coordinators—the most responsible and prestigious coaching positions below head coaching. Major league baseball has had only a handful of black managers to date, and presently only about 9% of the coaches and none of the general managers are black. Professional basketball has had the most black head coaches. In recent years as many as seven blacks have held these positions at once, but this is in a league with 80% black players. Fewer than five NBA general managers have been black (Lapchick, 1988).

Black coaches are equally scarce in intercollegiate athletics. Nearly all black college coaches are assistants, and most coaching staffs have only one black. As of 1989 fewer than 5 major university football and 10 basketball teams were coached by blacks. Other sports have even fewer black coaches.

Executive positions in professional and intercollegiate sports continue to elude blacks. In the commissioner's offices of pro sports, in the front offices of professional clubs, and among athletic directors of collegiate sports there are scandalously few blacks. Only about two dozen blacks hold collegiate jobs such as assistant or associate athletic director. The situation had come to be considered so disgraceful that in 1987 some of the sport governing bodies and civil rights groups formed committees and task forces to help seek out minorities for management and executive positions and to monitor team hirings. University of California sociologist Harry Edwards formed the National Organization on the Status of Minorities in Sports to monitor the hiring of black coaches and sport administrators. Substantial and meaningful results have been slow; the ranks of managers, head coaches, and front office personnel continue to be filled by whites, sometimes using thinly disguised ploys that eliminate blacks from serious consideration. For example, of 14 new general managers hired by major league baseball between 1987 and 1989, none was a minority. Of 18 new field managers, one was black. The one bright spot in this otherwise dim picture was the choice in February 1989 of Bill White, a black man, as the president of baseball's National League.

Summary and Preview

Class, gender, and race stratification are fundamental features of American society. There is dominance, exploitation, and discrimination of capitalists over workers, of males over females, and of whites over blacks. These systems of stratification are interrelated and equally important as enduring forms of oppression, but each has its own unique forms and consequences, which sometimes act independently of the others but sometimes in conjunction with them. Moreover, each alone and all in combination are played out in the world of sport.

Analysis of any segment of American society—including sport—that does not account for the importance of class, gender, and race stratification forms an incomplete foundation for understanding our historical traditions and our contemporary social organizations and relationships.

The political institution—or the state, as it is called in the social science literature—is the most prominent social institution in modern societies. This is true not only because of its omnipresent role in the lives of its citizens, but also because it is vested with society's ultimate power. It is a widely held myth that there is no relationship between sport and the state, manifested in pleas to "keep politics out of sport." In chapter 4 I describe the naiveté of such admonitions and examine how the state intervenes in American sport and physical recreation.

CHAPTER 4

Sport and
the State:
The Political
Economy of
American Sport

Sport and politics always have been institutional part-
ners . . . particularly where [a] society's reputation or
national pride are at stake. Although in the United States
the separation of sport and politics may be viewed as
the appropriate relationship, it is not the practiced one.

Arthur T. Johnson, political scientist,
and James H. Frey, sociologist

Every modern society has some system for promoting social order and
general welfare. The preamble to the U.S. Constitution provides a written
document articulating this system for our country. It states that "We the
people of the United States, in order to form a more perfect Union, establish justice, insure domestic tranquility, provide for the common defense,
promote the general welfare, and secure the blessings of liberty to our-
selves and our posterity, do ordain and establish this Constitution for
the United States of America." The network of administrative and
bureaucratic agencies that make up this system is often referred to by
social scientists as "the state" (which is not to be confused with one of
the 50 United States).

The state is both a social institution and a set of organizations (a *social
institution* is a set of relationships organized around a fundamental activity
or set of activities that sustain and maintain a society). The state is characterized by a socially constructed set of practices that address human
needs to stabilize the social order and promote the general welfare. It is
also the principal instrument of social control. In effect, the state is an
organized power structure, the functions of which are the management
and control of society (Giddens, 1987).

Typically composed of a great variety of organizations, the state includes government in all of its branches and levels, the military, the police
and the legal system, and the many public bureaucracies and agencies
whose authority stems from government; the public educational system
is also part of the state apparatus. As an institution coordinating and
integrating these organizations, the state is "the expression of an established and legitimate way of conducting the public's business" (Walton,
1986, pp. 176-177).

Most Americans feel there is little about the modern state—especially
democratic states, like their own—that they don't already know, for they
study government as a part of basic education. But there is typically little
effort to connect the state to other social institutions or to our capitalist
economy. It is almost as though the state were an independent entity.

But in fact the state is inseparably associated with all of America's social institutions as well as being part of a worldwide system of nation-states.

Power and Influence in the Modern State

The two images of society that were described in chapter 2—pluralistic and hegemonic—have much to say about the relationship between the state and its citizens. Pluralists see the state as attaining consensus and preserving social order by adjudicating the conflicts and demands of numerous social groups through a continuous sequence of bargaining processes. The state is equally accessible to all citizens and acts in the common interest, remaining outside particular interests but responding to diverse pressures. It is often contended by pluralists that the interests of the people and the policies of the state are the same. The state, then, is regarded as a benign and neutral set of agencies that have no direct involvement in either furthering or eradicating divisions and inequities of stratification because such things are regarded as being of little consequence in the overall operations of the state.

Gramsci did not articulate a clear conception of the state in his writings about hegemony, but the modern capitalist state has become a subject of lively discussion for social thinkers with ties to the hegemonic tradition. An organizing theme is the important changes that have occurred in Western capitalist countries—including the United States—over the past century through the expanding role of the state in both social institutions and cultural practices. Miliband's (1969) description of this trend is now a classic:

> More than ever before men [and women] now live in the shadow of the state. What they want to achieve, individually or in groups, now mainly depends on the state's sanction and support. But since that sanction and support are not bestowed indiscriminately, they must, ever more directly, seek to influence and shape the state's power and purpose, or try and appropriate it altogether. It is for the state's attention, or for its control, that [persons] compete; and it is against the state that beat the waves of social conflict. It is to an ever greater degree the state which men [and women] encounter as they confront other men [and women]. This is why, as social beings, they are also political beings, whether they know it or not. It is possible not to be interested in what the state does; but it is not possible to be unaffected by it. (p. 1)

One prominent sector of state expansion is the economy. In the hegemonic view, the state plays an indispensable role in ensuring the reproduction of capitalist social relations, and the powers of the state are used to sustain the general institutional framework of capitalist enterprise. The state is seen as intricately involved with supporting class differences and with protecting the overall continuity of dominant class interests against those of other classes. This is not to say that the dominant class is a unified social formation and that the state merely acts at the command of corporate capitalism. Miliband (1977) provided the appropriate perspective in noting that the pressure that powerful capitalist interest

> is able to apply upon the state is not in itself sufficient to explain the latter's actions and policies. There are complexities in the decision-making process which the notion of business as a pressure group is too rough and unwieldly to explain. There may well be cases where that pressure is decisive. But there are others where it is not. Too great an emphasis upon this aspect of the matter leaves too much out of account. (p. 72)

This perspective was recently reiterated by Vanneman and Cannon (1987), who claim that capitalist enterprise "does not dictate the minutiae of all class politics. Compromises and setbacks can readily be identified but do not by themselves disprove the fact of political dominance. . . . But dominant-class power, like all power, can be real without being omnipotent" (p. 303).

The notion that the state is reducible to the interests of a single dominant class, then, is too simplistic, because the state itself is the scene of class tension as well as gender and racial conflict. Consequently, the state "must force everyone to think alike (a rather difficult task that is beyond its power and would destroy its legitimacy) or generate consent among a large portion of these contending groups" (Apple, 1982, pp. 29-30). Thus, only by gradually and continuously integrating many of the interests of allied and even opposing groups under its banner can the state maintain its own legitimacy. But although there may be divisions and frictions within the dominant groups the society remains a class society with enormous differences in wealth and power, and the state is involved in reproducing the relations of production.

Though countries differ in how the state intervenes, there is no doubt about the existence and extent of intervention, especially in the United States (Castells, 1980). Here state intervention has become endemic, imposing on every aspect of citizen life from personal behavior to public policies.

The State and Private Accumulation

Gamble (1981) has noted that "whatever measure of state activity is taken, the importance of the state now lies not merely in securing the basic structure of law and establishing an acceptable form of money, but in actively subsidizing, supporting, and organizing industrial activity'' (p. 179). Parenti (1988) elaborated on this point:

> Behind capitalism there stands the organized power of the state. . . . Corporations can call on the resources of the state to rationalize and subsidize their performance, maintain their profit levels, socialize costs by taxing the many, and keep dissidents under control through generous applications of official violence. (p. 312)

The state provides conditions favorable to the accumulation of private capital by subsidizing it—directly through tax breaks, legal protection, protective tariffs, regulating markets, and loans and credits with favorable conditions and indirectly by providing essential equipment and services, such as roads, energy, and transportation, cheaply to capitalist firms. Miliband (1969) agreed, noting

> State intervention in economic life in fact largely *means* intervention for the purpose of helping capitalist enterprise. In no field has the notion of the "welfare state" had more precise and apposite meaning than here: there are no more persistent and successful applicants for public assistance than the proud giants of the private enterprise system. (p. 78)

A few examples will illustrate Miliband's point:

† In 1979 the Chrysler Corporation appealed to the federal government for a loan and received *$1.5 billion* in loan guarantees.

† In 1984, when one of the nation's largest banks, Continental Illinois, was on the brink of failure, it received $7.5 billion in federal aid.

† Some corporations completely escape federal income taxes. From 1981 to 1983 more than half of the largest and most profitable corporations paid no federal income tax in at least one of those years. General Electric, for example, earned *$6.5 billion* in profits from 1981 to 1983, yet paid no taxes and received refunds of $283 million. Even after the Tax Reform Act of 1986, giant, profitable corporations—such as General Motors, IBM, and Hewlett-Packard—have continued not to pay federal income taxes. In 1987, 16 of the huge corporations whose profits ranged from $42 million to $2.4 billion legally paid *no* federal income tax. General Motors, with a $2.4 billion profit, actually received a $742 million *refund* from taxes previously paid (Citizens for Tax Justice, 1988).

† In 1989 the federal government began a $166 billion bailout of the savings and loan industry—a bailout necessitated by widespread

corruption, outright cheating, stealing, and general mismanagement by the powerful and wealthy owners and managers in this industry.

This fact is clear: Our government at all levels favors corporate capital interests and is bound to corporate ideology and goals.

One of the major mechanisms by which the capitalist class enjoys favorable treatment by the state is through an interpenetration by members of that capitalist class into the state apparatus itself. In this way, economic wealth is translated into political power. Many elected politicians and top government officials are, in their primary occupations, business executives and lawyers who reflect the interests of the capitalist class. The highest levels of the state include many members of the corporate elite or people connected with them through kinship or social ties—all reflecting the close relationship and community of interests between the state and the capitalist class (Allen, 1987; Castells, 1980). One recent case illustrates well the confraternity between private and government sectors: Caspar Weinberger, Secretary of Defense under Ronald Reagan, was a director of Bechtel Group, Pepsico Inc., and Quaker Oats, all large corporations, before his Cabinet appointment. When he left this office in 1988, he was quickly hired as the publisher of Forbes, considered by many the leading business magazine.

A related mechanism of capitalist influence into the state apparatus is through the economic resources of corporations and their ability to influence politics. Pressure of economic interest groups is a pervasive condition under which the state must operate. A number of studies have shown that there is an inner group of large corporations that work together to ensure that public policies will not depart from their interests (Domhoff, 1983; D. Jacobs, 1988; Useem, 1984). A late-19th-century Republican senator from Pennsylvania, Boies Penrose, articulated this symbiotic connection in a frank—if crude—manner. In addressing a group of corporate businessmen, he told them,

I believe in a division of labor. You send us to Congress; we pass the laws under which you make money . . . and out of your profits you further contribute to our campaign funds to send us back again to pass laws to enable you to make more money. (Green, 1986, p. A35)

More recently, former Colorado Governor Richard Lamm made a similar observation:

Winning [public] office . . . comes down to money, not ideas. Even the most idealistic candidate must appeal to wealthy and powerful special interests to raise the huge sums required to run a campaign. Once elected, those we have put in office are frequently called upon to make decisions that affect the . . . interests that helped put them there. (Lamm, 1988, p. 9)

Results of political campaign-giving surveys convincingly show that corporate gifts dominate the large contributions to political candidates of both parties (Domhoff, 1983; Neustadtl & Clawson, 1988). Thus, behind benign symbols of solidarity—we the people, national security—the affluent and powerful legislate largely on their own behalf.

In spite of the bias of the state toward capitalist interests, it must be emphasized that the state is a contested terrain of conflict and compromise, which, although it largely serves to perpetuate the dominant social formations, does not simply obey their commands. As a result, working-class and underprivileged groups sometimes are able to wrest concessions from the state that are not supported by organized capital (Piven & Cloward, 1977), as exemplified in such welfare provisions as a minimum wage, social security, and other social services.

Capital Accumulation and Sport

Sport in American society is big business, and those who own and control it are wealthy and powerful. In 1989 twenty owners of professional sport teams were among the *Forbes* magazine list of 400 wealthiest persons; many of the others are just a notch below this. As a private business, professional sport is structured to maximize profit, and since its beginnings professional sport has benefited from actions of the state, sometimes by favorable legislation, other times by favorable court rulings, all the while with the insistence that sport is just fun and games and that owners are providing a philanthropic service to the public. Johnson and Frey (1985) have observed that "government policy as implemented through legislation, court decisions, and bureaucratic rules and regulations is [an] . . . important variable in defining the nature and dynamics of American sport" (p. ix).

Since World War II the state has taken on an increasing role in sport and physical recreation of all kinds and at all levels, from local to international. Because the state plays such a strategic role in the economy of sport, it is actually impossible to disentangle the two institutional strands. (In this chapter the primary focus is on the state; the connections between the economic institution and sport will be treated more fully in the next three chapters.)

The major means by which the state has protected the investments of professional team owners and has advanced capital accumulation has been the courts and Congressional legislation. As a part of the state, the law occupied a prominent position in Gramsci's (1971) thoughts about the hegemonic apparatus. He noted, "If every State tends to create and maintain a certain type of civilization and of citizen . . . and to eliminate certain customs and attitudes and to disseminate others, the Law will be its instrument for this purpose" (p. 246).

From its beginnings, the professional sport industry has benefited from favorable court decisions that have enabled owners to monopolize their industry, and in cases where their power has been threatened they have joined forces with the courts to crush opposition. All of the professional sport leagues operate as cartels (groups of firms that organize together to control production, sales, and wages within an industry), with team owners making agreements on matters of mutual interest. Although such agreements violate the intent of antitrust laws and are illegal in most businesses, the courts have consistently protected professional sports from antitrust accusations and have upheld their exemption from them. This protects each sports franchise from competition because the number of franchises is controlled by the team owners; no new franchise is allowed to locate in a given territory without approval of the owners. This protection from competition also eliminates price wars and frees owners to set ticket prices at will, thus maximizing their profits. Each league can also negotiate television contracts for the entire league without violating antitrust laws; indeed, this is protected by Congressional action in the 1961 Sports Broadcast Act.

Another advantage of cartelized arrangements for the owners is that professional athletes are drastically limited in choices of where they can play and in their bargaining power. An athlete who wants to play professionally in a particular sport must negotiate with the team that drafted him or her (or, in the case of veteran players, with the team that holds the contract). Team owners in all of the professional sports have taken advantage of their immunity from antitrust laws to implement practices and structures that serve their own interests (Closius, 1985).

Employment practices of owners in professional team sports have been protected by the courts and Congressional legislation, with the major results being the restraint of athletes' freedom of movement and of wages. Baseball was the first sport to adopt what is known as the reserve clause, but all the professional team sports have had some form of it. Historically, by the 1880s all major league baseball owners used a provision in every player's contract that enabled the owners to control the player's job mobility. Once a player signed a contract with a club, that team had exclusive rights over him; he was no longer free to negotiate with other teams because his contract had a clause that "reserved" his services to his original team for the succeeding year. The reserve clause specified that the owner had the exclusive right to renew the player's contract annually, and thus the player was bound perpetually to negotiate with only one club; he became its property and could even be sold to another club without his own consent. In all succeeding years, then, the player had to sell his services solely to the club that owned his contract, unless it released, sold, or traded him or he chose to retire. It was an effective device for holding down salaries because players were denied an alternative market for their services. As Dworkin (1985) noted,

> The major impact of the reservation system was to cause an extreme imbalance in bargaining power between owners and players. . . . The owners prospered, while the players toiled for wages much below the level they would have received had they been bargaining in a more competitive environment. (p. 25)

Resentment against the reserve clause was persistent from its beginnings, and twice challenges to its constitutionality reached the U.S. Supreme Court. In 1922 the Court upheld it, contending in essence that major league baseball was a sport, not a business, and therefore was entitled to immunity from antitrust laws. Again in 1972 when it was challenged, the court favored letting the 1922 decision stand. It was not until 1976 that the courts finally struck down the reserve clause, substituting in its place a limited player mobility plan (Lowenfish & Lupien, 1980).

Athletes in other professional sports have found themselves in much the same position as baseball players. In each case, the player's freedom of movement was restricted by some type of reservation system. With the approval of the courts and Congress, the NFL has been able to enforce a limited version of the reserve clause, the Rozelle Rule. This rule gave Pete Rozelle, former NFL commissioner, power to rule on the compensation a team signing a "free agent" must give the team losing the player. Thus, the apparent freedom of NFL players to negotiate with other teams is severely restricted, since the team buying a free agent must compensate the team losing the player, and the compensation has been loaded in favor of the losing team. Therefore a free agent does not, in reality, have full economic freedom. Other professional sports have worked out some form of compromise between owners and players, giving players limited control over their terms of employment (Freedman, 1987).

The extent to which the state protects capital interests against working class interests is illustrated in the various attempts that professional athletes have made to have their concerns and grievances addressed by forming player unions and engaging in collective bargaining. Unions of professional athletes go back to the 1885 creation of the National Brotherhood of Professional Ball Players. As other professional sports have emerged, most have formed players' unions, largely in response to low wages and the restrictive player reserve systems. Although player unions and collective bargaining have had some significant successes, owners have used their considerable personal wealth and influence in Congress and the courts to minimize the effectiveness of the player unions; the unions have not possessed equivalent legal and legislative clout to secure many of their needs.

Capital accumulation also accrues to professional-sports owners through tax breaks. Owners of professional franchises are given a number of ways to minimize taxable profits. One example is the depreciation of players. Most of the assets of a professional sport team are its players, so most of the cost of a franchise is player contracts. Owners can depreciate players the way farmers depreciate cattle and corporations depreciate company cars; the professional athletes' status is that of property. No other business in the United States depreciates the value of human beings as part of its business costs. The obvious beneficiaries of such tax breaks are the wealthy team owners.

The Social Costs of Private Enterprise

Another form of state intervention is its assumption of a large share of the social costs of private enterprise. These are costs that are not paid for by individual private businesses but are instead shifted onto the public via the state. The expenses include, but are not limited to, air and water pollution clean-up; toxic waste disposal; reclamation of wildlife, soils, and forest resources after their decimation for private profit; unemployment benefits; and health services (Feagin, 1984).

The state also bears the social costs of private enterprise in accepting much of the costs of public education and of training skilled labor and in subsidizing scientific research, the findings of which often benefit private capital. Federal and state governments often fund research and develop new technologies and then turn them over to private corporations for their profit. Indeed, corporate leaders demand it. John Young, president of Hewlett-Packard, recently asserted that "if the United States is to regain its competitive position, the public sector must encourage technical innovation, increased investment in research and development, and more emphasis on education of a highly trained workforce" (Seelmeyer, 1988, p. 3A).

Ralph Nader ("Alternatives for American Growth," 1979) noted with respect to the nuclear energy industry,

> The government funded the basic research, funded the technology, gave the designs to the utilities gratis, enriched the uranium, protected the utilities from liability under the Price-Anderson Act, and has now decided to pay the cost for nuclear wastes. From start to finish, it's a classic case of an industry that has been sponsored, shielded, and protected by the government. (pp. 12-13)

The same is true of a wide range of advanced technologies. As Chomsky (1987) explained, "The computer industry was subsidized by the public through the military system during the costly phase of research and development, then turned loose for profit-making when sufficient progress had been made for a market to become available" (p. 106).

Social Costs and Sport

Ubiquitous monuments to socializing the costs and privitizing the profits in sport are the numerous sport stadiums and arenas that have been built at public expense for the use of professional teams. Over 50 of these imposing facilities have been built or renovated at taxpayer expense in cities across the nation since the 1960s, and more than 20 cities in the U.S. and Canada have begun or are planning to build new stadiums or arenas. These lavish structures have come to symbolize a city's willingness to undertake ambitious projects, and they provide visible evidence, at least to some, of big league status in the competitive world of civic pride. But civic pride can carry a high price tag—the average cost of one of these publicly subsidized facilities has exceeded $50 million, with actual costs ranging from a low of $45 million for Houston's Astrodome, completed in 1965, to a high of an estimated $314 million for the twin-stadium complex planned for Baltimore.

About three fourths of these stadiums and arenas have been publicly financed, generally through revenue bonds issued by state, county, or city governments, and are allegedly to be paid off by revenues derived from the facilities. But whenever revenue bonds are used to finance a public project that cannot pay for itself—and so far all of these facilities have failed to make enough money to pay for themselves—the revenue bonds become an open-ended general obligation upon the taxpayers. Losses are so great that many facilities are considered successful if they generate enough income to pay half of the operating expenses, let alone payment on the bonds.

The reason that few pro sport team owners own the facilities in which their teams play is that when the government owns them, the owners are relieved of the burden of property taxes, insurance, and maintenance costs, not to mention construction. Owners pay rent on the facilities, of course, but this usually covers only a fraction of overall operating expenses. Local taxpayers actually wind up subsidizing professional team owners.

Another reason for team owners' not owning their facilities is that it makes it much easier for them to move franchises to other cities should they become unhappy with existing financial arrangements (one sportswriter calls this "stripmining" cities). In the 1980s, three NFL owners actually made such a move (the Oakland Raiders to Los Angeles, the Baltimore Colts to Indianapolis, and the St. Louis Cardinals to Phoenix), and the incidence of owner "extortion" appears to be increasing. An owner in this situation has very powerful leverage against a city and can extract very favorable leasing, concession, and parking agreements.

The pressures that encourage public officials to campaign for the construction of stadiums and arenas at public expense come from various sources, but it is the pro sport franchise owners supported by the local mass media that create local interest in and demand for these facilities. The symbolic and public purposes of sport and civic imagery merge with private economic goals. When faced with such pressures, local voters, city councils, and legislatures frequently accede to the demands for quality facilities (Baade & Dye, 1988). When Yankee Stadium was rebuilt in the mid-1970s, the New York Yankee owners encouraged a city on the verge of bankruptcy to contribute $100 million for the project. And there are more recent examples: In 1988 the citizens of San Jose, California, approved a referendum authorizing the sale of $67 million in municipal bonds for a sport complex. To prevent the Chicago White Sox from moving their franchise to another city in 1988, the Illinois state legislature passed a bill that includes financing the construction of a new stadium for the team. In the same year, funding for education in the state received a much lower increase than that which had been sought.

Professional sport team owners, and often local politicians, seek to rationalize the public expenditures in terms of public benefits, arguing that communities profit by increased revenues, business, and taxes. They also point to various intangible benefits, such as neighborhood redevelopment and enhanced civic pride. But these claims have never been well documented. In fact, most social and economic analyses have concluded that the prime beneficiaries of these sport facilities are a small group of wealthy individuals and that those most likely to bear the costs are low-income citizens (Baade & Dye, 1988; Lipsitz, 1984; Okner, 1974; Rosentraub & Nunn, 1978).

Economists Baade and Dye (1988) have studied the various benefits and costs for stadiums and arenas and concluded that ''in most of the cases we have examined, calculation of the . . . enumerated direct costs and revenues result in a net loss for the municipal treasury'' (p. 270). They further concluded that major league sports frequently have no significant positive impact on a city's economy, and in some ways may even drain funds from other municipal projects. Finally, with respect to the promised increased economic activity before and after building or renovating a sport facility, Baade and Dye's research led them to conclude that ''the positive impacts on area development touted by stadium promoters do not appear to be strong enough to show up in . . . measures of economic activity for individual cities that have built stadiums'' (p. 272). Those proclaiming economic benefit to a city appear to be blind to the myriad direct and auxiliary costs that diminish or eliminate positive economic impacts.

Socializing the costs and privitizing the profits in sport are not limited to sport facilities. Another example of what amounts to a public subsidy for both sport franchises and private, nonsport businesses is the purchase of game tickets by corporations, which can be deducted from taxes as a business expense. A large proportion of the season tickets for professional sports are purchased by businesses. In effect, then, taxpayers are subsidizing the costs for corporate executives and their friends to see professional sport contests. When this deduction was threatened by the Internal Revenue Service, professional sports and businesses combined their lobbying efforts to retain the subsidy.

The State and Its Ideology

One of the traditional functions of the state is that of fostering and preserving social harmony. It does this by creating and maintaining social stability and support for the reigning hegemony. A united society is unified within a common system of goals, values, and beliefs, and it is this consensus that supplies the cohesion on which a society stands. The most formal mechanism for carrying out this task is enforcement agencies, such as the police and the armed forces, that ensure that laws are observed. But states typically try to avoid using legitimated violence—via the police and armed forces—because this involves force and has the potential of antagonizing citizens and causing rebellion. Instead, hegemony is maintained through ideological inculcation, which socializes people to internalize and accept the current social arrangements. Poulantzas (1978) argues that

> the state cannot enshrine and reproduce political domination exclusively through repression, force, or "naked" violence, but directly calls upon ideology to legitimize . . . and contribute to a consensus of those classes and fractions which are dominated from the point of view of political power. (p. 28)

Public education is a primary avenue for the state's hegemonic ideological work in socializing people to accept the status quo, to see the government and all of its branches as right. Two notions underlie this educational promotion of hegemonic ideology: Citizens must be taught loyalty and patriotism so that they will, one, support their political leaders and, two, fight to defend their country. History and civics, both required by law, are the primary school subjects through which these ideas are taught. Of course, the school, through its organization and social milieu, tends to sustain and reproduce the existing hegemonic relations. Ideological work is actually carried out in several social institutions, not just the schools, with the encouragement, support, and approval of the state.

For example, the mass media play a decisive role in the ideological sphere (this will be described in chapter 6).

Sport and Nationalism

Sport is one of the means by which a state socializes its citizens. The sport world inculcates values and norms that bolster the legitimacy of the American political system. National loyalty and patriotism are fostered through sport rituals and ceremonies that link sport and nationalism; indeed, our entire society has a propensity for employing ritual for transmitting the symbolic codes of the dominant culture. We have developed sport rituals that influence citizens toward conformity to beliefs and values that prevail in the wider society. National symbols and pageantry are often woven into sport events. Reciting the Pledge of Allegiance, singing the national anthem, performing patriotic half-time shows, and displaying emblems and insignias like flags all ideologically celebrate national unity and the legitimacy of the existing social order. Probably nothing provokes stronger emotions than activities tied to patriotism.

Important national and international events like the Super Bowl and the Olympic Games are incorporated into a panoply of political ritual that serves to remind people of their common destiny. Such events help to create and support an effective dominant culture because they convey messages about norms, values, and dispositions that contribute to the ideological hegemony of dominant groups. They are also a means of social control in that the coaches, athletic directors, broadcasters, and so forth, limit the version of ideological perspectives presented. Anything that is not in agreement with the reigning hegemony is censured; all that is seditious is removed or explicitly condemned (Frankfurt Institute, 1972).

Most sport organizations and officials go to great lengths to emphasize national loyalty and patriotism, and in almost every political controversy the sports establishment can be counted upon to line up behind the reigning political leaders. Any stand on social or political issues is typically supportive of the current consensus about what constitutes a social or political problem and what to do about it. One example is exhortations to athletes to shun drugs and proclamations favoring random drug testing of athletes (Hargreaves, 1986).

Occasionally, dominant structures and values are contested in the sports world. In recent years the occasions of political resistance have centered around gender and racial politics. One of the most memorable political displays by athletes occurred at the 1968 Mexico City Olympic Games. As an attempt to call dramatic attention to America's pervasive racism, black American Olympic athletes Tommy Smith and John Carlos raised gloved, clenched fists and bowed their heads during the playing of the national anthem. They paid a heavy price for their commitment to racial justice. The U.S. Olympic Committee stripped them of their medals and banned them for life from further Olympic competition.

Title IX of the Educational Amendments Act of 1972 contained a provision that opened up sport opportunities previously denied females in educational institutions. However, women's sports groups could not get the government to force universal compliance with the law; indeed, the Reagan administration and various branches of the government coordinated efforts to avoid enforcing Title IX. After the 1984 U.S. Supreme Court decision in *Grove City College v. Bell* (described in chapter 3) that Title IX applied only to specific programs or departments receiving federal funds, numerous women's groups immediately began lobbying Congress to pass legislation to restore the civil rights lost in the ruling. Their efforts were successful. In March 1988, Congress overrode President Reagan's veto and passed the Civil Rights Restoration Act. Here was an example of successful political resistance against the dominance of the state.

The State and International Affairs

Contemporary state interests extend far beyond national boundaries. Technological and industrial advances as well as political events of the past century have transformed relations between nations to the point that people of the world are interdependent in unprecedented ways. We live in a world system of interacting and interdependent nations. Since World War II, the dominant features of this world system have been struggle—first, an economic struggle between capitalism and socialism, with each side trying to favorably influence the other as well as "uncommitted" countries, and, second, a geopolitical struggle in which the leading capitalist and the leading socialist countries (the United States and the Soviet Union) have been military adversaries, each fighting to get the advantage. One consequence of these developments is that both the U.S. and the U.S.S.R. engage in ideological work to protect and maintain the hegemonic conditions in their state and to extend their influence worldwide.

From its beginning, there has been what Marx called "an expanding character" to capitalist production, and Wallerstein (1974) has noted that "capitalism as an economic mode is based on the fact that the economic factors operate within an area larger than that which any political entity can totally control" (p. 348). Early merchant capitalism gave way to colonialism, which in turn in the 20th century has given way to post-colonialism, the current era of development of the world capitalist economy. The current period is so called because all the major territories subject to direct colonial rule have won their independence as new nations. The demise of direct colonial rule has been accompanied by a significant development in the nature of international capitalism: the rise of the multinational corporation. This form of capitalist organization has become a leading influence in the world economy. Some social scientists have called multinational corporations "the modern colonial powers."

Multinational corporations are a network of privately owned firms unified by common ownership that have extended their marketing and production into countries outside their origins. Most of the world's multinationals are American in ownership and origin. As with any capitalist firm, the major driving force behind multinationalism is the profit motive.

Multinational corporations bring investment into countries throughout the world, thus stimulating the local economies and linking the economies of the world's nations, laying the groundwork for a world economy. But they also exploit many countries, especially in the Third World, by many of the same methods of colonialism (paying low wages, not training local leadership, exporting local products, and returning profits to the modern country). Regardless of their other effects, multinational corporations are extremely profitable; some exceed in annual net income the gross national product of many countries.

The Soviet Union and other socialist countries explicitly affiliated with Marxism have principally been on the margins of the world economy. By organizing planned economies based on the suppression or strict limitation of privately owned capital, these countries have largely insulated themselves from the trade and commercial relations between capitalist countries and the rest of the world. But the Soviet Union and some Eastern European countries do have strong enough economic ties with the West that they cannot be wholly isolated from factors influencing capitalist economic development.

For capitalism or socialism to grow and prosper worldwide, a congenial climate must be created to encourage other nations to purchase the products and services of these systems. At the same time, capitalist and socialist states attempt to persuade other nations about the viability of their political-economic systems, spending significant state resources on ideologically based activities designed to demonstrate their indisputable superiority.

Analyses of the state have tended to focus on internal political operations or on the state's economic role—as though the state's significant influences in the world system were only domestic politics and the production and exchange of goods. Consequently, the state has often not been perceived as a potential aggressor toward other nations. But the major geopolitical fact since World War II has been the disharmony between the two "superpowers," the United States and the Soviet Union. Although the U.S. emerged from World War II as the most powerful military nation on earth, its advantage was lost within a few years as the Soviet

Union achieved military parity, especially in the form of nuclear weapons. Since the 1950s the two nations have confronted each other throughout the world in what has been called the Cold War. But in place of armed conflict the superpowers have waged a war without weapons in the form of political and diplomatic strategies designed to win support from the world community for their political economic system.

Sport as an Instrument of International Politics and Diplomacy

One of the fastest growing cultural practices throughout the world is organized sports. The unmistakable preoccupation with sports is illustrated by the increasing number of national sport programs, which develop elite athletes for international competition in such events as the Olympic Games, the Pan-American Games, the British Commonwealth Games, the Asian Games, the African Games, and the Third World Games. In all of these events, competition takes place in many different sports. In addition, each sport has its own World Championship competition. The result of this worldwide interest and competition is a large, immensely popular, international sport industry.

Commercialization and professionalization have firmly established themselves permanently in international sport, and competition between athletes representing different nations offers those countries free media publicity. Television has stimulated the incredible interest in the world's sport events and now binds them together. Because access to television is nearly universal, people in every part of the globe can follow the achievements of "their" athletes: Billions of viewers watch World Cup play-offs, Olympic Games, and other international sport events. Sport has assumed significance in linking participants and observers throughout the world. The past 50 years have brought a skyrocketing ascension for sport as an international cultural practice.

The high visibility of international sport events has fostered a favorable climate for state intervention. Countries are increasingly using sport to promote national unity and pride and to reflect the accomplishments of their political-economic systems. Entire books are devoted to the many dimensions of international sport (e.g., Espy, 1981; Redmond, 1986; Shaikin, 1988). I examine here the ways and means by which state intervention is used in the ideological construction of dominant class consensus. My focus will be broader than just American involvement, for such a worldwide phenomenon is more appropriately examined from a wider vantage point. From this framework American actions and policies can then become clearer.

Sport to Advance National Unity

✗ A widespread use of sport on the international level is to assert national prestige and promote a sense of national unity. The United States and other large countries do not have to depend on sport for recognition and respect, but the achievements of their athletes can provide temporary emotional surges of national unity. Anyone who witnessed the 1980 U.S. Olympic hockey team victory over the Soviet Union and the wild flag-waving spectacle that followed can probably recall the outpouring of nationalistic enthusiasm. Similar feelings are engendered on many occasions when athletes from one's own country prevail over those from other nations. Gerald Ford, when he was president of the United States, said,

> A sports triumph can be as uplifting to a nation's spirit as a battlefield victory. . . . If we want to remain competitive, and I think we do, we owe it to ourselves to reassess our priorities, to broaden our base of achievement so that we again present our best in the world's arenas. From a purely political viewpoint, I don't know of anything more beneficial in diplomacy and prestige. (Ford & Underwood, 1974, pp. 17-18)

For the smaller—sometimes new—nations seeking national pride and recognition and respect in the world community, triumphs in international sport competition can serve this purpose well. A relatively unknown country can gain worldwide attention when one of its athletes or teams wins an important event. For a few days at least, a country can bask in the limelight of the world's mass media. Invariably, such achievements become a focus of conversation within a country, and feelings of national pride are enhanced as people sense a common bond among the athletes, themselves, and their nation.

East Germany, perhaps more than any small country, has undertaken a deliberate program to use sport for national promotion. A nation of only 17 million people (about the size of California) placed third in the Summer Olympics in 1972, second in 1976 and 1980, and second in 1988 (with other socialist countries, East Germany did not take part in the 1984 Games).

Canada and Australia are two countries small in population who have undertaken systematic programs to develop elite athletes for international competition. Their governmental actions began as efforts to provide greater opportunities for mass sport and physical fitness, but turned rather quickly toward the promotion of high-performance sport because of its perceived potential for much more attractive political payoffs, especially in unifying nationalist needs (Baka, 1986; MacIntosh, Bedicki, & Franks, 1987). In a recent book describing sport and politics in Canada MacIntosh, Bedicki, and Franks (1987) describe the massive federally funded sports program as an instrument "to promote national unity" (p. 4).

The most populous country in the world, the People's Republic of China, has revised its national sport policy from "friendship first, competition second," once advocated by Mao Tse-tung, to an all-out quest for global recognition and status. China's political and sport officials openly acknowledge that they view sport as one instrument for promoting national pride and identity, which is a primary motivation behind the expenditure of over $300 million annually for sports (Deford, 1988; W.O. Johnson, 1988).

Of course, when chauvinistic sentiment becomes wrapped up in athletic achievements, athletic failures can bring national embarrassment. The poor showing by the U.S. team at the 1988 Calgary Winter Olympics caused hand-wringing among political and sports officials and numerous mass media odes to the national disgrace of the quality of American sport. Even more embarrassing to Canada, though, was the ignominious disclosure that sprinter Ben Johnson, the gold medal winner of the 100-meter dash at the 1988 Seoul Summer Olympics, failed the postrace drug test. One Canadian television announcer described it as "a tragedy for the country and the Canadian Olympic movement." And from a Canadian magazine publisher: "What he achieved . . . gave me a great deal of pride. Now I feel shame" (Jolidon, 1988, p. 7E).

There are certainly those who question pouring money and resources into the training and material welfare of elite athletes for international competition, money and resources that could be used elsewhere. Every country of the world has social problems involving the poor, hungry, homeless, sick, and oppressed. In the U.S., for example, millions of poor and homeless people are in need of basic human necessities, and conditions are much worse in other countries, especially in the Third World. In the face of such reality, American expenditures of an estimated $1 billion per year for promoting national unity through sport raises the specter of distorted priorities. It is possible that national unity could be more appropriately promoted by raising the standard of living of the downtrodden. That would certainly contribute more to the advancement of the human condition and social health than does supplying sports entertainment to the masses, diverting their attention, however briefly, from their government's neglect.

International Dominance Through Sport

Historically, international political dominance has been pursued through military threat (or action), economic embargoes, increased tariffs, or severed diplomatic relations. International sport has become another instrument for political dominance and diplomatic coercion. Because international sport has such high visibility, actions taken against other countries gain worldwide attention. Thus, countries have come to use sport to sanction recalcitrant nations and pressure them into complying with their wishes.

Official Recognition.   When a nation chooses to compete athletically with another, this is interpreted as a recognition of that country and its government. Conversely, refusing to engage in sport events with another country or denying its athletes visas or travel documents has become equivalent to severing diplomatic relations. The history of international sport, especially the Olympic Games, is filled with examples of this tactic. Germany and Austria were denied participation in the 1920 Olympics at Antwerp because of their role in World War I. Germany, Japan, and Italy were banned from the 1948 Olympics because of their actions in World War II. South Africa has been excluded from the Olympic Games since 1964 because of its apartheid policies. Although these actions were all officially taken by the International Olympic Committee, they were endorsed and supported by national governments; indeed, in some cases the actions were taken in direct response to governmental threats of various kinds.

Inviting countries into the world sport community, on the other hand, is a way of showing approval of their policies. Japan's hosting of the 1964 Olympics gave that country a chance to stage the Games while at the same time be welcomed back into the family of nations. Japan could show the world that it was a modern, peace-loving, democratic country and that it had put the legacy of World War II behind it. The 1972 Munich Olympic games did much the same for West Germany, although the Arab terrorist massacre of 11 Israeli athletes destroyed much of the positive image West Germany had hoped to receive from the Games.

Sport has occasionally been used to open channels of diplomatic recognition. The most well-known example of this is the "Ping-Pong diplomacy" carried out by the U.S. and the People's Republic of China in the early 1970s. From 1949, the beginning of the Mao socialist government in China, until 1971 the U.S. government had no diplomatic relations with the P.R.C. By the early 1970s, it had become increasingly clear that this policy needed changing, so President Nixon arranged for groups of American and Chinese table tennis players to play a series of matches. This Ping-Pong diplomacy, as it came to be called, opened channels that ultimately resulted in the renewal of diplomatic relations between the two countries.

Renewed or improved diplomatic relations are the harbinger of expanded economic relations. Multinational corporations are major beneficiaries of expanded international relations because new markets are opened up and capital accumulation is fostered for the products and services of these huge firms. Sport, then, serves to lubricate the international political economy.

Boycotts. The enormous popularity of sport insures that much of the world's population will be aware of the existence, or lack, of sport competitions between particular countries. International athletic contests have thus become a public forum; countries can express disagreement with other countries' policies by refusing to compete with them. Governments have increasingly used the boycott to express political disapproval with other nations' policies. Perhaps the most long-standing and worldwide boycott has been enforced against South Africa for its state system of apartheid. South Africa has been boycotted from the Olympic Games since 1964, and since then almost every major international sport event has denied South Africa participation.

The incidents Americans are undoubtedly most familiar with are the U.S. boycott of the 1980 Moscow Olympic Games because of the Soviet Union's military intervention in Afghanistan and the Soviet Union's retaliation in boycotting the 1984 Los Angeles Games. Although these instances are well known, the boycott has been used frequently by other countries at various times.

Sport in Promoting Political-Economic Systems

Nations have increasingly forged direct propaganda links between sport triumphs and the viability of social systems. In this strategy, sport is an instrument of state policy that ties achievements of the nation's athletes to the country's political-economic system to promote the system's superiority. This has been called *sports diplomacy*, and the athletes used for this purpose have been labeled *diplomats in sweat suits*.

One of the early and blatant examples of sport as a platform for demonstrating political superiority was Adolf Hitler's use of the 1936 Olympic Games "to strengthen his control over the German people and to show-case Nazi culture to the entire world." The Games "were a dazzling charade that reinforced and mobilized the hysterical patriotism of the German masses" (Mandell, 1971, frontispiece). More recently, both capitalist and socialist states have used sport to promote their causes. Riordan (1977), in his well-documented *Sport and Soviet Society*, says that the Soviet government views the successes of its athletes as having "particular political significance. . . . Each new victory is a victory for the Soviet form of society. . . . It provides irrefutable proof of the superiority of socialist culture over the decaying culture of capitalist states" (p. 364). A similar ideological pride is found among Americans. Olympic fencer and modern pentathlete Rob Stull asserted that international sport sets the stage for "system versus system. And I believe we should show them that the capitalist system just beats the living hell out of [the socialist] system" (Woodward, 1988, p. 2C).

In comparison to the Soviet Union, the U.S. government carries out limited direct involvement in sport. This does not mean, however, that our government and its many branches and agencies are not committed to using sport for the advancement of our political-economic system. Indeed, concern about America's international image prompted former president Gerald Ford to create a President's Commission on Olympic Sports. The Commission spent $1 million and took a year and a half to investigate and analyze U.S. elite amateur sport with a view toward helping American athletes perform better in international competition. The Commission's recommendations ("Final Report," 1977) resulted in the Amateur Sports Act of 1978, reorganizing amateur sport and committing the government to a continuing investment in international sport. At the same time, the report strongly recommended that capitalist firms provide the major funding for American sports, suggesting that it was in their interests to promote the American political economy throughout the world.

The massive and growing corporate sponsorship since that time for elite athletes and teams that compete in international sport can be seen as a response to the President's Commission report. It is especially noteworthy that many of the corporations that sponsor sports are multinationals. A number of benefits flow from their investment in sport. First, it supports the ongoing strategy of using sport to promote the American political economy. Second, corporate sponsorship offers companies image enhancement, high visibility, name recognition, and, perhaps, increased sales. As the athletes and teams who are sponsored compete worldwide, the sponsor's name becomes associated with the athletic achievements; thus, assuming that consumer behavior is related to advertising, capital accumulation for the multinational firm is enhanced worldwide.

The extent of the overall financial investment in the American Olympic movement can be seen through the $250 million 1988-1992 quadrennial budget of the U.S. Olympic Committee (which does not include an expected $50 million from the sale of 1988 U.S. Olympic coins). This $250 million will come from many public and private sources: a projected $90 million to $100 million in sponsorships, a projected $60 million from the USOC's television rights for the 1992 Olympic Games, and anticipated federal legislation for an ongoing coin program and tax checkoffs.

Promoting international sport as an instrument of ideological warfare turns out, on close examination, to be also solidly grounded in economics. It integrates the interests of the dominant economic and political nexus and is a particularly good way of stimulating capital accumulation in the gigantic world marketplace, which is driven to innovate new products, services, and industries. Manipulating competition between athletes to make it seem to represent competition between countries stimulates widespread interest in the events and their outcomes.

The enormous industry that has emerged to satisfy the needs of this competition includes building construction, transportation, clothing, sporting equipment, coaching, education, and medicine, and it involves some of the world's largest multinational corporations—all to the end of staging sport competition among athletes from different countries. The major material beneficiaries of this competition, however, are the sport entrepreneurs, managers, and executives who plan and stage the events and who own or manage the ancillary industries.

Summary and Preview

This chapter highlights the partnership between the state, capital, and sport in American society—the political economy of sport. As the state has expanded its intervention into social institutions and cultural practices, once fairly independent of the state, it has become a key link between corporate capitalism and modern organized sport. The state has nurtured and stimulated capital accumulation of sport business while using sport as an instrument of national policy, bolstering and consolidating the state's role in the management and control of American society.

On this foundation, I now take up a more extended analysis of commercialized sports. In chapter 5, the growth of commercialized sport over the past century is described and analyzed. An underlying theme is that with the commercialization of sport, hegemonic features have increasingly come to define and regulate our understandings of what sport is and how it should be played.

CHAPTER 5

Commercialization of Sport

[Cultural practices, such as play, games, and sport] have been vital, indeed necessary, features of human experience from earliest times. What distinguishes their situation in the industrial-capitalist era . . . are the relentless and successful efforts to separate these elemental expressions of human creativity from their group and community origins for the purpose of selling them to those who can pay for them. . . . The common characteristics of cultural products today are the utilization of paid labor, the private appropriation of labor's creative product, and its sale for profit.

Herbert I. Schiller, professor of communication

Demonstrating that contemporary American sport is a massive commercialized enterprise poses little problem. The sport economy has recently been quantified as a portion of the nation's $4.52 trillion gross national product (a figure describing the total value of the country's output and services); according to figures compiled by *Sports inc.* magazine, the gross national sport product was $50 billion in 1987 (Sandomir, 1988). This makes sport the 23rd largest general business enterprise in the United States. Sports directly contribute over 1% of the value of all goods and services produced in the U.S.

Gate receipts alone accounted for $3.1 billion in sport revenues, and the television and radio industries paid over $1.2 billion in rights fees. The professional sport industry, with over 140 major franchises spread throughout the country, is perhaps the most salient aspect of commercialized sport. These franchises are owned by some of America's wealthiest persons, and professional athletes are some of the highest-paid wage earners. Figure 5.1 delineates some of the categories that make up the gross national sport product and their estimated contributions.

The current status of commercial sport needs to be understood as a historical moment; commercial sport is not a cultural universal. It is the

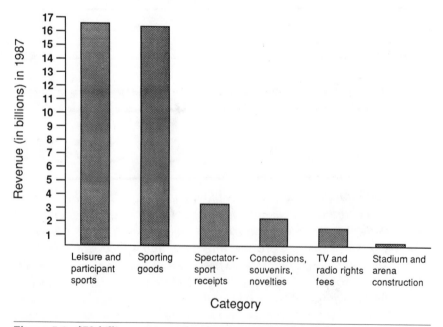

Figure 5.1 $50 billion gross national sport product breakdown. *Note.* Data from Sandomir (1988).

result of social and economic events extending over the past two centuries, and it has evolved hand in hand with the growth of commercialization of modern society. This in turn has occurred as an outgrowth of advances in technology, industrialization, urbanization, a population boom, and development of a capitalist and a wage-earning class.

Forming a historical sensitivity—one component in Mills's (1959) sociological imagination (chapter 1)—can help one grasp just how different sport once was and how dramatic have been its transformations. A historical review can help one to realize that current sport practices and conditions are firmly rooted in events of the past. Readers wishing more extended coverage than can be offered here can find a number of excellent books (e.g., Lucas & Smith, 1978; Rader, 1983; Spears & Swanson, 1988; Vincent, 1981).

The Foundations of Modern Sport

Technological and economic changes since the mid-19th century have transformed the United States from a preindustrial, largely rural population of about 4 million people widely scattered along the Eastern seaboard into a nation with a mostly urban population of 246 million, one of the world's most modern and industrially advanced economies, and one of its most highly commercialized sport industries.

Pre–19th Century

Prior to the 19th century, the overwhelming proportion of America's working population were small, independent farmers, with some skilled artisans and craftsmen, small retail shopkeepers and merchants, and shippers and traders to be found in the scattered towns. During the presidency of George Washington about 80% of white families had property and worked for themselves. Day-to-day economic activities were structured around the regularity of seasons and harvests and bonds of social interdependence. A social aristocracy based on wealth (plantation owners in the South; large landholders, rich merchants, and shippers in the Middle and Northern colonies) occupied the top of the social ladder.

There were no organized participant or spectator sports during this era of American history. Our early settlers had little time or opportunity to engage in sport. Wresting a living from the environment necessitated long and arduous work, and people who did not devote most of their efforts to it could not hope to survive. Moreover, religion was a powerful social institution in the American colonies, and all of the religious groups strictly restricted games and sports, with the Puritans in New

England being the most extreme. Attacks were directed at almost every form of amusement: dancing for its carnality; rough-and-tumble ball games for their violence; maypoles for their paganism; and sports in general because they were often played on the Sabbath. Honest labor was considered the greatest service to God and a moral duty; any form of play or amusement took on the badge of time-wasting and idleness and was therefore defined as a vice. Lucas and Smith (1978) in their *Saga of American Sport* explained: "That everyone should have a calling and work hard at it was a first premise of Puritanism. . . . Not leisure and enjoyment but activity only served to increase the glory of God" (p. 8).

Religious and legal strictures failed to eliminate the inclination to play, however, and indeed during the latter 18th century the harsh religious attitude toward sport "was muted with the decline of Puritanism, the economic growth of the colonies, and the more secular and liberal spirit of the age" (Adelman, 1986, p. 269). Although frequently done in defiance of local laws, people participated in games and sports for fun, sociability, and relaxation; horse racing, shooting matches, cockfights, footraces, and wrestling matches were popular throughout the colonies to break the monotony of life. They were local, unorganized, and subject to the natural rhythms of the seasons (Rader, 1983). Other common recreations were those associated with the taverns. The tavern was a social center, primarily for drinking but also for all manner of popular pastimes, such as cards, billiards, bowling, and rifle and pistol shooting.

On the frontier, religious strictures against sport were not very effective, and the frontiersmen enjoyed a variety of competitive events when they met at barbecues and camp meetings. They gambled on horse races, cockfights, and bearbaiting. The sports and games that marked these infrequent social gatherings were often rough and brutal.

The 19th Century

A series of technological inventions in England during the late 18th century made possible large-scale manufacturing and began to transform the lives of Americans during the first decades of the 19th century. These inventions made possible the use of machines, large-scale production, and, gradually, business consolidation. They also ushered in two of the most significant developments in human history—industrialization and urbanization.

The industrial revolution, which began in England in 1760 and then spread to the United States, involved a fundamental change in the system of production, changing human labor in important ways: First, employers organized the work process into an extensive division of labor, separating the making of a product into simpler and simpler tasks that could be learned quickly and performed at higher speeds; second, work operations that once were performed by human hands increasingly were performed by machines; and third, vast amounts of nonhuman power were used to drive machinery. These changes, and others, greatly increased the control that the owner of a productive enterprise could exercise over workers.

The major characteristics and social consequences were that a capitalist mode of production grew in prominence and a factory system was developed and quickly expanded. The initial impact of the industrial revolution was on the textile industry. Spinning thread and weaving cloth had traditionally been done at home on spinning wheels and hand looms, but these tasks could suddenly be done in factories by power-driven machinery. By 1820, the Lowell loom had been developed, making it possible to spin and weave cotton in the same factory. The sewing machine of Elias Howe revolutionized the making of clothes, shoes, and various leather goods.

Other industries quickly emerged. The successful smelting of iron with the aid of anthracite coal was perfected about 1830; by 1850 improved methods of making steel had been developed. Steel production became the harbinger of industrial development because the machinery for factories was made primarily from steel. Moreover, the rapidly growing railroad system depended on steel for track and for railcars. Beaud (1983) explained that "with water power and steam engines, which allowed mechanization to reach its full potential for productive output, and employment of a plentiful, cheap, and totally disarmed labor force, levels of production increased dramatically" (p. 84).

By the mid-19th century a growing, flourishing industrial capitalism existed in the Northeast. A rural society based on plantation slavery and cotton production characterized the South, and a society of farming, ranching, and mining spread out into the West. Both the South and West contributed raw materials and other necessities to keep industrialization expanding.

Industry needed a plentiful supply of labor near plants and factories, so population shifts from rural to urban areas began to change our demographics. In the first U.S. census (taken in 1790), about 6% of the population was classified as urban; by 1850 some 23% were urban, and by 1900, 35%.

The gathering storm of dissension over slavery in the South eventually erupted into civil war in 1861. The stimulus the war gave to manufacturing and industrial expansion served as the economic basis for subsequent rapid advances in industrialization and urbanization during the latter 19th century. Before 1860, U.S. industry was largely concentrated in New England and the mid-Atlantic states, but after the Civil War industrialization and manufacturing spread to all parts of the country. Especially noteworthy was the movement of industry westward. Now industries were created: The meat-packing industry developed in Chicago and Kansas City, while in the Plains States raising cattle and producing farm crops became prominent.

Developments in one field stimulated changes and growth in others. As noted, the steel industry was enhanced by the expanding railroad network that used steel rails for the lines being built in the West. Railroads, in turn, were stimulated by the need of the steel industry for iron ore, coal, and other materials that had to be transported by rail to the factories. Between 1869 and 1873—just 4 years—the length of completed railroad lines increased by 50%. Railroad development encouraged the westward movement, and new and fertile areas of the West produced farm crops and cattle that required transporting to markets, further stimulating railroad building. Simultaneously, industry produced the farm machinery that made it possible to raise more crops. Finally, the new methods of communication promoted the growth of all kinds of businesses and were in turn stimulated by that growth.

As technology increased the means of industrial production, more and more people gave up farming and came to the cities to work in the proliferating factories and offices. They were joined by a seemingly endless stream of immigrants who sought a better life in North America. Factories multiplied, and towns and cities grew rapidly. Chicago's population tripled between 1880 and 1900, as did Boston's—from 177,840 to 560,892— between 1860 and 1900. From 1860 to 1910, the number of American cities with populations over 100,000 increased from 9 to 50. New forms of social, economic, political, and intellectual organization evolved from these trends.

By the 1890s, corporations produced nearly three fourths of the total value of manufactured products in the United States. The large corporations were able to develop mass-production methods and mass sales, the bases of big business, because of the huge amounts of money that they controlled. Consequently they were able to drive out small businesses and acquire control over production and the price of goods and services in particular fields. For example, by 1880, the Standard Oil Company controlled 90% of the country's petroleum business. When the U.S. Steel Corporation was founded near the turn of the century, it controlled some 60% of the iron and steel production of the nation—from mining the ore to distributing the finished products (Edwards, 1979). In the 20th century, the corporate form of business has expanded and extended into virtually every form of goods and service operation. As of 1989, 91% of total sales receipts of American businesses were from corporations.

Capitalism and Social Relations of Production.   Any discussion of the industrial revolution is incomplete without considering the major social class configurations that arose from it, namely an industrial capitalist class and an industrial working class. During the first half of the 19th century, factories were small, and the most common forms of business organization were the partnership (two or more owners) and the proprietorship (a single owner). But as the factory system took root, an industrial capitalist class began to emerge, eclipsing former business configurations. Labor power to run the factories and carry out the semiskilled and manual tasks that kept industries growing was supplied by wage workers, who became the backbone of the modern working class.

The American capitalist class had its origins in the landed gentry, merchants, shipowners, and moneylenders who dominated commerce during the colonial era and the first few decades of the 1800s. During the Civil War and in its aftermath, a new generation of capitalists formed and asserted themselves. They built the framework for monopolistic control of the economy and became a powerful influence over cultural practices, a development that has characterized American capitalism since. In the 1880s Andrew Carnegie gained control of the steel industry, until it was acquired by J.P. Morgan in 1901 and organized as the United States Steel Company, further consolidating control. Cornelius Vanderbilt, the railroad magnate, secured a monopoly of the railroads. John D. Rockefeller formed the Standard Oil Company of Ohio in 1870 and by 1878 "controlled 90 percent of the American refineries, and by 1904 controlled 85 percent of the domestic business and 90 percent of the export business as well" (Beaud, 1983, pp. 136-137). These represent only a few of the most noted of the expanding wealthy and powerful capitalist class of this era.

Growth of corporate monopolies in the 1880s and 1890s gradually wiped out large sectors of independent business. By the early 20th century competitive struggle between small businesses and the ruthless and powerful monopoly capitalists reduced the number of firms in virtually every industry to a relative handful. By 1900, large percentages of American businesses were represented by the huge corporations, called trusts (see Figure 5.2).

At the beginning of the 19th century over 90% of the population was economically independent (self-employed). Before the 1840s most manufactured goods were produced in the home or by individual artisans and craftspersons paced by the natural rhythms of seasons and their own motivation, but 50 years later most manufactured production was done in factories under a specified production schedule. A major consequence of this change was the requirement of long hours—60- to 70-hour work weeks were not unusual—under harsh conditions as owners strove to best the competition in the various expanding commodity markets. (Remember, a commodity is something whose value is defined in monetary terms; in commodity production, goods and services are produced to be sold.)

Another consequence was that workers became divided into a mass of relatively unskilled manual laborers or machine operators; many artisans and craftspersons were transformed into an industrial, wage-labor

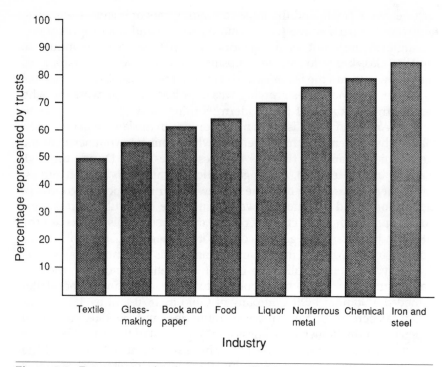

Figure 5.2 Percentages of industries controlled by trusts in 1900.

work force under the direction of capitalist ownership. Wage labor increasingly became the central life activity of the new industrial worker.

The introduction of machinery housed in factories meant that workers had to be employed by owners of the productive forces and brought to the factories to carry out the work. Many farmers and their families left the farms to work in the factories and city businesses that were being created. As Beaud (1983) noted, "Industrial development inaugurated and then accentuated the end of a millennia of primarily agricultural production in overwhelmingly rural societies" (p. 85). The proportion of the labor force engaged in wage labor steadily increased from approximately 20% in 1840 to 52% in 1870 and 72% in 1910 (Gordon, Edwards, & Reich, 1982).

As industrial capitalism gained strength, its overriding logic took shape: private ownership of the means of production, profit maximization, market competition, and a minimum of state intervention. In this system capitalists were the owners of the means of production, and they used their capital to buy commodities in the market and sell them for profit; the underlying purpose behind this system was, of course, capital accumulation. Industrial capitalist enterprises were (and still are) sustained by workers with no material goods, only their labor power, to sell.

Their labor, in effect, became a commodity that they sold to capitalists to get money to live.

From the beginnings of industrial organization, workers labored under the direction, supervision, and control of capitalists. Directions and orders in the production process were communicated to workers from above. There was a hierarchical organization between those who had power (the capitalists) and those who did not (the workers); Karl Marx, an astute analyst of the 19th century industrial workplace, described this relationship as the despotism of the workplace. Capitalists held power over workers because they had purchased the right to dispose of the workers' ability to perform labor. Workers had no property rights in the production of whatever resulted from their activity. They were only a means to an end—the growth of capital (Lebowitz, 1988). Alt (1976) articulately elaborates on the capitalist-worker relationship:

> The historical significance of industrial capitalism was that it transformed social relationships into relationships mediated by exchange. Labor and its products thus took the form of commodities: things whose value was defined in monetary terms reflecting market processes and class relations. (p. 57)

Industrial laborers, Beaud (1983) has related,

> were employed with the intention of extracting the maximum, and it was in conditions of misery and unbearable oppression that the original core of the modern working class was formed. This movement was an extension of what had begun in England during the previous century, but with a definite acceleration [in the U.S. after 1860]. (p. 83)

The development of industrial capitalism ensured as priorities the economic, the instrumental, and the technical to the point that it involved every aspect of social institutional patterns and cultural practices (Giddens, 1987).

Sport in the 19th Century.   In the first few decades of the 19th century, Americans enjoyed essentially the same recreation and sports as they had during the colonial period. But industrial expansion necessitated dramatic changes in daily life as the working class accommodated to factory exigencies, the long work day, and urban living. The city's growing number of sedentary workers and the conditions of urban life became prominent concerns of the press, medical practitioners, and educators. Also, drinking and debauchery among the expanding urban working class were viewed as socially disruptive and detrimental to job performance by factory owners and business employers. Thus, the dominant class sought to discourage such behavior.

It became increasingly obvious that industrialization and urbanization were creating needs for new forms of leisure activity. As conditions changed from a rural to an urban population and from home trades and individualized occupations to large-scale industrial production, there was neither the space nor the opportunity to engage in traditional forms of leisure. Urban dwellers, especially the working class, progressively turned to watching sports for entertainment, especially horse racing, rowing, prizefighting, footracing, and similar activities. The occasional, informal, and social community form of sport participation diminished as highly organized commercial spectator sports became the structural and cultural principle in the period after the Civil War, setting the stage for revolutionary developments in leisure pursuits, mass popular sport, and professional sport.

By the latter three decades of the 19th century an orchestration of expanding industrialization and urbanization, enhanced by the revolutionary transformations in communication, transportation, and other technological advances, provided the framework for the rise of commercial sport. No transformation in the recreational and sport scene was more startling than the sudden burgeoning of organized sports, which, according to Spears and Swanson (1988), diffused "from the wealthy and upper class outward to the upper-middle, the middle, and also the working class" (p. 152). Increasingly concentrated city living and monotonous and wearisome repetition of factory and other industrial work created a demand for more sport and recreational outlets. In accounting for the rise of organized sports, Betts (1974) argued that "urbanization brought forth the need for commercialized spectator sports, while industrialization gradually provided the standard of living and leisure time so vital to the support of all forms of recreation" (p. 232).

In addition to the long-standing interest in horse racing, yachting, and prizefighting, new sports gained popularity. Lawn tennis, croquet, golf, and polo were pioneered by the wealthy as games for "polite society." But none of these sports grew as rapidly as baseball and American football. From an informal children's game in the early 18th century, baseball developed codified rules in the 1840s, and groups of upper-class men organized clubs, taking care to keep out those of the lower social class. The Civil War tended to wipe out this upper-class patronage of the game, and a broad base of popularity existed in 1869 when the first professional baseball team was formed. This was followed in 1876 by the organization of the first major league, and baseball became firmly entrenched as a popular spectator sport—indeed, the national pastime—by the end of the century (Rader, 1983).

Intercollegiate athletics began in 1852 with a rowing match between Harvard and Yale, but it was not until the 1870s and 1880s that intercollegiate sports became an established part of higher education and contributed to the enthusiasm for athletic and sporting diversions. During this era, football was a sport for the upper classes rather than for the masses, because it largely reflected the interests of the college crowd; nevertheless, the sport developed into a national one by 1900 (Smith, 1988).

Towns and cities were natural centers for organizing sports. Betts (1974) noted, "Millionaires who ventured into yachting, office girls and young ladies of leisure who turned to cycling, and prizefighting enthusiasts who backed their favorite challengers were largely from the town or city." He went on to summarize the influence of the city: "Urban areas encouraged sport through better transportation facilities, a growing leisure class, a higher standard of living, more available funds for purchase of sporting goods, and the greater ease with which leagues and teams could be organized" (p. 172). The popular sport of horse racing centered in New York, Charleston, Louisville, and New Orleans, while the first organized baseball clubs were founded in such communities as New York, Boston, Chicago, St. Louis, and Toronto. Yachting and rowing regattas, footraces, billiard matches, and even the main agricultural fairs were held in or near the larger cities.

One of the ways city dwellers replaced some of the traditional social functions of the village community and the church was through voluntary associations, in which they could interact and form friendships with people of common interests. Rader (1977) explained that "sports clubs, as one type of voluntary association, became one of the basic means by which certain groups sought to establish subcommunities within the larger society. . . . [And they] provided a tremendous impetus to the growth of American sport" (pp. 356-357). Some of these urban sport clubs were founded and patronized by ethnic groups—the Scottish Caledonian clubs and the German Turner societies are examples—and others were organized on the basis of social status and patronized by the wealthy commercial, professional, and social elite. These latter clubs were the predecessors of country clubs, which began to flourish in the early 1900s. Although clubs were overwhelmingly dominated by men, they were on the forefront of providing expanded sport opportunities for women. It was, of course, a very restricted menu of sports—golf, tennis, archery, croquet.

One major purpose of the metropolitan sport clubs was social rather than competitive, but during the late 19th and early 20th centuries they became key in dominating amateur agencies. The Amateur Athletic Union (AAU) and the U.S. Olympic movement were both primarily under the sponsorship of socially elite members of sport clubs.

Opportunities for participatory sport and leisure for the growing urban working class were restricted in several ways. Space was at a premium; city building closed off open play areas at an alarming pace. Work weeks of 50 to 60 hours left little time for physical recreation.

Ideological discourse by religious and capitalist leaders often promoted a hostility toward the concept of free time and disparaged sport and playful activities for the working class. Local laws often prevented the playing of sports at certain times.

Mass production of goods and corporate organization developed in sport just as in other industries. The first major sporting goods corporation was formed by Albert G. Spalding, a former pitcher for the Boston and Chicago baseball clubs, in 1876. Beginning with baseball equipment, he branched out into various sports, and by the end of the century the A.G. Spalding and Brothers Company had a virtual monopoly in athletic goods. Spalding was "the monarch of the business in the late years of the century" (Betts, 1974, p. 205). Department stores began carrying sporting goods on a large scale in the early 1880s, led by Macy's of New York City. Sears, Roebuck devoted 80 pages of its 1895 catalog to sporting equipment.

The Cult of Manliness and Women in Sport.   Along with the social and occupational changes of the 19th century arose a concern about the impact of modernization on male roles and behavior. Rapid change was altering institutions of socialization and drastically eroding traditional male roles and responsibilities. Writers, educators, and influential national leaders expressed fear that men were losing "masculine" traits like courage, ruggedness, and hardiness to effeminacy. There was even concern about the future of the nation if men lost their traditional characteristics. A host of organizations—the Boy Scouts, YMCAs, and athletic clubs—were created to promote a broadly based devotion to manly ideals, to toughen up boys for life's ordeals.

Within this context, sport, with its demands for individual competition and physical challenge, was promoted as an important proving ground for manhood. As towns and cities spread over the continent, sport blossomed as an escape hatch from effete civilization, a kind of sanctuary from the world of female gentility; it catered to men who felt a need to certify their manhood. Involvement in sports became a principal source for male identity and a primary basis for gender division.

The cult of manliness became widely pervasive in the upper and middle classes and rapidly trickled down to working-class social life. According to Adelman (1986),

> The frequency with which writers began to assert that sport could serve as a means of promoting manliness was in direct response to both the impact of modernization on urban society and the role of modernization in redefining the masculine role and creating a new middle-class view of proper sexual behavior. (p. 283)

Defining sport as an inculcator of manliness had the obvious effect of excluding women from all but a few sports, and those only when done in moderation. Although women were encouraged to participate in recreational sports for health reasons, they were given no rationale for competing with one another. Indeed, women who wished to participate in competitive sports and remain "feminine" faced almost certain social isolation and censure. "Since competitive sport was a place were manhood was earned, women had nothing to gain and everything to lose by trying to join in" (Adelman, 1986, p. 286).

Of course, it was not just the cult of manliness that discouraged female involvement in sport. Responsibility for domestic labor and child rearing weighed heavily against women's engaging in sport as either participants or spectators. Victorian attitudes and religious moral codes also militated against sport for women. The net effect of all these influences on the concept of femininity was to demand docility, domesticity, and subordination of women.

In spite of these obstacles, upper class and college women were often ardent participants in croquet, archery, lawn tennis, rowing, and bicycling. In fact, the bicycle was an important agent of social change, revolutionizing lifestyles for women, especially middle class women, who were denied by social status, money, and lack of leisure time participation in most physical recreation. It was one of the most significant factors in liberating attitudes of women and men toward the capabilities and needs of females. In order to comfortably ride bicycles, women were allowed to experiment with shorter skirts or some type of "bloomer" costume—both very daring for that period—which gave them a new sense of freedom. Bicycling also gave young women opportunities to escape everpresent parents or chaperones and to test independent social relationships (Spears & Swanson, 1988).

The 20th Century

Enormous, multifaceted changes have taken place at a bewildering pace in America during the 20th century, changes greater than in any other period in human history. Scientific discoveries and the new technologies they spawned have been appropriated by business interests to build new industries and reorganize old ones, especially in transportation, communication, and electronics. These industries and others, which have done much to shape 20th century society, have been the offspring of the marriage of science and technology to the business world. They have been fundamental to what has been called the "scientific-technical revolution" by some and the "second industrial revolution" by others (Edsforth, 1987). Regardless of the name, they are fundamental to the social, economic, and cultural trends of the 20th century.

As important as the steam engine was to improving transportation and stimulating industrialization, its impact on the social life and transportation habits of Americans was slight compared to that of the internal combustion engine. This invention made possible the automobile and the airplane, modes of transportation that completely revolutionized travel and numerous other aspects of American life. The automobile and airplane created totally new industries, involving billions of dollars of annual capital and employing millions of workers. Together they spawned the growth of many ancillary industries (including oil, rubber, and steel) and occupations. Garages, filling stations, hotels, airports, and numerous highway businesses are a few of the myriad by-products of the motor age.

The automobile also changed social habits; cities were expanded by suburbs, allowing people to live away from commercial and manufacturing centers of the city, and the automobile gave them greater opportunity for personal travel. The airplane has become the most common means of long-distance transportation. Air travel has in effect shrunk our world.

Improvements in communication kept pace with developments in transportation. The telegraph and telephone, inventions of the 19th century, were supplemented by radio and then television. Commercial radio broadcasting began in 1920, and by 1940 broadcasting companies claimed that 98% of American homes had at least one radio. The television boom occurred in the early 1950s; by the mid-1960s TV sets were a fixture in over 90% of American homes.

The electronics industry has been another revolutionizing force in the 20th century. Electricity turns the wheels of industry; without it the gigantic increases in industrial output would be impossible. Electricity lights up everything from homes to billboards, and it has led to the production of countless new manufactured products, many of them labor-saving ones.

Entrepreneurial capitalism was overshadowed by monopoly capitalism in the latter 19th and early 20th centuries. The first was characterized by ownership of business by an individual or partnership who organized and managed the enterprise; the second took the form of control by a few corporations of entire industries or markets, such as steel production. In the corporate model, the functions of ownership and management tended to be separated, and the primary agents of capital accumulation became salaried managers who replaced the self-made entrepreneurs. The transformation toward monopoly capitalist organization brought a wave of capitalist expansion that is still going strong.

Before 1860 American industry was largely concentrated in New England and the mid-Atlantic states, but by 1900 industrialization and manufacturing spread out to all parts of the country, and the U.S. had become the world's leading industrial nation. Large corporations expanded and extended into virtually every form of goods and service operation. These megacorporations were able to develop mass-production methods, mass merchandising, and mass sales because of the huge amounts of money they controlled.

The second industrial revolution shaped our economic system so that greater and greater concentrations of economic wealth and power are being held by fewer and fewer capitalist enterprises. Influence by one corporation (monopoly) or several (oligopoly) became the dominant form of market organization as older industries modernized and new industries grew. In the 1980s, the largest corporations had assets of 50 to 100 *billion* dollars, more than the gross national product of most countries of the world (Szymanski, 1983). In 1989, the 100 largest industrial corporations, out of over 200,000, controlled over 60% of the total assets held by all the corporations, an increase from 39.8% in 1950 (see Figure 5.3).

The decisions of the megacorporations influence prices, unemployment, prosperity, and the very character of the work and occupational structure in the U.S. Although the megacorporations operate in a competitive capitalistic infrastructure, they monopolize their industries and are able to monopolize supply; through their large-scale advertising and other sophisticated marketing techniques, they create consumer demands for their goods and services. Small businesses are often driven out of the market.

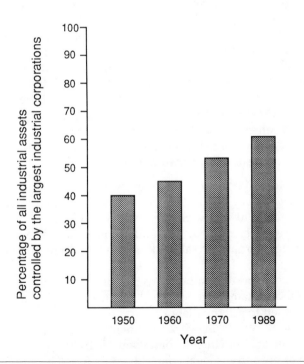

Figure 5.3 The percentage of all industrial assets controlled by the nation's largest industrial corporations continues to rise rapidly.

As developments in the economic sector led to further needs for workers and further centralization of production, this in turn led to further urban development. In 1890 about 35% of the population lived in cities or towns; by 1989 the proportion had grown to around 78%. Modern cities have a different social texture from preindustrial towns and cities, which were more of a collection of neighborhoods than industrial labor markets. Modern cities tend to be places to live in order to find work rather than places to live one's life; a sense of community, though present in varying degrees, tends to have lost importance (Ingham, Howell, & Schilperoort, 1987).

A second economic mutation of the second industrial revolution has been the advent of a national consumer-goods market. The combination of cheap raw materials, cheap energy, cheap labor, and mass production methods has enabled capitalist enterprises to keep prices relatively low and still make good profits. Thus millions of Americans can afford automobiles, radios, refrigerators, television sets, and hundreds of other consumer items. Of course, unless millions of consumers keep buying, these products cannot be made in great quantities, be sold at such low prices, or bring in such attractive profits. To hold and extend their markets, companies spend tremendous sums on nationwide advertising and skillful sales techniques. Installment buying—buying out of future income—has been widely encouraged.

Because the domestic market has been unable to absorb the endless stream of products, corporations have gone after foreign markets as well. Throughout the world people have been eager to buy American products. International trade has become vital to American industry, and multinational corporations have been established to control these expanding markets. This dependence on the mass consumption of goods and services by both consumers and producers (who are actually workers who in turn become consumers) has become a way of life that has spawned what social scientists call a consumer culture.

The 20th-Century Work Force. Occupational trends that began under entrepreneurial capitalism in the 1800s have continued. Whereas early in the 19th century 10% of working people were employed (meaning that over 90% were self-employed), presently some 90% of the working population are wage earners or salaried employees, increasingly in service occupations.

The average worker is rather powerless in the occupational structure. Workers without material goods to sell or the material means of producing goods are left to sell their labor power, their ability to work. This system of relations results in workers' having no property rights in the product that results from their labor (Lebowitz, 1988). Inherent in capitalist ownership of property is legal control over its use. The employee faces, Steinberg (1982) says, "inequality in the labor market armed only with a set of legal rights more appropriate to a preindustrial society in which work was carried out by independent entrepreneurs and skilled craftsmen" (p. 4). We have a political democracy but an economic dictatorship. As Carnoy and Shearer (1980) have observed, "The work place [is] governed by the laws of private property, not the Bill of Rights" (p. 12).

The systematic adoption of rationalization in the workplace is another outgrowth of the second industrial revolution. The early social processes of labor, emphasizing kinship, family patterns, and personal relationships, have been gradually transformed by a highly structured bureaucratic approach to production, emphasizing specialization within the division of labor, rigid control by management, and a socially private existence mediated by consumerism. As part of a program of economic hegemony, industrial capitalists reorganized the workplace according to the principles of what was called "scientific management," with far-reaching social and economic implications for workers. The scientific management movement, which emerged from the studies and writings of Frederick Taylor, was based on cost efficiency in the productive process. The mass production assembly line exemplifies the Taylorist approach to production.

Taylor believed that an organization could reach its production goals only by achieving an optimal cost-efficiency ratio. The resulting system of management treated workers as a tool, assuming that they would cooperate and work only when forced to do so. Workers were reduced to an instrument of the organization, functioning under a hierarchical authority relationship. Relations between managers and workers were closed and inflexible; there was little opportunity for change initiated by the workers (Edsforth, 1987). Alt (1976) argued that "the combined result of these processes is the cultural devaluation of the role of labor as the determinant of class experience and the subsequent valuation of consumerism as a major mechanism for shaping consciousness and reproducing capitalist hegemony" (p. 69).

In other words, the 20th-century transition to a monopoly capitalist society has moved the source of social relations, culture, and ideology from a class culture of work to a mass culture of consumerism. For most American workers, working in capitalist hierarchies is alienating—workers feel powerless and isolated from products they make—but one's occupation is perceived as the way to support one's lifestyle outside of work. Workers have accepted the dominant capitalist norms because the domain for self-expression and pleasure has come to be away-from-work activities and consumerism rather than occupation.

Sport in the 20th Century.   The prosperous years before World War I and the tumultuous 1920s were especially important periods in the rise of commercial sport. The growth of the city and the rising standard of living were important social forces that combined with numerous other conditions to promote the expansion of organized sport at an unprecedented rate. Shorter working hours and higher wages resulted in discretionary time and money for leisure activity, one form of which was sport.

Commercial spectator sport became one of the most engrossing of all social interests. By the 1920s, it was a bandwagon around which rallied students and alumni, business and transportation interests, advertising and amusement industries, and the mass media. The '20s are still looked upon by some as sport's golden age. A number of America's most famous athletes were at the height of their careers during those years: Babe Ruth, the "Sultan of Swat," in baseball; Knute Rockne and the "Four Horsemen of Notre Dame" in college football; Jack Dempsey, "The Manassa Mauler," heavyweight boxing champion; Bill Tilden and Helen Wills Moody in tennis; and Bobby Jones and Glenna Collett in golf.

The contours and meanings of commercialized sport were quite different for men and for women. Although there were progressive changes in attitudes toward female involvement in sport and physical recreation in the first 2 decades of the 20th century, the dominant viewpoints about the female body had not changed dramatically. In the 1920s American women slowly pushed into competitive sports; some became noted in such arenas as tennis, golf, ice skating, and swimming. The presence of women in the Olympics became acceptable.

The emergence of competitive female athletes represented a changing conception of women's bodies. But, as Stephanie Twin (1979) argued,

This growing awareness of women's physical potential had, significantly, another dimension. The female form was becoming a marketable item, used to sell numerous products and services. . . . The commercialization of women's bodies provided a cultural opening for competitive athletics, as an industry and ambitious individuals used women to sell sports. (p. xxix)

The female athlete was being used—reflecting traditional patriarchal stereotypes of women as sex objects—as yet another tool for the generation of capital accumulation rather than being accepted for her athletic achievements. Nevertheless, although women's physical marketability did profit commercial markets, the opportunity for women to compete in a range of sports created a limited means of liberation through an expanded use of their bodies.

Contemporary Sport as a Commodity

From the 1920s onward, commercial sport has been pervasive in American society, penetrating every sphere of social life and becoming one of the most popular cultural practices. Two major trends have characterized recent commercial sport development: the phenomenal expansion of amateur and professional spectator sports and the boom in participatory sports.

Youth sport, high school, and college programs are the backbone of amateur sport. Although these programs are all classified as amateur, they are closely tied to the spread and penetration of capital production, and they have grown at an astounding pace in recent years. Baseball and football were once about the only sports sponsored for youngsters, but there are now over 25 organized youth sport programs—from swimming to motorcycling—and it is possible for children as young as 6 to win national championships. And high school and collegiate programs once limited to a handful of sports for males only have expanded to 12 to 15 sports for both males and females.

The professional sport industry has been a growth industry in recent decades. Indeed, professional sport has such a dominating presence in America that I devote an entire chapter (chapter 7) to it.

Participatory sport, the second major trend of the past generation, has been the product of increased leisure and income and of a concerned awareness about sedentary lifestyles and related health problems. One national poll reported that approximately 7 in 10 American adults engage in some form of exercise or sport each week (Miller Lite Report, 1983). It is estimated that in one year 72 million persons swim, almost 23 million play golf, 12 million water ski, and 14 million ski downhill; bicyclers far outnumber all but swimmers. Other sports have their devotees as well. Perhaps most remarkable is the running boom that has swept the nation since the early 1970s (U.S. Bureau of the Census, 1989).

The growth of sport participation is also closely linked to the commodity world of goods and services. Equipment, facilities, and sundry services are provided for participants by sport industries as diverse as sporting goods manufacturers and conditioning spas. Participatory sports have been penetrated by diverse and aggressive businesses whose primary goal is selling their products and generating profits, and they have been successful. Some $16.4 *billion* is spent annually in leisure and participant sports (Sandomir, 1988). This commercialization of participatory sport is one aspect of the wider consumer culture, structured in accordance with the priorities of the interests that own and control it.

The rise of a monopoly capital society, with its concentration of power, wealth, and influence in corporate giants that not only dominate economic life in their incessant search for markets and profits but also dominate personal social relations, has transformed sport and mass informal leisure into a huge, commodified industry that more and more dominates the everyday life of the average American. Sociologist T.R. Young (1986) captures the essence of this trend: ''The most significant structural change in modern sports is the gradual and continuing commodification of sports. This means that the social, psychological, physical, and cultural uses of sport are assimilated to the commercial needs of advanced monopoly capital" (p. 12). Leisure time has left most people dependent on the marketplace as a source of gratification, providing increased incentive for the full-scale commodification of sports. Working people are enjoined to purchase much of their sport and leisure involvement with their own wages. The commodification of sport and other leisure activities, as Adorno (1975) has noted, "transfers the profit motive naked onto cultural forms" (p. 13).

One can study the connection between commodification and sport in several ways: The two I will examine are

- the dimensions of the commodified sport industry and
- the meanings and ethos (values, ways of thinking) of sport as a commodity.

The Dimensions of the Commodified Sport Industry

The industry of commodified sport has multiplied into a variety of organizations and occupations. The major categories that I will describe will provide you with a basic understanding of the multifaceted nature of the phenomenon.

First, a significant portion of the sporting industry is organized as profit-maximizing enterprises. Here, capital investors own, organize, and control a business with a goal toward capital accumulation. An example of this is the professional sport industry, composed of owners, athletes, coaches, and ancillary workers.

A second form of sport is organized with all of the trappings of commercialism but does not function strictly for profit; the objective is to balance the books so as to seem to be breaking even. Examples of this are high school and intercollegiate athletic programs and some elite amateur programs. In order to maintain a nonprofit status with the Internal Revenue Service, these programs must give the appearance—in their accounting practices—of not making a profit. In reality, many members of these organizations profit handsomely.

Third, commercial sport creates a market for associated goods and services, so numerous businesses accumulate capital indirectly by providing those goods and services. Some examples of this are the sporting goods industry (mostly manufacturers and retailers), the sport component of the mass media (including television, newspapers, and magazines), businesses that benefit from sport events (hotels, airlines, restaurants), and advertisers (those buying sport advertising or sponsoring events). A less-clear example is gambling; although one's immediate response may be that gambling and sport are unrelated, this is wrong.

Some $2.8 billion is legally wagered annually on sporting events, and it is estimated that illegal wagers exceed $50 billion.

The Meanings and Ethos of Sport as a Commodity

The commercial sport industry seeks to organize events on strict market principles—namely, the pursuit of capital accumulation—rather than the satisfaction of individual personal and social needs. Although the industry goes to great lengths in advertising and public relations to make the public think it is nurturing play forms and traditional values, it actually has little to do with the human play impulse and traditional conceptions of personal development, family, and community. Recreation expert Richard Kraus (1988) recently noted that "the continued growth of spectator sports, involving the buying and selling of athletes, and of franchises, have undercut much of the genuine meaning behind athletics as a form of recreation or entertainment" (p. 86). Braverman's (1974) observations about how monopoly capitalism has transformed all social practices into a huge marketplace illuminate Kraus's observations. Braverman said this:

In a society where labor power is purchased and sold, working time becomes sharply and antagonistically divided from nonworking time, and the worker places an extraordinary value upon this "free time," while on-the-job time is regarded as lost or wasted. Work ceases to be a natural function and becomes an extorted activity, and the antagonism to it expresses itself in a drive for the shortening of hours on the one side, and the popularity of labor-saving devices for the home, which the market hastens to supply, on the other. But the atrophy of community and the sharp division from the natural environment leaves a void when it comes to the "free" hours. Thus the filling of the time away from the job also becomes dependent upon the market, which develops to an enormous degree those passive amusements, entertainments, and spectacles that suit the restricted circumstances of the city and are offered as substitutes for life itself. Since they become the means of filling all the hours of "free" time, they flow profusely from corporate institutions which have transformed every means of entertainment and "sport" into a production process for the enlargement of capital. . . . So enterprising is capital that even where the effort is made by one or another section of the population to find a way to nurture sport . . . through personal activity . . . these activities are rapidly incorporated into the market so far as is possible. (pp. 278-279)

There is compelling historical evidence that as human practices undergo changes in form and content, they inevitably experience transformations in meaning, and this has certainly been the case with modern leisure and sport. Alt (1976) observed that "one of the great cultural transformations of the twentieth century is the disappearance of traditional forms of industrial working class leisure and the emergence of socially-privatized leisure related to the products of the consumer industries" (p. 74). Playful activities emphasizing autonomous and nonutilitarian values in sport have been increasingly incorporated into the instrumental culture of capitalism. Social relations of sport and leisure have become grounded in relations of capital domination, with individuals cast in the role of consumers by businesses that shape them to promote their own interests. A survey of the leisure activities of suburbanites concluded that "leisure and recreation are indeed to a large extent coming to be regarded as commodities to be purchased rather than as experiences to be lived" (Alt, 1976, p. 75).

Even when people do pursue active leisure they cannot break free of the values of the hegemonic culture. Kraus (1988) argued that when Americans do engage in leisure activities on their own, they

> shape their free time so it becomes as much like work as possible— segmented, mechanical, purposeful, busy and routinized. They commit themselves to a host of scheduled classes, leagues, rehearsals and meetings and beyond this, often see leisure as a means of gaining status by doing things that are popular or that contribute to career success. (p. 86)

Hegemonic influence is mediated through various ideological avenues throughout the social formation (e.g., schools, mass media); they are the means of transmitting and elaborating on the dominant ideology. In commodified enterprises the ethics and standards of profit making dominate. This is nicely characterized by the term "the bottom line," which in business language defines the ultimate consideration: Is it profitable? The same value is manifested in commodified sport by the common attitude that "winning isn't everything, it's the only thing." National Hockey League president, John Ziegler, when asked in a television interview if he thought that the fighting in NHL hockey should be eliminated, answered,

> It doesn't matter to me. What matters to me is providing a product that people enjoy and want to see . . . because I am in the entertainment business, and the measure to me is, Are people going to pay money to see . . . [fighting]? And they are saying yes to it. . . . So, if it ain't broke, don't fix it.

In an essay on modern sport, Kliever (1988) suggested that commodified sport has subverted the *ethics of play* with an *ethics of work*. While both center on competition, they are worlds apart, he argues. In competitive play one strives to win within the rules of the game and to perform to the best of one's abilities, whereas in competitive work one pursues a very different goal, namely striving to succeed by whatever means are necessary. He says,

> In an ethics of play, competing to win does not mean that winning is everything. In play, the test is ultimately more important than the contest. But in an ethics of work, competing to win does mean that winning is everything. (p. 567)

Rationalization, Bureaucracy, and Sport. The values and norms of the work world have increasingly come to define and characterize the sport world. This is a trend that could have been anticipated, given Max Weber's (1922/1978) insightful analysis of bureaucratic organization. For Weber, the expansion of capitalism is closely linked with bureaucratic administration. He argued that large, industrial, capitalist firms depend upon training the work force to accept strict control and discipline in order to enhance production and maximize profit. Furthermore, he suggested that because social life under capitalism is dominated by it, this bureaucratic model of rational discipline would extend beyond the boundaries of the workplace.

The fulfillment of Weber's prophecy is evident in contemporary sport. Even the language of the bureaucratic work world has become prominent in sport—productivity, hard work, sacrifice, loyalty. Some critics of modern sport contend that it has increasingly come to resemble a workplace. One has argued that sport has become a sector for the rationalization of work—a copy of the world of work—and that individual athletes have become merely objects in the production of sports performance (Rigauer, 1981). According to another, commodified sport mirrors industry, with the same formal functional rules and standards of valuation (Brohm, 1978). It is revealing that coaches who want to praise athletes call them "hard workers."

The rise of industrial capitalism and mass production brought standardization, objectivity, and impersonality to the workplace. Organization is authoritarian, hierarchical, and rational. Under a system of rationality, organizational goals are to be achieved as completely and cheaply as possible. Rational organizations are designed to minimize the discretionary behavior of individuals by making organizational processes more routine and predictable (Weber, 1978).

Central to capitalist production is the belief that employers hold the right to decision making and that workers must subordinate their wills to the organization. Because the central ideology supports technology and the domination of humans and their environment by bureaucratic techniques, science, organization, and planning are all prime values.

The influence of corporate power is so strong and so pervasive that the values and behaviors it engenders have become core ones for American society. They so permeate the fabric of every social institution that the socialization process is largely devoted to conditioning youth—particularly males—to this ideology. As commodified sport has grown prominent and powerful, it has clearly adopted the assumptions and values of large private and public organizations. Sociologist Charles Page (1973) has persuasively argued that

> the social revolution of sport, viewed in historical perspective, has been in large part the transition from both folk-rooted informal contests and the agonistic recreation of elites to its bureaucratization—or, in simple terms, from player-controlled "games" to the management-controlled "big time." . . . There has been the decreasing degree of autonomy of the athlete . . . whose onetime position as a more or less independent participant has been largely replaced by the status of skilled athletic worker under the strict discipline of coaches, managers, and, in the case of the pro, the "front office." This large-scale bureaucratization of sport, it should be stressed, is by no means confined to its professional version: rules and routine, the ascendancy of work over play, and the rise of the coach's authority within and beyond the athletic realm have penetrated deeply into collegiate and high school sports and even into the adult-controlled, highly organized "little leagues" in baseball and football. (pp. 32-33)

The emergence of a bureaucratic ethos in sport has been dependent on many of the same factors that were responsible for its growth in other areas of organizational life—for example, the expansion of a money economy, larger administrative units, the growth of occupational specialization, and the prominence of the profit motive.

Commodified sport at all levels has assumed an acceptance of the priorities of sport organizations and a belief that individuals must subordinate their wills to them. Individual players are expected to do their best to meet the needs of the organization. This is vividly exemplified by a popular locker room slogan: "There is no 'I' in team." Systems of incentives and rewards (e.g., letter awards, helmet decals, player-of-the-week designations) are instituted to motivate athletes to perform. Decisions are made by the management (the coach) after a thorough cost-efficiency analysis, and the players are expected to carry out the will of the coach for the accomplishment of organizational goals (Sage, 1985).

In sport, as in other complex organizations, authority is rigid. Strict hierarchies control more and more of workers' and athletes' lives both on and off the job or the field of play. "The bureaucratization of top-level sports implies a system of social roles like that existing in the world of work," argues Rigauer (1981). He continues,

Within a sports [team], as in an industrial enterprise, every active person acquires a rank that fixes his area of activity. . . . Every social role is linked on the basis of objective determinations to expected behavior on the part of those who fill the role. Top-level sports have copied this model of ordered status and roles in their elementary forms of social organization. (p. 48)

Coaches typically structure relationships with athletes along authoritarian lines; they analyze and structure team positions for precise specialization, and they endeavor to control player behavior not only in practices and contests but around the clock, with rules for grooming, training, dating behavior, and so forth. Under this form of management, the athletes are the instruments of organizational goals. In most cases they are not consulted about team membership, practice methods, strategy, or any of the other dynamic functions of a team. In a biting critique of modern sport, Jean-Marie Brohm (1978) stated that

sport is basically a mechanisation of the body, treated as an automaton, governed by the principle of maximizing output. The organism is trained to sustain prolonged effort and maintain the necessary regularity of pace. . . . In the guise of a game which is supposed to freely develop the strengths of the individual, sport in fact reproduces the world of work. (p. 55)

Because coaches are the authorities of organized sport teams, athletes learn dominant-subordinate relationships within the social relations of the sport productive process. Thus the structure of contemporary society is learned by athletes through understanding the hierarchy of power within the structure of modern sport.

Scientization and Technology in Sport.[1]   Just as science and technology were appropriated by dominant economic interests to create new and influential industries, they have been appropriated to serve commodified sport interests. There is a flourishing industry of so-called sport sciences whose primary goal tends to be performance enhancement, that is, getting athletes to run faster, jump higher, and throw farther.

These sport sciences tend to treat individual athletes as machines, or as though they ought to be machines. Training methods are designed to achieve maximum performance from the human body. When athletic performance is not up to expectations, solutions are sought in science

---

[1]I am indebted to John Hoberman (1987a, 1987b) for a number of the ideas in this section.

and its companion technology. A newspaper article entitled "Training Becomes a Science" described the Sports Science Program of the Olympic Training Center at Colorado Springs. The article noted that

> the Sports Science Program operates year-round, poking and prodding at top athletes in 38 sports to determine their strengths and weaknesses. From the knowledge gained, programs are built to fine-tune each person's athletic abilities. . . . The sports scientists become masters at fine-tuning. (Jones & Crewell, 1987, pp. 13-M–14-M)

In describing the training of ice skaters, the authors of the article state that "on the ice, the skaters are put through 'kill drills' to test their stamina" (p. 14-M). As bizarre as this might sound, this manipulation of athletes in the name of better and better performance is not uncommon in the world of sport science.

High-performance sport has increasingly become a project in human engineering whose objective is producing levels of performance with seemingly little understanding of—or even interest in—what the consequences may be for the personal and social development of the athlete. This approach to sport tends to implicitly validate enhancing performance, employing scientific findings, and using technological techniques as unproblematic—there is an unreflecting and uncritical attitude about *ends* in sport.

There seems to be a manipulative solution for every problem athletes might encounter. Athletes who suffer from anxiety are taught stress management techniques. If motivation seems to be languishing from months of hard training, a behavioral modification program is employed to reward athletes for meeting the coach's goals of performance, or a goal-setting program is established whereby the coach can manipulate athletes to set goals for themselves that are congruent with the coach's goals. Drugs (legal and illegal) and nutritional supplements are administered to elicit sustained training regimens that would not be possible without them.

Sport scientists, and coaches who employ them, seem to be unconcerned with the social consequences of their programs and socially naive about the complexities and contradictions of contemporary sport. They seem unaware of the connection between sport and the broader society, especially as it is manifested in ideological, political, and economic arenas. Although sport scientists may not believe their field to lie within the political and economic contexts of modern society, this does not exempt their work from ideological meaning (Mills, 1959).

Some observers have noted the glaring absence of outspoken critiques of modern sport by sport scientists—critiques of coaches who psychologically and physically abuse athletes, of dangerous equipment, of unproven psychological intervention techniques, or of the ethos of performance enhancement. One observer said this:

> Look at those aspects of domestic sport that American discourse avoids recognizing and talking about: the denial of individual person-hood to athletes in favor of making them abstract embodiments of sociopolitical ideology; the absence of ordinary civil and political rights among them; the power of large organizations over them; anorexia/bulimia, emotional disorders, steroid abuse, and blood-doping tied directly to the pressure for sport success and either directly encouraged by or insufficiently discouraged by coaches and officials; the concealing of medical data, the social approval, and desire for family advancement which lead, as in the case of gymnastics, to the victimization of their own children by dominant class and status groups. (MacAloon, 1987, p. 114)

Although sport scientists can rightly claim that they are not solely responsible for all of these practices and that they cannot be held fully accountable, few speak out forcefully against any of them. In their desire for status, recognition, and entry into the rarefied environment of elite sports, sport scientists have been unwilling to criticize what coaches and athletes are doing in the name of achieving records and winning championships.

Relevant oppositional perspectives to the thrust of scientization in sport are difficult to muster. As Hoberman (1987a) has said,

> We should be honest enough to realize that at this point in its history our civilization provides us with very little in the cultural mainstream which can match the performance principle in mass appeal. . . . The inexorable logic of the performance principle will demand improved performances, which in turn require the use of scientific techniques which challenge—or appear to profane—certain traditional ideas about what human beings are and should remain. (p. 8)

Though the popularity of high-performance sport will undoubtedly continue to pressure sport scientists to help coaches, trainers, and athletes achieve new performance records, one might hope for a contrary predilection among some to direct their efforts toward nurturing, promoting, and studying athletic participation that is evaluated by qualitative criteria rather than by quantitative efficiency criteria.

Although any real critique of the dominant ethos of commodified sport interests has been very minimal and spasmodic up to now, there is hope on the horizon. An awareness of this dominant ethos and a desire to stem its influence are growing, and various forms of resistance are beginning to mobilize in word and in deed.

Summary and Preview

Contemporary sport and physical recreational forms in the United States are historically and culturally rooted in the development of our country since its birth. Traditional play and games of preindustrial American life were community-based expressions of pleasure and ceremony. They were unorganized, episodic, and localized, and they were governed by particularistic rules and customs. Today, a massive commercial industry is the driving force behind sport and physical recreation forms. Sport has experienced a transformation in meaning as it has undergone changes in form and content; hegemonic features and dominating interests in commercialized sport have increasingly come to define and regulate our understandings of what sport is and how it should be played (Gruneau, 1988).

A major pillar for stability and maintenance—one could say the lifeblood—of commercial sport is the mass media. The media are the main advertising forum for modern sports, but at the same time commercial sports are an important source of revenue for the media. The various connections and mutual dependencies between the mass media and contemporary sport are examined in chapter 6.

CHAPTER 6

Mass Media and Sport: Managing Images, Impressions, and Ideology

Television buys *sports. . . . Television tells sports what to do. It is* sports *and it runs them the way it does most other things, more flamboyantly than honestly.*

Leonard Shecter, sports journalist

The term *mass media* refers to all of the technically organized means of communication that reach large numbers of people quickly and effectively. This system of communication falls into two major groupings: print media, such as newspapers, magazines, and books, and electronic media, such as radio, television, and movies. Each media form has unique aspects, and although most of my attention is devoted to newspapers and television, considerations specific to other media are discussed where appropriate.

The mass media comprise one of the most powerful social institutions in American society. Their power is derived from two main sources: constitutional protection, and corporate organization. The First Amendment of the United States Constitution, or freedom of the press (which has come to include the electronic media), gives the media almost unlimited public license. Although freedom of the press is unarguably fundamental to the maintenance of a free and open society, the enormous power in this freedom can be abused. The media have direct access to the public and are instrumental in directing attentions and shaping attitudes, values, and beliefs. In addition to their constitutional power, the media hold the power inherent in their ownership by giant corporate conglomerates. The mass media, then, are "an institution with a dual social identity. They are both an economic . . . and a cultural institution; they are a profit-making business and at the same time a producer of meaning, a creator of social consciousness" (Hallin, 1985, p. 141).

Ownership and Control of the Mass Media

All mass media in the United States are privately owned. But the forms of ownership and management have changed dramatically since the end of the 19th century. The trend over the past few decades has been for fewer and fewer companies to acquire control. As a consequence, most media firms are now owned by corporations comparable to huge manufacturing and financial conglomerates in size. Despite the fact that, in the U.S., there are some 25,000 mass media outlets—newspapers, magazines, radio stations, television stations, book publishers, and movie companies—just 29 corporations control more than 50% of the business (Bagdikian, 1987).

In the 1890s most newspapers were owned by individuals or partnerships, and publishers were not particularly wealthy. At the end of World War II more than 80% of the daily newspapers were independently owned; by 1989 only 27% were independently owned. Today the prevailing pattern for newspapers is transcontinental "group" ownership. Indeed, newspaper chains own over half of America's daily newspapers, which account for some 70% of daily circulation. The Gannett Corporation, publisher of *USA Today*, is the largest newspaper chain in the U.S.; other large chains include Scripps Howard and Times-Mirror. Concentration of power in the news industry is reflected in another way: Behind most of the news in our hundreds of papers are but a few highly centralized organizations that feed stories to the locals—the wire services of the Associated Press (AP), United Press International (UPI), the *New York Times*, the *Los Angeles Times*, and the *Washington Post*.

The broadcasting industry displays a similar trend. The big-three TV and radio networks are part of massive corporate conglomerates. NBC is owned by General Electric, one of America's largest corporations; GE's total revenue in recent years has been about $37 *billion*, 3 billion of which comes from broadcasting. ABC is owned by Capital Cities Communications, with an annual revenue over $4 billion. CBS, while not a subsidiary of a larger corporation, has expanded well beyond broadcasting into such areas as book publishing; its revenues are about $5 billion (Bagdikian, 1987; Herman & Chomsky, 1988).

The concentration of ownership and centralized control of the mass media parallels that in other sectors of the corporate economy, and, collectively, the mass media are a forum for the most powerful corporate interests in the United States. Overlap of the mass media elite and the economic elite is considerable, with perhaps as many as half of their members being part of both groups. And even those only in the media have characteristics resembling the economic elite. Chomsky (1987) noted that

> the media represent the same interests that control the state and private economy, and it is therefore not very surprising to discover that they generally act to confine public discussion and understanding to the needs of the powerful and privileged. . . . Their top management (editors, etc.) is drawn from the ranks of wealthy professionals who tend naturally to share the perceptions of the privileged and powerful, and who have achieved their position, and maintain it, by having demonstrated their efficiency in the task of serving the needs of dominant elites. (p. 125)

Together, then, the economic and media elite largely represent the same upper class (Allen, 1987; Dye, 1986). As a result, the dominant economic class exerts a major influence on the mass media, directly through ownership and indirectly through buying advertising.

Ideological Hegemony and the Mass Media

Basic to hegemonic theory are the premises that a main source for creating and perpetuating ideological hegemony is the dominant class and that it is through the successful extension of their material control to the cultural sectors that the dominant class can reinforce and sustain that control. Because the dominant class controls the economic and political institutions, it tends to have privileged access to the major institutions for fostering ideology, such as the mass media. Through its privileged access, the dominant class is in a favorable position to control important societal resources that shape the beliefs and thought patterns that explain and justify existing social arrangements; this enables it to cultivate values that reinforce the status quo. "Such propagation," emphasized Sallach (1974), "involves not only the inculcation of its values . . . but also and especially the ability to *define* the parameters of legitimate discussion and debate over alternative beliefs, values, and world views" (p. 41).

That the mass media comprise one of the most salient cultural institutions is illustrated just by the time people devote to them; one survey found that Americans spend an average of 7 hours per day in front of a home TV set ("We're Watching," 1988). The media, then, are part and parcel of our daily life, investing it with particular meanings. They have become an extremely powerful source for forming values and organizing consensus within American society. Television, especially "through its use of a powerful language comprising images, words, gesture, clothing, settings, music, and sounds, has become one of our society's principal repositories of ideology" (Himmelstein, 1984, p. 3).

A great deal of the mass media's ideological work is impression management. One of the forms this takes is shaping the images people hold of the media itself. One of the primary pictures the mass media like to draw of themselves is that they are looking out for all of us: The slogan of the The New York Times, for example, is "All the news that's fit to print." A second impression purports that media versions of events are unfiltered, objective reality; witness common slogans like "and that's the way it is," "eyewitness news," and "brought to you live." Another favorite media cliché is that they write and broadcast what the public wants. According to a top executive officer at CBS, "All TV does is reflect the taste of the American public" (Moore, 1989b, p. 2A).

Actually, mass media claims of looking out for everyone, reproducing reality, and giving the public what it wants are questionable—one might even argue dangerous and misleading—half-truths that conceal how the media can indeed constrain and shape public impressions and beliefs. "It is not the vast pluralistic range of voices which the media are sometimes held to represent, but a range *within certain distinct ideological limits*" (Hall, Crutcher, Jefferson, Clarke, & Roberts, 1978, p. 61). However, many people do see the mass media as objective reporters of the news and events that are worthy of note. They are unaware of the highly mediated and politicized nature of the process by which information is conceived, produced, and disseminated in reaching us. Media content that is perceived as objective news or simply innocent entertainment will not be understood as laden with hegemonic ideology.

The salience and power of the mass media, particularly television, and its interpretative nature also enable it to play a crucial mediating and connective role in forming public opinion and in orchestrating that opinion in concert with the dominant ideology. The media are a conduit for ideologically encoded messages. Goldsen (1977) argued that

> the power to dominate a culture's symbol producing apparatus is the power to create the ambience that forms consciousness itself. It is a power we see exercised daily by the television business as it penetrates virtually every home with the most massive continuing spectacle human history has ever known. (p. 14)

Mass media, in effect, engage in the social construction of information that conveys and promotes dominant political-ideological agendas— agendas that appear to be the authoritative interpretation of events, persons, and values. The variety of techniques used to carry this out are numerous and complex. One in particular is frequently used in news reporting: the "expert." Supposed experts commonly are quoted to suggest *the* authoritative view of issues and events; some radio and television stations have even endowed certain reporters with specialist status in areas like business, the arts, crime, and education. The impression meant to be conveyed is that such spokespersons have access to more accurate or more specialized information than the average person. The subtle message is, of course, that the "experts" and "specialists" will tell us what is good, right, or true. But even where these experts and specialists are indeed knowledgeable, they tend to be the servants of the media industry, elaborating and defining the dominant consensus.

There has been an increasing interest in the media and an increasing awareness of the role they play in shaping people's understanding of the world. Their influence has been analyzed by social scientists from several theoretical standpoints. Most analysts have found that the media are biased toward maintaining the status quo and promoting dominant group interests (Himmelstein, 1984; Meyrowitz, 1985). In discussing the role of the media, Altheide and Snow (1979) proposed that "social reality is constituted, recognized and celebrated with media, thus supporting the idea that media present to us what is 'normal' " (p. 12). And Snow (1983) has suggested that our cultural norms and values, our knowledge and understanding of the world are derived more and more through our experience with the mass media. Stein (1972) has put it a little stronger by proposing that by shaping our picture of the world the media determine what we think, how we feel, and what we do about our social and political environment. In producing *their definition* of social reality, the media tend to construct an image of society that represents dominant class interests as the interests of all members of society.

Image Versus Reality

The relationship between media presentations and reality has been pursued by Gerbner and his colleagues (Gerbner, Gross, Signorelli, & Morgan, 1980). Their analyses suggest that the message of television is distinctive and deviates from "reality" in several compelling ways. Evidence supporting their theory has been compiled through content analysis of American television showing persistent and consistent distortions of reality in the areas of the family, education, sex roles, work roles, aging, death and dying, and violence and crime (Ferguson, 1983; Fishman, 1978; Gerbner, 1964; Gerbner & Gross, 1976; Gieber & Johnson, 1961; Glasgow Media Group, 1976; Tuchman, 1978).

An explicit implication of this line of research is that "the culture industry produces its goods, tailoring them to particular markets and organizing their content so that they are packaged to be compatible with the dominant values and mode of discourse" (Gitlin, 1987, p. 240). Even though the mediated images may be distortions of reality, we eventually come to believe them as truth because the media relentlessly present them as such. Thus, in addition to wielding the power inherent in the enormous economic foundations of the mass media, the media—especially television—are our culture's most potent instrument for articulating the dominant ideology, helping "to reproduce and sustain the definitions of the situation which favor the powerful" (Hall et al., 1978, p. 65) and thus integrally serving a larger system of social control.

In attempting to connect the economic realities to the ideological potential of the mass media, it is easy to discern their inherent capacities for hegemonic work, because they are the forum for the most influential commercial interests in America. Contrary to conventional wisdom and the claims of the TV industry, televised events are not a neutral product. Indeed, the television industry is not a neutral communicator of messages in any of its programming. It is instead an industry of complex organizations involved in the everyday production and marketing of mass cultural products. Its traditions, norms, and practices belong to a broad system for interpreting and promoting culture and consciousness (Himmelstein, 1984; Meyrowitz, 1985). Television directs attention and shapes cognitions that "cultivate the dominant image patterns. It structures the public agenda of existence, priorities, values, and relationships" (Gerbner, 1973, p. 569). Because television is such a powerful force in the presentation and interpretation of information it helps to shape our perceptions of social reality. Sullivan (1987) has said that

> if we learn anything from Gramsci's (1971) *Prison Note Books*, it is that capitalism is held together by consent from within a populace . . . rather than through coercion. The main organ of this consensus in our contemporary period is the mass-media communications systems. (pp. 60-61)

The media tend to reinforce the established social order and reigning consensus, not necessarily out of a cynical self-interest or subservience to particular group interests, but certainly as an instrument for the promotion of dominant meanings and ideas. However, the media do not merely dispatch the ideology of the dominant class in a conspiratorial manner—the control of ideology in society is a much more contingent process than that. Moreover, media credibility and legitimacy are maintained by their lack of complete agreement on all issues and controversies and by their occasionally even opposing the dominant political and economic perspectives. But the media's structural affinity with the economically and politically powerful plays a key role in propagating the definitions of dominant groups. As already emphasized, securing consent to the dominant ideology does not necessarily require force or threats of force because it is flexible enough to assimilate, co-opt, undermine, or override potentially contradictory notions; this is its genius (Williams, 1977).

Media Sport Coverage

Both print and broadcast media devote significant attention to sport issues and events. Contests themselves are broadcast on TV and radio, with interpretive commentary; daily newspapers have sizable sport sections to report on local and national news; and sport has spawned myriad specialty publications to offer even more extensive coverage.

Newspapers

Although it is difficult for those under 40 to imagine, prior to 1950 there were no home television sets, and only 30 years earlier no home radios. So it is only since 1920 that electronic media have been a part of daily living. The only prior mass medium was print—newspapers, magazines, and books. In the mid-19th century, American newspapers began periodic coverage of sport events, but it was not until the 1890s that a sports section first became a regular newspaper feature. It was William Randolph Hearst, publisher of the *New York Journal*, who developed the modern sports section. Today, some 30% of the public say they buy the newspaper for the sports section. In some of the most popular newspapers almost 50% of the nonadvertising space (a sizable proportion of any paper) is devoted to sports, which has five times the readership of any other section.

The Electronic Media

Wireless transmission of information was developed in the 1890s, and in the early 1920s radio broadcasting began. Reports and broadcasts of sport events quickly became one of radio's most popular functions. Today, radio stations broadcast more than 400,000 hours of sport annually. The newest innovation is 24-hour sport stations, by which serious fans can stay abreast of what is happening in sport (Meadow, 1988).

The technology to produce telecasts was developed during the 1930s, but large-scale growth was delayed until after World War II. In the early 1950s commercial TV, developed by private capital in the context of an expanding consumer culture, immediately made a union with sport. Since then the two industries have developed a symbiosis; indeed, it is often claimed—and with good reason—that commercial sports could not exist without television and that television would have a lot tougher time generating revenue without commercialized sport.

Spectators consume sport to a far greater extent indirectly through television than directly through personal attendance at events. Almost 1,600 hours of televised sport is programmed per year by the three major networks, and cable TV provides an additional 6,000 hours. The Entertainment and Sports Programming Network (ESPN) alone broadcasts over 4,400 hours of live sports each year. Other cable networks are now emphasizing sport programming, and there is a rapidly growing industry of regional cable sport channels, representing about 17.5 million cable subscribers in 1988 (Gloede & McManus, 1988; McManus, 1988b).

Over half of the 25 top-rated television programs of all-time are sport events (Eitzen & Sage, 1986). An estimated 3 billion people worldwide tuned in to at least some of the televised coverage of the 1988 Olympic Games. The World Cup, involving 24 soccer teams playing 52 games in a month-long tournament, drew 12.5 billion viewers in 1986 when it was telecast from Mexico.

Media Influence on Sport

The first objective of the mass media is profit. The television industry, for example, is primarily an advertising business, not a journalistic one.

Its profits accrue from selling advertising; its major guiding principle is the highest rate of return on investment. Sporting events provide some rather high returns; it is estimated that NBC made an $82-million profit on its coverage of the 1988 Seoul Olympics.

Sport programs are merely bait for selling advertising; that is how the media uses sport. And television sells a lot of advertising for sport events. As a percentage of all network TV advertising by corporations, sport accounts for about 25%. Advertisers are willing to spend huge sums of money—more than $2.5 billion annually—because "advertising uses the drama and mythic power of sports to generate [consumer] demand and to realize profit for advanced monopoly capital" (Young, 1986, p. 20).

The media have no inherent interest in sport. It is merely a means for profit making. For newspapers and magazines, sports sell the publications. For TV and radio, sports get consumers in front of their sets to hear and see commercials; in effect, TV and radio broadcasts rent their viewers' and listeners' attention.

Sport and television have become mutual beneficiaries in one of capitalism's most lucrative associations. The networks sell advertising to corporations who are selling a product and wish to advertise it. Because so many people are interested in sport, which is more exciting and suspenseful than many other programs, it is a natural setting for advertising. Motivated by their mutual desire for financial gain, commercialized sport and the mass media both profit—because sport is something the public wants, the media can sell time for advertising and commercial sport gets free publicity. Indeed, with respect to professional sport, no other privately owned, profit-making business receives as much free publicity for its product. Media exposure is in itself enough to promote pro sports, but typically the sports are reported in a blatantly booster fashion designed to hype interest in the athletes and teams. Of course, the reciprocal nature of this is quite clear: The more interest is generated in sport, the greater the profits for the mass media (Klatell & Marcus, 1988).

Because TV sports are particularly popular, the networks have been able to set phenomenal advertising fees; for example, NBC sold time for the 1989 Super Bowl for an average of $675,000 per 30-second commercial—$22,500 per second! Knowing about the advertising fees that television is able to command, the sport industry can negotiate large contracts for the rights to televise events, which in turn helps make commercial sports wealthy. Take a few examples:

† A 3-year NFL television contract that ends in 1990 totals $1.43 billion ($17 million per year for each of 28 teams); thus, about 65% of all revenues of NFL teams comes from television.

† The national TV rights to major league baseball for 4 years (1990 to 1994) were sold to CBS for $1.1 billion and to ESPN for another $400 million over 4 years, making the annual income from these

two contracts over $15 million for each team. More than half the teams can pay their entire 1990 player payroll just from national TV revenues. This does not include local broadcast rights, which total over $185 million annually. The most lucrative of these contracts to date was a 12-year, $500-million deal signed in 1989 between the New York Yankees and the Madison Square Garden Network.

† CBS and NBC will pay $644 million in rights fees to televise the 1992 Winter and Summer Olympic Games.

† In 1989 CBS signed a 7-year TV contract with the NCAA for $1 billion for the Division I men's basketball tournament; this was an increase of 260% over the previous deal.

Contracts like these have made the commercial sports industry very wealthy, resulting in expanded franchises, higher salaries, and all-round plush lifestyles for many in the industry.

Prior to the marriage of television and professional sports, pro sport franchises were considered to be permanent fixtures in a city. In the past 25 years, however, franchise-jumping has become commonplace. One reason in almost every case has been the potential for additional TV revenues in the new city (see chapter 7 for more detail).

The relationship between the media and professional sports goes beyond simple mutual interests; they have intimate business connections. Several owners of professional sport teams are also owners, or major shareholders, of media corporations. Ted Turner, owner of the Turner Broadcasting empire, owns the Atlanta Braves baseball team and basketball's Atlanta Hawks. Ed Snyder, owner of Spectator Communications, also owns the NHL's Philadelphia Flyers. Jerry Buss, a principal owner of Prime Ticket Network cable TV, owns the Los Angeles Lakers of the NBA. The owners of the New York Knicks, Paramount Telecommunications, also own the Madison Square Garden Network. These examples illustrate well the tight business associations between the media and sport.

Another linkage between professional sport and capital arises from the employment by the media of former professional athletes. A growing pattern is to hire former sport stars to report play-by-play coverage or serve as commentators for sport events. Some of these former athletes have even ascended to management positions.

Sport Adaptations for TV

To enhance spectator appeal and accommodate programming needs, the television industry has been increasingly permitted to manipulate the structures and processes of sport. In NFL football, certain rule changes—

moving the sideline hash marks and the kickoff spot, reducing defensive backs' contact with receivers, liberalizing offensive holding—have been implemented to open up the game and make it more attractive to television viewers. Other modifications have been introduced to permit more commercials—official time-outs at the end of each quarter, time-outs at the discretion of television officials, and, of course, the 2-minute warning. The sudden-death tie-breaking rule and the extended play-off system are further means of increasing spectator interest.

In both professional and collegiate basketball, the shot clock, the slam dunk, and the 3-point shot have been adopted to enhance viewer interest. In televised golf, match play, where the golfers compete hole by hole (with the golfer winning the most holes being the winner), has been completely replaced by medal play, where golfers play the field (and the one with the lowest score over the course wins), and the Skins Game (a variation of match play where large sums of money ride on the outcome of each hole) because these forms of play are more compatible with television coverage. To accommodate television scheduling, tennis officials established a tie-breaker system of scoring when sets reach six games for each contestant, thus making it easier to complete matches within a designated time period.

For the same reason of viewer interest, major league baseball introduced the designated hitter and lowered the strike zone, and there is strong suspicion—denied by baseball executives and ball manufacturers—that in recent years the baseball itself has been modified to make it more lively. All of these changes have stemmed from a view toward producing what spectators like to see: a steady barrage of extra base hits and home runs. The time-honored afternoon World Series and All-Star games have been switched to evenings to accommodate the interests of television. The 1988 addition of lights at Chicago's Wrigley Field was a pure and simple concession to TV.

Another bow to TV involved rescheduling events in the 1988 Summer Olympics. To maximize its revenue from the sale of television rights, the Seoul Olympic Committee agreed to reschedule championship events to accommodate NBC's desire to show them during America's prime time. In contrast with previous Olympic Games, the finals of many events were shifted from the afternoon in Seoul to early in the day so that they could be seen from 8:00 p.m. to 10:00 p.m. in New York (9:00 a.m. to 11:00 a.m. Korean time). This radical change, made for American commercial television interests, was a first in the history of the Olympics (Min, 1987).

These and other sport adaptations, modifications, and concessions are tied directly to enhancing the action for the television viewers so that a bigger audience will see the advertising being shown. This illustrates how capital accumulation priorities go hand in hand with cultural practices that have become commodified.

Trash Sports

One of the most disturbing influences of televised sport for those who cherish traditional sport forms has been the creation of various pseudo-sport events, popularly and appropriately called *trash sports*. This form of trivialized sport began in 1973 with *Super Sports*, an ABC program in which outstanding athletes competed in events other than their specialty. The idea was to find the "best" athlete and discover which sports had the "best" athletes. Once *Super Sports* became a television success, other trash sports followed: *Challenge of the Sexes*, where top male athletes compete against top female athletes, with the males given handicaps to heighten the uncertainty of the outcomes, and *Super Teams*, where members of professional teams in two different sports compete in contrived events.

The ultimate in the demeaning of sports was the introduction of programs like *Battle of the Network Stars* and *Celebrity Challenge of the Sexes*. Previous trash sports at least involved real athletes, but in these, television and movie entertainers competed against each other in "sporting" events. Thus, sport was blatantly exploited to promote show business personalities and the programs they represent.

The popularity of such programs has been the subject of much speculation, but no firm resolution. Some social scientists contend that the public has become so hooked on the media-created celebrity status of athletes and other entertainers that they will tune in to see their admired stars regardless of what they are doing. For other social scientists, the popularity of such shows indicates an alienation from everyday existence, a craving for excitement, perhaps even a pathological desire to escape from the realities of daily life.

A new form of event is on the horizon: made-for-sponsor sports. These will be a variant of trash sports, but nearly every aspect will be aimed at making them appealing to corporate sponsors. Sid Morris, who has already launched one of these sports, ProSail, said, "It is a marketing tool, purely and simply, geared to deliver results to its sponsors. Unlike sports and sanctioning bodies that were already there, we have the luxury of making it up all fresh" (Murphy, 1988, p. 38). ProSail's format will be 3 days of racing in two classes, 21-foot and 40-foot catamarans. The boats will stay close to shore to assure that the sponsors' signage they carry will be visible to spectators. A harbor festival including booths for sponsors, radio commentary on the races, souvenirs, a boat show, and other promotional activities will be part of the event (Murphy, 1988).

The U.S. Olympic Committee, in an effort to generate revenue and interest in Olympic sports, has approved the formation of a U.S. Olympic Cup Series. The USOC hopes to interest both network and cable television in the multisport, multievent series. They are making an un-disguised attempt to package sport specifically to attract television sponsorship (Rosner, 1988).

Ideological Hegemony, the Media, and Sport

Although the televising of sport events may seem a neutral activity, it is in reality a forum laden with opportunity for dominant interests to shape the very meaning of sport and to cultivate their ideology among generally unsuspecting viewers. Sport telecasts, carefully chosen and orchestrated, have become symbol-bearers, with the choices of what is shown and how being guided by the hegemonic agenda.

Defining Sport

Media sport has been assimilated into media culture, meaning that its form and content have been altered to suit the interests of the mass media (Altheide & Snow, 1979). Television redefines the meaning of sport in many ways, but one of the most prominent is through selection—the decisions both to televise some sports and not others and to accentuate certain aspects of each sport for viewers. Alan and John Clarke's (1982) insightful description of this deserves to be quoted at length:

> [Television] selects *between* sports for those which make "good television," and it selects *within* a particular event, it highlights particular aspects for the viewers. This selective highlighting is not "natural" or inevitable—it is based on certain criteria, certain media assumptions about what is "good television." But the media do not only select, they also provide us with definitions of what has been selected. They interpret events for us, provide us with frameworks of meaning in which to make sense of the event. To put it simply, television does not merely consist of pictures, but also involves commentary on the pictures—a commentary which explains to us what we are seeing. . . . These selections are socially constructed—they involve decisions about what to reveal to the viewers. The presentation of sport through the media involves an active process of re-presentation: what we see is not the event, but the event transformed into something else—a media event. This transformation is not arbitrary, but governed by criteria of selection, which concentrate and focus the audience's attention, and, secondly, those values which are involved in the conventions of television presentation: concentration and *conventionalism*. (pp. 69-71)

In his book *Creating Media Culture,* Snow (1983) illustrated how the selective presentation of a televised sport event influences the meaning of some aspects of it for viewers:

When the strategy of television stresses the offensive or scoring character of [an NFL] game, people involved in organizing, playing, and watching the game come to take for granted the idea that offense should be the primary characteristic of the game. (p. 11)

So television does not merely nonchalantly report sport events. TV sport presentation is the culmination of a complex process of sorting and selecting events and topics according to a socially constructed set of values and assumptions.

The selecting, screening, and filtering of sport events by television professionals through the images shown and the commentary given has the effect of presenting games as entertainment, and in essence that is what televised sport is all about—commodified entertainment. Consequently, the basis for interest in sport is changed from the traditional appreciation of the beauty and style, the skill, and the technical accomplishments of the performers to a primary concern for provocative excitement and productive action, usually meaning scoring.

Furthermore, the spontaneous, creative motive to participate in sport for the love of the game has been overshadowed by an obsession with victory above all else. Broadcast sports tend to be unbridled odes to winning (we frequently hear commentators say that an athlete will do "whatever it takes to win"); almost any action in the pursuit of victory is justified. Indeed, players sometimes are lionized for illegal play. In one NFL play-off game, the instant replay showed an offensive lineman clearly and deliberately throwing a vicious elbow into the face of an opponent, which was followed by a comment from one of the sportscasters: "Nobody said this was going to be a tea party!" The competition is waged not only against opponents but also against the rules—to see how often and how thoroughly they can be stretched and outright violated, in letter and spirit, without getting penalized, all in the pursuit of victory.

Camera crews, sportscasters, and viewers are not attuned to the aesthetic nuances of a well-executed play. Christopher Lasch (1977) eloquently described one of the consequences of televised sport directed to a mass audience:

As spectators become less knowledgeable about games they watch, they become more sensation-minded and bloodthirsty. . . . What corrupts an athletic performance . . . is not professionalism or competition but the presence of an unappreciative, ignorant audience and the need to divert it with sensations extrinsic to the performance. (p. 26)

A similar point was made by Robert Hughes and Jay Coakley (1984):

Commercialization does not destroy the acclaim given to hits in a baseball game but it does encourage placing extra emphasis on the meaning of home runs; nor does commercialization destroy everyone's appreciation of offensive line play in football, but it leads people to focus their attention on touchdown runs and long pass completions rather than who blocks whom on the line of scrimmage. (p. 60)

Hegemonic Work in Sport

In principle, the televised sport event has no manifest ideological content. Basically, it is a tool for attracting viewers to the screen so television corporations can show the commercials they have sold to advertisers. A common assumption of the public is that a broadcast sport event is an objective mirror of the reality of the contest, and that the camera angles and commentary are neutral conduits for presenting "the facts" of the event. But actually a broadcast game is a commodified entertainment spectacle sold in the marketplace. Sportscasters and the entire apparatus involved in producing programs have become the definers of the subculture of sport, the interpreters of its meanings, and, most important, a crucial means by which hegemonic ideology is propagated and reproduced.

Televised events become mediated experiences for viewers. Ostensibly, sportscasters simply keep viewers apprised of essential information. But they do much more. Because of sportscasters' mediation, a game becomes a media-defined event, a collage of happenings and thus a "reality" socially constructed by the sportscasters, who decide what to reveal to viewers and how. This supposed reality becomes, in effect, the "event," and the way viewers experience it becomes their reference point for its very existence—but it is a manufactured version of reality. As Clarke and Clarke (1982) have noted,

Between us and the event stand the cameras, camera angles, producers' choices of shots, the commentators' interpretations—the whole invisible apparatus of media presentation. We can never see the whole event, we see those parts which are filtered through this process of presentation to us. It locates us as watchers in a very different position from the spectator at the event itself. (p. 73)

And Comisky, Bryant, and Zillmann (1977) add, "Whereas the viewers in [a] stadium perceive the event as is, the home viewers are exposed to a 'media event' that is the product of a team of professional gatekeepers and embellishers" (p. 150).

That the televised sport event is mediated and different than the actual event is illustrated through pregame shows that at one level are mostly a contrived mix of hoopla, banal interviews, network promos, and puff pieces (e.g., theme building, "match-ups"). The rhetoric focuses viewer attention on the overall importance of the competition, individual athletes' (and coaches') personalities, statistics, records, and team styles of play. Integrated with this, however, is the major purpose of these programs—to frame and contextualize the game by artificially building dramatic tension and solidifying allegiances, thus convincing viewers to stay glued to their sets and preparing them for how they should see and understand the contest.

Sportscasters.   Announcers and commentators are carefully selected with an eye to their ability to command credibility; indeed, the media rely heavily on the personas of these men and women, so former professional and elite amateur athletes with high name recognition are often selected. Presenting accredited "experts" is a prime purpose behind this selection process because their statements will convey objectivity and authority. Once the expertise of the personnel is established, the impression conveyed to viewers is that they have privileged access to knowledgeable opinion about the event and preferred interpretation of its meanings. The fact that most sportscasters are male contributes to the impression of authority and expertise our society continues to associate with men.

Viewers are expected to rely on the judgment of these "experts" and to accept their opinions as absolute. Thus, exclusive access through certified experts serves to legitimize media interpretations (Hargreaves, 1986). Although employing former athletes to describe the technical skills, strategy, and tactics used during a game may seem reasonable enough, it is important to understand that sportscasting does not act only to report on the action of the contest. Perhaps more importantly it also acts "to prescribe moral values and to comment prescriptively on social relationships" (p. 145). Former sport stars are uniquely qualified for this task because they are survivors—even models—of the competitive meritocracy. By and large their social consciousness is congruent with hegemonic perspectives; they are fully integrated into the dominant value and belief system.

One of the basic jobs of announcers and commentators is to sell their sports. Much game commentary is actually commercial hype for the league and sport being televised—and an advertisement for sport as a commodified product. For example, sportscasters use slogans to develop name recognition and get viewers to identify with teams or athletes—Orange Crush, Doomsday Defense, America's Team, "Too Tall" Jones, "The Three Amigos" (three wide receivers for the Denver Broncos). The audience is unaware it is being subjected to advertising—advertising that is independent of commercials that periodically appear during the program. In *Television Myth and the American Mind*, Himmelstein (1984) contends that a more appropriate term for sportscasters would be "sport public-relations agents" (p. 241).

Political and Moral Ideology

The media are an ideological system of symbols sharply honed to promote political hegemony. The strong relationship that has evolved between sport and the mass media has not merely enhanced the mass appeal and popularity of sport but has also bolstered both the range and depth of sport's influence on political consciousness (Aronowitz, 1973). Hargreaves (1982) has contended that

> in their working assumptions and practices—the type of commentary, the use of verbal and visual imagery—the media re-dramatize and re-present what are already potent dramatic spectacles within a framework of interpretation, which facilitates the passing of ideologically coded messages, that is, preferred ways of seeing sport and society. (p. 127)

He further notes that

> media sport often reads like a handbook of conventional wisdom on social order and control. There are homilies on good firm management, justice, the nature of law, duty and obligation, correct attitudes to authority, the handling of disputes, what constitutes reasonable and civilized behavior, on law and order and on the state of society generally. (p. 145)

The annual Super Bowl, for example, utilizes numerous symbols—technology, competition, individual achievement, flag, nation—within this one event for a national celebration of the "American way of life" (Bailey & Sage, 1988; Sullivan, 1987). Riordan (1987) has argued that

> by making a fetish of ritualized sport, a political regime may thereby draw a veil over the realities of the manipulation of people's imaginations and so make opaque what would clearly be seen as intolerable if social relations were transparent. A society in which the popular media supply the public with enough pabulum of pseudo-events and plastic personalities in the field of phony sport can therefore operate by consensus. (p. 378)

Even though the mass media have no inherent interest in sport per se, they become the definers of its subculture, the interpreters of its meanings, and thus the crucial means by which the normative culture is transmitted. Mass media entertainment conveys information about moral boundaries like public hangings once did—as largely a symbolic act directed at the rest of society (Scattenberg, cited in Macaulay, 1987). Although TV sport bears little resemblance to the real world, this does not detract from its symbolic usefulness in spreading information about meanings and moral boundaries in sport and in the wider society. Media's influence ranges far and wide, communicating messages with hidden content. The hidden, or latent, content is something that has to be consciously sought to be identified.

Gender, Race, and the Mass Media

Gender and racial discrimination in sport is widespread and deeply rooted, and media sport is one of the foremost arenas for the reproduction of dominant, traditional gender and racial images and of inequality between the sexes and races. It is in media coverage and reporting and occupational opportunities that this is most notably manifested.

In television women's sports continue to struggle for coverage. With the exception of women's professional tennis and golf, there is little regular programming. No women's professional team sport league has ever secured a network TV contract. Undoubtedly, there are multiple reasons for this, but certainly a major one was expressed by the president of the largest regional cable company, the Madison Square Garden Network. He said, "Advertisers don't buy sports to get women. . . . If you want to reach women, there's a better way to do it. [Advertisers] are not convinced that women watch women" (Comte, Girard, & Starensier, 1989).

Reportorial and pictorial images of females and female athletes often belittle and trivialize their athletic efforts and achievements. Sports journalists have contributed to the condescending attitudes and stereotyping of female athletes; coverage of women's sport constitutes under 15% of the sports section of most newspapers, and when females do get media attention the emphasis is frequently on them as sex objects. Recent manifestations of this have been the selection by the media of a "sweetheart" in multisport events like the Olympics or an emphasis on female athletes in their roles as wives, mothers, or girlfriends rather than as skilled performers. In studies in the 1980s of newspapers and popular sport magazines, investigators found that sexist language was still being used in portraying women athletes, and an overwhelming proportion of articles were male-oriented; in other words, the image of female athletes is largely constructed by males (Duncan & Hasbrook, 1988; Hilliard, 1984; Lenskyj, 1986; Rintala & Birrell, 1984).

Mary Jo Kane (1988) analyzed the content of feature articles in *Sports Illustrated*, a potent and commanding creator of sport images, from 1964 to 1987. She found that although the proportion of feature articles about females in athletic roles increased over this period, many more articles were written about females in "sex-appropriate" sports (tennis, golf, figure skating) than in "sex-inappropriate" ones (basketball, softball, weightlifting), and this pattern remained constant over the period. In interpreting her findings, Kane suggested they reveal a continued conventional and restricted view of female athletic participation. She further argued,

> If the amount and type of coverage is any indication of the kind of image a publication wants to project, then *Sports Illustrated* is sending a clear message as to which sports are considered acceptable or valued within women's athletics. When the vast majority of coverage still focuses primarily on "feminine" and therefore non-threatening female sport behavior, how much progress has actually occurred in challenging traditional stereotypes of what it means to be a female and an athlete? (p. 96)

In a study of a U.S. newspaper, Theberge and Cronk (1986) utilized data from fieldwork and reported that the limited coverage devoted to females in the media is not simply due to journalists' bias against women's sports but that it is "woven into newsworkers' beliefs about the contents of the news and their own methods of uncovering the news" (p. 195).

Trivializing women's athletic achievements or treating them differently from men's promotes and reproduces traditional cultural gender relationships. Although there are definite signs that the marginalization and trivialization of female athletes are diminishing and that media recognition of female athletes is likely to increase, this may turn out to be a mixed blessing, because as females increasingly compete in male-defined sports their performances can be objectively measured against males. As Messner (1988) has emphasized, because the major media sports

> are organized around the most extreme potentialities of the male body, "equal opportunity" as the sports media's dominant framework of meaning for presenting the athletic performances of women athletes is likely to become a new means of solidifying the ideological hegemony of male superiority. (p. 206)

In this context, equal opportunity will provide compelling evidence for the "natural" superiority of male performances, thus justifying the predominant coverage of male sport by the media.

Because black and minority male athletes are *male*, their presence in sports is considered legitimate at least in the patriarchal scheme of things, so they have not suffered the same stigmatization as female athletes. Moreover, the long history of outstanding black athletes in American sports has established a tradition of reporting their performances in the mass media. Nevertheless, subtle racial stereotyping has been present. The most blatant examples are the frequent attributions of black athletes' achievements to their "natural" abilities to run fast and jump high and their "instincts" to react fast; at the same time—and sometimes during the same game—white athletes' achievements are typically attributed to their "intelligence" and superior "thinking ability." Historical stereotypes of blacks are coded into characterizations of this kind.

Sports journalism and broadcasting were virtually all-white occupations until the 1980s, closely mirroring the hierarchical racial division of labor so evident in the broader American occupational structure. Blacks simply have not had the same opportunities as whites when their playing careers are finished. In 1987 there were only five blacks in network radio and television sportscasting and only four black baseball journalists (as well as one Hispanic and one Asian) among the 254 full-time writers covering the major leagues' 26 teams (Shuster, 1987). In a 1988 *MacNeil/Lehrer News Hour*, sociologist Harry Edwards called the mass media "the most segregated corner in sport," and in a *New York Times* article columnist Ira Berkow said, "The hiring practices within the media have been deplorable" ("Edwards," 1988, p. 2C; see also Shuster, 1988).

Because sport has traditionally been viewed as a male preserve, the message to females interested in sports reporting or broadcasting has been clear: Women do not understand sport, so they certainly could not know how to report it. Despite the indignities and discrimination that female sports journalists and broadcasters have experienced and the relatively few women in the field, impressive gains have been made since the late 1970s. Perhaps the most significant event in legitimizing the improved status of women sports journalists was the appointment in November 1978 of LeAnne Schreiber as the first woman sports editor in the history of the *New York Times* ("New York Times," 1978).

That appointment came only after a decade-long struggle by women to be given equal opportunity and access to sport news. During this period they had to overcome policies of sport officials that excluded them from stadium press boxes and locker rooms. In one celebrated case, Melissa Ludtke, a young female reporter for *Sports Illustrated*, brought a suit claiming that her exclusion from locker rooms was based solely on her sex and thus violated her right to pursue her profession under the equal-protection and due-process clauses of the Fourteenth Amendment ("Sharing the Best," 1979). By the end of the 1970s, Ludtke and other female sports journalists had won access to locker rooms, press boxes, and any other facilities that pertained to their work.

Two significant events at the end of 1987 signaled improved opportunities for women in sports broadcasting. Gayle Gardner, an ESPN *SportsCenter* host, was hired by NBC as the first full-time female sports anchor, and Gayle Sierens, a news anchor and former sportscaster at Tampa's WXFL-TV, became the first female play-by-play broadcaster in NFL history in a game between the Kansas City Chiefs and the Seattle Seahawks (Martzke, 1987a, 1987b).

Many barriers have fallen by the wayside as women have gained increasing respect for their sports reporting and broadcasting skills, but there are still very few females in the field. The subordination of women continues, and each new breakthrough in media sport requires concerted struggle against the persistent, male-dominated sexual division of labor.

Summary and Preview

A symbiosis exists between the mass media and contemporary sport. Media sport is another arena for accumulation of capital and expenditures for leisure. But media sport is not just about the economic interests of the corporations that own the media. Because the media are effective and powerful organizations for promoting hegemonic ideology, media sport is also an arena for the advancement and reproduction of dominant interests.

Professional team sport, the focus of chapter 7, is a major form of modern commercial sport, and it is an industry with close ties to the mass media. Indeed, the mass media is the financial foundation that drives professional team sport. Without the television rights fees paid to the various professional sports leagues, they could not continue to function in their accustomed manner.

CHAPTER 7

The Professional Team Sport Industry

Sport . . . has become one more site for capital accumulation and leisure expenditure. . . . This new dominant social definition of sports practice—and the full incorporation of professional sport as a part of sport's modern institutional structure—has become a constitutive part of the consolidation of capitalist hegemony in the modern world.

Richard S. Gruneau, sport sociologist

Professional team sports comprise a commercial industry with a commanding place in contemporary American life. They dominate significant portions of our lives through print, radio, television, and just daily conversation. Following the fortunes (and misfortunes) of one's favorite teams is one of the most popular forms of leisure and entertainment for a broad spectrum of Americans. Seventeen million people attend professional football games each year and 48 million attend major league baseball games; the National Hockey League has averaged 12 million in recent years and NBA basketball 15.5 million.

But television is the medium through which most people are directly involved with professional sports. Up to 25 hours of professional team sports are beamed to home television sets per week by the major networks, and hundreds of additional hours are provided by cable networks spread across the country. Some of our most popular programs are professional sport events—the Super Bowl, the World Series, the Stanley Cup play-offs, the NBA World Championship play-off. The Super Bowl is usually the highest-rated single TV program each year.

Professional athletes and coaches are some of the best-known celebrities in the U.S., and they are held up as role models by many people, young and old. Becoming a professional athlete is something to which millions of young boys—and increasingly girls—aspire because pro athletes are viewed as society's heroes by many.

The professional team sport industry is also one in which capitalist productive relations hold sway and in which power, dominance, and subordination are fundamental. In many ways it reflects the material and ideological foundations of contemporary American social and economic life (Sage, 1984). The premise of capital accumulation is the foundation on which this industry is built: Professional team ownership is privatized, and team owners want to make money. Competition in this industry, though present, is primarily against other forms of popular entertainment; in effect, competition among team owners within a league is intentionally muted (more on this later) so that franchises within a professional league do not compete directly against each other. Sport leagues and team owners want a minimum of government interference, while at the same time getting unique local and national government protections.

In trying to understand the professional team sport industry it is important to recognize it as a *business*—it is made up of incorporated enterprises whose major purpose is the accumulation of profits. A sport corporation like the New York Yankees or the Denver Broncos is as real a business as General Motors, Exxon, or Paramount Pictures, and the profit motive drives professional sport just as it does the auto industry, the gas and oil industry, or the movie industry. The products in the case of professional sport are sport events, just like the products in the auto industry are automobiles and the products in the movie industry are films.

Professional sports are a component of the economic processes of production and consumption. In owning or controlling the means of athletic production, team owners, commissioners, and league organizers represent the interests of the dominant class, through acting as agents of it as well as belonging to it.

The average American does not view or perhaps refuses to view professional sport in this way. Instead, professional teams are seen by many as a kind of extension of the local high school team, with the players thought of like a group of local boys who, through their achievements, boost civic pride and promote solidarity and community. A local professional team is viewed as having been brought to the city by a public-spirited citizen, instead of a wealthy entrepreneur making another investment. Because most people do not understand the pecuniary driving forces of professional sport, the pro sport owners, the league commissioners, and the mass media nurture the public's gullibility about professional sport franchises because such an attitude is good for the pro sport business.

Not only is professional sport concerned with business, but its leaders go to great lengths to conceal this fact from the public. Jerry Jones, owner of the Dallas Cowboys, said, "I don't feel I own the Dallas Cowboys. . . . All I . . . do is use my talents to husband the Cowboys for our fans. That's who owns the Dallas Cowboys" (Caulk, 1989, p. 17S). Advertising suggests that the local team is owned by the public and operated on their behalf. Professional teams are named after cities rather than owners solely for commercial purposes. Team advertising and hype from the mass media sell civic identity and community involvement through terms like "Your Denver Nuggets." In reality, a pro sport team is no more "yours" than is Sears or Wal-Mart. Through such tactics, professional sport mimics other forms of capitalist enterprise that employ ideological techniques to provide socially sanctioned justifications that legitimate money making.

Actually, celebration over the successes of a privately owned, profit-making business that calls itself by its city's name is naive. But the public take very seriously the assertion that they are the owners of pro teams in their cities, and the real owners consider it essential to encourage this belief—after all, it's good for their business. This public attitude has enabled professional sport team owners to extract very favorable subsidies for their businesses from the public sector (as was described in chapter 4).

Development of Professional Team Sports

Although the evolution from amateurism to commercial professional teams has occurred at a different time and different pace in each of our four major men's sports, in every case the process has produced a group of franchise owners, dependent on television for the growth and health of their financial interests.

Baseball

Professional team sports had their beginnings just before the Civil War with the formation of the National Association of Base Ball Players, but it was during the last three decades of the 19th century that professional baseball boomed. Between 1869 and 1900, some 850 professional baseball clubs were founded; most perished within 2 years. Only the Cincinnati Red Stockings, launched in 1869, survive from the era before the establishment of the National League in 1876. The Cincinnati team was a touring team—there was no professional league—that traveled throughout the country playing local teams. The Red Stockings established an enviable record in their inaugural year, winning 64 of their 65 games (Vincent, 1981).

Within 2 years of the Red Stockings' initial season, a group of baseball players formed the National Association of Professional Baseball Players, and in the summer of 1871 they began operating as professional baseball's first major league. This "players' league" lasted 5 years before it folded, to be replaced in the summer of 1876 with the National League. A second league, the American League, began in 1900, completing the two major leagues that still exist today, though in a much expanded form.

Football

What is now the sport of football had its beginnings in the latter 1800s. The first intercollegiate game was played in 1869, and football quickly gained popularity in colleges. During the 1890s and through the 1920s noncollege football games were played in which the players were paid. Most of the teams represented a town or city, and most players came from the local community, supplemented by current and former collegiate players who were paid by the game to play. There were no leagues and no regular schedule of games. However, in 1921 a group of interested parties organized the American Professional Football Association, with membership set at $100. A year later the association was reorganized and the name was changed to the National Football League (Roberts, 1953).

From its beginnings, private commercial interests have had a hand in the development of the NFL. The Acme Packing Company in Green Bay, Wisconsin, sponsored a local team, fittingly called the Packers; and in Decatur, Illinois, the A.E. Staley Manufacturing Company started the team now known as the Chicago Bears. From these humble beginnings, professional football is a $600-million-a-year business, and each franchise in the NFL is worth over $60 million. The editor of *Sports inc.*, Craig Reiss, estimated (1988) that the total value of the 28 teams in the league is $2.4 billion!

Ice Hockey

Professional ice hockey paralleled the development of professional football in many ways, but its early development took place in Canada. By the end of the 19th century it was played throughout Canada. The first professional hockey team was formed in 1903; soon after, other professional teams were organized and the first professional league, the International Professional Hockey League, was formed in 1904. In 1917 the National Hockey League was organized (Isaacs, 1977).

All of the original NHL franchises were located in eastern Canada, but in 1924 a franchise was granted to the city of Boston, thus making professional ice hockey available to American audiences. Two years later New York, Chicago, and Detroit gained franchises.

Following World War II the NHL settled into a league composed of 6 teams. In 1967 a major expansion took place and the league doubled the number of franchises; by 1972 it had expanded to 16 teams, and there are now 21 teams. Despite the admission of more and more American teams into the NHL, Canadian players have always vastly outnumbered Americans.

Basketball

The last of the major professional team sports to develop, basketball was born in 1891 when James Naismith wrote a set of rules for the game and had his students at Springfield College play it for the first time. The sport caught on immediately in colleges, especially women's schools, and by World War I there were teams made up of players who were professional in the sense that they received money for playing; in most cases they were getting a cut of the gate receipts. After a number of false starts between the world wars, the NBA was founded in 1946.

During its history the NBA has had a great deal of unrest, especially with franchise relocations. At first some NBA franchises were located in smaller cities, including Sheboygan, Wisconsin, and Waterloo, Iowa, with limited potential for generating the necessary revenue to support a professional sport team. As the franchises moved to larger cities during the 1950s, the popularity of professional basketball grew, and increased gate receipts throughout the league consolidated its stability.

During the 1960s the NBA was confronted by two rival leagues, the American Basketball League (ABL) and the American Basketball Association (ABA). The ABL lasted only 2 years; the ABA merged with the NBA in 1976.

Recent Expansion

Although professional sport teams have existed now for over 100 years, the rise of professional sport to its present visible, powerful, dominant position in American life is a development of only the past 30 years. In the mid-1950s major league baseball was a struggling business with 16 teams (now 26). The NFL was a modest sandlot league of 12 teams (now 28). The NBA had 7 or 8 franchises of little note—the best basketball was played in the AAU by company-sponsored teams. The NHL has grown from 6 teams to 21. The boom in professional sport and the number of teams has been the work of television. The foundation of current professional sports is the rights fees paid by the broadcast industry, as discussed in chapter 6.

Although male professional team sports have been a growth industry, women's professional team sports have generally been unsuccessful. As noted in chapter 3, the most popular professional sports for women are individual sports, especially golf and tennis. Women's professional softball and basketball leagues have tried and failed to win approval. The only women's professional team sport with any success in recent years is volleyball. Several other countries have women's professional basketball leagues, and many of the best American women basketball players are going abroad to play.

Sport Cartels

Commenting on the organization of professional team sports, Freedman (1987) noted they "have in general operated apart from normal business considerations, and their rules of business conduct have not been subject to governmental scrutiny to the same extent as any ordinary business" (p. 31). Actually, the basic organizational unit of professional sport teams is the league, not the individual franchise. As such, professional leagues are effectively cartels. A cartel is an organization of independent firms that has as its aim some form of restrictive or monopolistic influence on the production or sale of a commodity as well as the control of wages. Obviously, cartels increase the benefits for the powerful few at the expense of the many. As economist Roger Noll (1974) has argued, the purpose of cartel organization in pro sports is that "of restricting competition (for athletes) and dividing markets among firms in the industry" (p. 2). Whatever other functions a professional sports league performs, it serves as a network of power.

The Consequences

A cartel acts to constrain individuals to behave in the interests of the group of firms as a whole. The actual consequences of cartelized industries are varied and complex, depending upon such factors as the commodity produced and sold and the amount of the market actually under the control of the cartel. But in most cases the negative consequences impact labor and consumers most heavily. With respect to labor, cartels are able to hold down wages, and with respect to consumers cartels typically restrict production and control sales and thus can set prices as high as they wish. The beneficiaries of cartel-wide control of wages and production should be obvious. The major benefits accrue to owners of individual firms through the maximization of joint profits. In the case of professional team sports, the cartel members are the owners of the various team franchises, all of whom are wealthy. One does not have to be an economist to understand that the advantages of cartel organization in sport go overwhelmingly to the powerful owners, while the powerless laborers (athletes) and consumers suffer the burdens of such organization.

Professional sport leagues operate as cartels in three major ways (Freedman, 1987):

1. They restrict interteam competition for players by controlling the rights of workers (players) through player drafts, contracts, and trades, thereby reducing competitive bidding between teams for player services.
2. They act in concert to admit or deny new teams, and they control the location and relocation of teams.
3. They divide local and regional media markets as well as negotiate, as a single entity, national media rights fees.

Most people recognize the economic and political power inherent in collective corporate organization, and they believe that there are laws prohibiting cartels, monopolies, and trusts. It is true that beginning in the late 19th century the U.S. government took steps designed to thwart large corporations who organized to restrict trade through such tactics. The Sherman Antitrust Act of 1890 forbade every contract, combination in the form of trust, or conspiracy in restraint of trade and all attempts to monopolize any part of an industry. Since then, much additional legislation has been passed in the government's effort to outlaw corporate conspiracies. Unfortunately, it has had limited effect in the corporate world. And, more importantly, in the case of professional team sports it has been judged generally not to apply.

In spite of numerous challenges to cartelization by athletes and rival leagues extending over the 20th century, professional sports have been able to sustain their position that a sport league is a single entity—some have called it a joint venture—and that there can be no restraint of trade as defined by the Sherman Act because that would require two independent firms. Several arguments have also been consistently advanced to justify collective organization:

- Teams have to cooperate in scheduling and playing games.

- Commercial sport events must involve fairly evenly matched teams to maintain uncertainty about the outcome of games and league championships (without evenly matched teams there will be no marketable competition, so the league needs control over the distribution of athletic talent).
- Revenue sharing is necessary to regulate economic competition between teams and to equalize the distribution of money, thus enabling resources to be similar among the various franchises and equalizing competition on the field.

Pete Rozelle (1964), the Commissioner of the NFL for over 25 years, spoke articulately concerning the essential need for a cartel system in professional sports. In what has become a classic defense of this system, he said this:

On the playing field, member clubs are clearly competitors—and every effort must be made to promote this. But in their business operations, member clubs of a league are less competitors than they are partners or participants in a joint venture. There is nothing comparable to this relationship elsewhere on the American scene. Because of it, the application of ordinary antitrust principles to sports league operations is more likely to produce confusions and distortions than sound results. (p. 94)

Although there are certainly ways in which professional team sports differ from most business enterprises and thus they need to structure their organization differently, it is the enormous advantages in terms of power and accumulation of profits that foster cartelized arrangements.

Restriction of Interteam Competition for Players.   When professional team sports were in their formative stages, team owners and promoters competed with each other in an open market, vying for athletes and spectators. But it became gradually evident to a few promoters and potential owners of professional baseball teams that such competition was counterproductive to the interests of controlling sport labor and capital accumulation. They realized that labor and consumer issues could be better stabilized and joint profits more consistently realized by a collective, or cartel. Accordingly, they took the lead in bringing order from the chaos with the formation of the National League, which set a precedent for business organization in professional sports that ultimately became the standard.

Founders of the National League established cartelized practices in the marketplace, and within a few years they expanded this to include a practice that economists call *monopsony*, which merely means a one-buyer market. In the case of professional baseball, this meant that all rights to a player were held by one team and one team only. Once a player signed a National League standard player contract with a team, he was bound to that team for his entire playing career unless it sold him. Under this reserve clause system (chapter 4), competitive bidding among teams for player services was forbidden. The reserve system was, then, basically an agreement among owners not to compete with one another for players.

A 1922 challenge to the reserve clause, standard in major league contracts, was settled by a U.S. Supreme Court ruling in favor of the baseball owners. Freedman (1987) has summarized the court's action in this way: "Professional baseball . . . was granted an exemption from the application of the federal antitrust laws upon the ground that this professional sport was not engaged in interstate commerce or trade, and furthermore baseball was in essence not a commercial activity" (p. 32). By default other professional sports have used that decision, and more recent ones, to define their own special legal and economic positions; all have adopted monopsonistic practices as they have evolved.

The Franchise Market

Control of the number and location of franchises is one of the important advantages of cartel organization in professional sports; all of the leagues have policies that allow the owners to do this. By controlling the number of franchises within a league, the owners make them scarce commodities, which means their worth appreciates much faster than other investments (Goodman, 1988). Consider these financial returns:

- Edgar Kaiser bought the Denver Broncos in 1981 for $35 million and sold the franchise just 3 years later for $70 million.
- Larry Weinberg paid $3.5 million for the Portland Trail Blazers as an expansion franchise in 1970 and sold the franchise in 1988 for $70 million.
- Edward B. Williams paid $12 million for the Baltimore Orioles in 1979; Eli S. Jacobs bought the franchise in 1988 for $70 million.
- In 1984, the Murchison family sold the Dallas Cowboys to a group of Dallas investors for about $60 million. Five years later the franchise was sold to Jerry Jones for $140 million.
- In 1985 "Red" McCombs sold the Denver Nuggets to Sidney Shlenker for $20 million. In 1989 Shlenker sold the Nuggets to a group of businessmen from Chicago for $65 million.

Another example illustrates how scarcity has worked in the franchise market: The Seattle Mariners of major league baseball were bought for $13 million in 1981 by George Argyros; as of January 1, 1988, the franchise was appraised for $58.6 million, despite 12 straight losing seasons (Whitford, 1988). In 1988 the editors of *Sports inc.* estimated the value of all NFL franchises and claimed that "no NFL team is valued at less than

$70 million" ("Buying low," 1988). Table 7.1 shows the figures for some of the franchises along with the incredible appreciation that has occurred with them. *Sports inc.* estimates of some franchise values of major league baseball teams are shown in Table 7.2. Predictions are that the values of franchises will continue to appreciate in the 1990s.

Franchise Expansion

Team owners exercise great control over league expansion. Applicants for new franchises must secure the permission of three fourths of the existing owners in a particular league. Such permission is difficult to obtain because owners are typically reluctant to expand the league and further share athletic talent and profits. Moreover, the scarcity of existing franchises and the difficulty of securing permission for a new franchise drive up the cost of expansion franchises—when they are approved. For example, applicants for each of the four newest NBA franchises (Miami, Charlotte, Orlando, and Minneapolis) had to pay $32.5 million to obtain the franchise. The cost is made more burdensome for the applicant because he or she is often required to pay an indemnity fee if the new franchise is to be located near an existing one.

The only alternative for someone who wants to establish a professional sport franchise is to start a new league, and all four established professional team sports have experienced challenges from upstart rivals. The established leagues have used their enormous political and economic power to either destroy the new league or incorporate some of the teams into the established league on terms that were very favorable to the established team owners. In 1986 the USFL brought a suit against the NFL challenging several of the monopolistic advantages the NFL enjoyed over any new league. Although the court ruled that the NFL was indeed a self-regulating monopoly committed to crushing rival leagues, the court set damages at $3, making it clear that it had no intention of changing this antitrust exemption.

Franchise Relocation

In addition to controlling the number of franchises within a league, each league has policies about the movement of franchises. The basic policy is that a franchise may not be moved without the approval of at least three fourths of the owners. All the leagues have fought fiercely to maintain control over franchise movement or relocation. As Freedman (1987) noted, the reasons for this are that

> the stability of each franchise is important to the overall financial success. If franchises were permitted to move freely, such as a move into

Table 7.1 Approximate Values of Selected NFL Franchises

Team	Principal owner	Last major transaction ($/year)	Team worth ($)
Atlanta Falcons	Rankin M. Smith	8.5 million/1965	75 million to 80 million
Cincinnati Bengals	John Sawyer	7 million/1968	80 million to 85 million
Cleveland Browns	Art Modell	3.925 million/1961	75 million to 80 million
Dallas Cowboys	Jerry Jones	140 million/1989	140 million to 160 million
Denver Broncos	Pat Bowlen	70.5 million/1984	80 million to 85 million
Detroit Lions	William Clay Ford	4.5 million/1963	75 million to 80 million
Green Bay Packers	Publicly owned since 1922	—	70 million to 75 million
Houston Oilers	K.S. "Bud" Adams, Jr.	25,000[a]/1959	75 million to 80 million
Indianapolis Colts	Robert Irsay	19 million/1972	75 million to 80 million
Kansas City Chiefs	Lamar Hunt	25,000/1960	75 million to 80 million
Los Angeles Rams	Georgia Frontiere	0[b]/1979	90 million to 95 million
New York Giants	Tim Mara, Wellington Mara	2,500/1925	95 million to 100 million
New York Jets	Leon Hess[c]	1 million/1963	95 million to 100 million
Phoenix Cardinals	Bill Bidwill	50,000/1932[d]	75 million to 85 million
Pittsburgh Steelers	Dan Rooney	2,500/1933	75 million to 80 million
San Diego Chargers	Alex Spanos	41 million/1984[e]	80 million to 85 million
San Francisco 49ers	Edward DeBartolo, Jr.	16 million to 18 million/1977	100 million to 120 million
Tampa Bay Buccaneers	Hugh F. Culverhouse	16 million/1976	70 million to 75 million
Washington Redskins	Jack Kent Cooke	15 million[f]/1985	80 million to 85 million

Note. Adapted from "Buying Low, Selling High" (1988).

[a]Includes AFL membership fees. [b]Inherited. [c]One of five buyers together paying $1 million. [d]Inherited in 1972. [e]Bought 57%. [f]Paid over many years.

Table 7.2   Approximate Values of Selected Major League Baseball Teams in 1988

Team	Value (millions of $)
National League	
Atlanta Braves	65 to 70
Chicago Cubs	70 to 80
Houston Astros	70 to 80
Los Angeles Dodgers	110 to 120
Montreal Expos	70 to 80
New York Mets	105 to 115
Pittsburgh Pirates	55 to 65
San Francisco Giants	60 to 70
St. Louis Cardinals	85 to 95
American League	
Baltimore Orioles	65 to 75
Boston Red Sox	75 to 85
California Angels	90 to 100
Cleveland Indians	50 to 60
Detroit Tigers	70 to 80
Kansas City Royals	70 to 80
Minnesota Twins	65 to 75
New York Yankees	100 to 120
Oakland Athletics	65 to 75
Texas Rangers	60 to 75
Toronto Blue Jays	80 to 90

Note. Adapted from Wendel (1988).

an existing franchise market or to a distant franchise market, the franchise movement or relocation could jeopardize the existing financial security of all professional teams in that league. Stability of franchise operations is also important to cities and states which support those franchises; public bonds are often utilized to construct stadiums and arenas for use of professional sports teams. (pp. 78-79)

Although these may sound like good defenses, the fact is that when faced with economic considerations, the hypothetically valid reasons for franchise stability have frequently been jettisoned. As shown in Table 7.3, since 1953 there have been over 60 franchise relocations in baseball, football, basketball, and hockey, attesting to the leagues' power to accomplish what they consider beneficial to the business of professional sports (Freedman, 1987). This movement of franchises vividly reveals the lie in the "your team" rhetoric advanced by pro team owners. During the 1980s,

Table 7.3   Professional Team Sport Franchise Movement Since 1953

Major league baseball
1953 Boston to Milwaukee (Braves)
1954 St. Louis (Browns) to Baltimore Orioles
1955 Philadelphia to Kansas City, MO (Athletics)
1958 Brooklyn to Los Angeles (Dodgers)
     New York to San Francisco (Giants)
1961 Washington (Senators) to Minnesota (Twins)
1966 Milwaukee to Atlanta (Braves)
     Los Angeles to Anaheim, CA (Angels)
1968 Kansas City, MO, to Oakland (Athletics)
1970 Seattle (Pilots) to Milwaukee (Brewers)
1972 Washington (Senators) to Arlington, TX (Rangers)

Professional football
1953 Dallas (Texans) to Baltimore (Colts)
1960 Chicago to St. Louis (Cardinals)
1961 Los Angeles to San Diego (Chargers)
1963 Dallas (Texans) to Kansas City, MO (Chiefs)
1971 Boston to Foxboro, MA (Patriots)
     Dallas to Irvine, TX (Cowboys)
1973 Buffalo to Orchard Park, NY (Bills)
1975 Detroit to Pontiac, MI (Lions)
1976 New York to Rutherford, NJ (Giants)
1980 Los Angeles to Anaheim, CA (Rams)
1982 Bloomington, MN, to Minneapolis (Vikings)
     Oakland, CA, to Los Angeles (Raiders)
1984 New York to Rutherford, NJ (Jets)
     Baltimore to Indianapolis (Colts)
1988 St. Louis to Phoenix (Cardinals)

Professional basketball
1956 Milwaukee (Blackhawks) to St. Louis (Hawks)
1958 Ft. Wayne, IN, to Detroit (Pistons)
     Rochester, NY, to Cincinnati (Royals)
1961 Minneapolis to Los Angeles (Lakers)
1963 Philadelphia to San Francisco (Warriors)
1964 Chicago (Zephyrs) to Baltimore (Bullets)
     Syracuse, NY (Nationals) to Philadelphia (76ers)
1969 St. Louis to Atlanta (Hawks)
     Anaheim, CA (Amigos) to Los Angeles (Stars)
     Teaneck, NJ (Americans) to Commack, NY (Nets)
     Minneapolis (Muskies) to Washington (Caps)
1970 Houston (Mavericks) to Charlotte, NC (Cougars)
     Minneapolis (Muskies) to Pittsburgh (Pipers)

(Cont.)

Table 7.3   (Continued)

Professional basketball (continued)
1971   New Orleans (Buccaneers) to Memphis (Pros)
          Los Angeles to Salt Lake City (Stars)
          Washington (Caps) to Norfolk, VA (Squires)
1972   San Diego to Houston (Rockets)
1973   Cincinnati (Royals) to Kansas City, MO (Kings)
1974   Baltimore to Landover, MD (Bullets)
1975   Charlotte, NC (Cougars) to St. Louis (Stars)
1976   Memphis (Tams) to Baltimore (Claws)
1978   Commack, NY, to Rutgers, NJ (Nets)
1979   Buffalo (Braves) to San Diego (Clippers)
1980   New Orleans to Salt Lake City (Jazz)
1983   San Diego to Los Angeles (Clippers)
1985   Kansas City, MO, to Sacramento, CA (Kings)

Professional hockey
1973   Philadelphia to Vancouver (Blazers)
          Ottawa (Nationals) to Toronto (Toros)
          New York (Raiders) to Cherry Hill, NJ (Knights)
          Boston to Hartford, CT (Whalers)
1974   Detroit (Stags) to Baltimore (Blades)
          Cherry Hill, NJ (Knights) to San Diego (Mariners)
1975   Denver to Ottawa (67s)
          Oakland, CA (Seals) to Cleveland (Barons)
          Kansas City, MO (Scouts) to Denver (Rockies)
1976   Cleveland (Barons) to Minneapolis (North Stars)
          Toronto (Toros) to Birmingham, AL (Bulls)
1978   Houston (Aeros) to Winnipeg (Jets)
1980   Atlanta to Calgary (Flames)
1982   Colorado (Rockies) to Rutherford, NJ (Devils)

---

efforts by fans of football's Oakland Raiders, Baltimore Colts, and St. Louis Cardinals to petition and plead to keep "their" teams fell on deaf (but powerful) ears, blatantly exposing the community facade promoted by the professional sport industry.

The dynamics of franchise movement are quite complex, involving owners, politicians, business leaders, and the mass media, to name only the major participants. In each specific situation, at the heart of the phenomenon is the exercise of subtle power by different combinations of these groups. A frequent underlying issue in franchise relocation, or threats of relocation, is the complaint by an owner that existing facilities are inadequate or that financial arrangements with the city for facility rental, division of concessions, and parking are unacceptable. Owner complaints are usually accompanied by threats to move the franchise: "Build a new facility/improve the existing one/give us a better financial package, or we will move" is the way the demands and threats are usually phrased. Sportswriters have begun to refer to this tactic as *sportmail* (a play on blackmail). Whatever it is called, it must be taken seriously by cities housing professional teams because there exist many examples of the mobility of pro franchises; a number have relocated when their demands were not satisfied; three teams in the NFL alone relocated during the 1980s. Furthermore, the threat to move is especially ominous because communities know that it will be extremely difficult to secure another franchise if one is lost. All in all, then, owners have considerable leverage for extracting concessions from cities desperate to retain their franchises.

Add to the instability of the franchise market the fact that some cities have appointed commissions whose sole task is to try to lure professional franchises. These commissions and their backers resort to an incredible array of enticements that exacerbate sport-franchise hopscotch. Encouraged by the success of Indianapolis, Indiana, which built a football stadium before the city had a professional football franchise and, once it was built, went out and lured the Baltimore Colts to move there, other cities are constructing facilities—most publicly financed—as bait to attract sport franchises.

Publicly Owned Facilities

Loss of a professional franchise is viewed by many people as having adverse consequences for a city, but another issue is frequently part of the relocation equation. Since the 1950s, cities have spent close to a *billion* dollars building municipal stadiums for professional sport teams; about 70% of professional sport stadiums and arenas have been built with public funds. This issue of public subsidies for professional sport owners was discussed in some detail in chapter 4, but a few additional points deserve elaboration here.

Many cities are financially burdened with debt on municipal facilities built to accommodate local franchises. As I pointed out earlier, most of these public facilities have become a financial liability because rental income from pro teams typically covers only a fraction of the actual maintenance and construction costs, let alone debt reduction on the municipal bonds the community sold to build the facility. When a professional franchise leaves a city, an additional load is thrust on taxpayers by a facility with no tenant to provide income. A public trust given to franchise owners through provision of a playing facility comes back to burden the taxpayers, who all along have been subsidizing the accumulation of private capital by owners (Baade & Dye, 1988).

Professional Team Owners

Owners of franchises in the early years of professional baseball, football, hockey, and later basketball included a menagerie of promoters, local politicians, small manufacturers, and local business owners. They were a far more financially diverse group than the men and women who presently own and control the major sport franchises. With few exceptions, professional teams have always been owned and controlled by private interests; most owners have been white males with considerable accumulated wealth, either through inheritance or their own financial investments.

In the only book wholly devoted to sport team owners, Kowet (1977) said that

> some of today's owners were lured by the glamour that pro athletes radiate; others are dyed-in-the-wool fans; many have bitten the bait of tax writeoffs and antitrust exemptions. Some are benevolent dictators; others, outright despots. Some live in baroque elegance; a few absolutely detest showiness. But despite their differences one common bond sets them apart from the masses of ordinary [people]. The poorest of the pro sports owners is very rich. (p. 5)

Kowet's statement, made in the late 1970s, is as true 10 years later; owners are definitely among America's capitalist elite. To illustrate, near the end of 1988 Eli S. Jacobs reached an agreement to buy the Baltimore Orioles for $70 million, and Victor Kiam became the majority owner of the New England Patriots, which he and a partner bought for $85 million. Jacobs is chairman of the board of Memorex Telex Corporation, the world's second-largest manufacturer and distributor of computer peripheral equipment; he has controlling interest in companies whose revenues exceed $5 billion. Kiam is chief executive officer of Remington Products and a very wealthy man indeed.

Each year *Forbes* magazine compiles a list of the nation's 400 wealthiest individuals. Those on the 1989 list have an average personal wealth of $672 million. In recent years between 20 and 30 of the "Forbes 400" have owned sports franchises. In 1989 the richest sports owner was Ted Arison, the majority owner of the Miami Heat of the NBA. He is one of the 10 richest men in the U.S., with an estimated worth of $2.86 billion. Edward John DeBartolo, owner of the Pittsburgh Penguins of the NHL, has an estimated personal worth of $1.4 billion. Baseball's richest owner is Ted Turner, who owns the Atlanta Braves; his worth is estimated at $1.76 billion. In the NFL Jack Kent Cooke, who owns the Washington Redskins, has a personal fortune of $1.25 billion. In 1989 at least 9 of the 28 NFL owners had personal fortunes estimated to be at least $200 million.

In examining the sources of the wealth of sport team owners, Flint and Eitzen (1987) found that almost 50% of team owners have primary business interests in communications, oil production, and real estate and land development, and more than two thirds (68%) of the wealthiest owners' interests lie in these same industries. Table 7.4 presents the primary business interests of the 141 professional sport team owners that Flint and Eitzen identified.

The Green Bay Packers are the major exception to the overwhelming pattern of private ownership in professional sports. The Packers have been a publicly owned corporation since 1922; about 1,800 stockholders own some 4,700 shares of stock, and no individual can own more than 200. The stock pays no dividends and is redeemable only for the original purchase price of $25. Stock ownership entitles one to attend the annual

Table 7.4 The Primary Business Interests of Sport Team Owners

Business arena	#	%	% by category
Entrepreneurial capital (private ownership)			
Communications and publishing	12	8.5	
Oil and energy development	10	7.1	
Real estate and land development	44	31.2	
Transportation and distribution	1	.7	
(Subtotal)	67	47.5	47.5
Professional occupations			
Law partnership	7	5.0	
Medical practice	1	.7	
(Subtotal)	8	5.7	5.7
Franchise operations and management			
Sport executive	14	9.9	
(Subtotal)	14	9.9	9.9
Monopoly capital (public corporation)			
Automotive industry	5	3.5	
Banking, finance, and insurance	9	6.4	
Brewing and liquor industry	5	3.5	
Industrialist and manufacturing	4	2.8	
Sales and merchandising	5	3.5	
(Subtotal)	28	19.7	19.7
Residual			
Inheritance	4	2.8	
Unknown	20	14.2	
(Subtotal)	24	17.0	17.0
Total sample	141		99.8

Note. From "Professional Sports Team Ownership and Entrepreneurial Capitalism" by W.C. Flint and D.S. Eitzen, 1987, *Sociology of Sport Journal,* **4**(1), p. 20. Copyright 1987 by Human Kinetics Publishers, Inc. Reprinted by permission.

stockholders' meeting, which elects the team's board of directors and conducts general oversight of team business. Whereas relocation of privately owned franchises requires only a decision by the owner (and approval of other league owners), moving the Green Bay Packers would require the approval of its 1,800 shareholders, 90% of whom live in the Green Bay area.

Motivations for Owning a Professional Team

In one of the few attempts to analyze the motivations of those who invest in professional sport franchises, Brower (1976) suggested two basic reasons: fun and capital accumulation. Brower says that people "who own professional athletic teams originally go into the venture with the intention of having fun. . . . Almost without exception, owners are superfans rather than merely prudent financial investors" (p. 17). Pat Bowlen, owner of the Denver Broncos, agrees; he was quoted as saying, "A lot of people who own sports teams live vicariously through their players. I get a lot of thrills from this. Making money is one thing, having fun is something else" (Brown, 1988, p. 2C). Victor Kiam, majority owner of the New England Patriots, at first turned down offers to get involved in buying the Patriots but changed his mind "because of the fun factor" (p. 2C).

Even though owners may seek the fun factor of being a part of the immensely popular world of pro sports, once owners acquire franchises, they also want to make a profit. As Brower (1976) says, "These owners, successful business[people] neither accustomed to, nor comfortable with, losing money in business ventures, want to succeed financially with their investment even when the impetus for entrance is primarily nonpecuniary" (p. 25). And indeed there are various ways in which sport team owners can add to their already considerable wealth. First are the number of tax advantages available to them; one of the most significant is depreciation allowances. Second are direct profits from annual revenues and, more importantly, resale of the franchise. Finally, important promotional opportunities enhance profits and the value of other investments the owners have.

Player Depreciation. Sport franchise owners can depreciate professional athletes just like ranchers and manufacturers depreciate cattle or aging machinery; from the standpoint of pro sport owners, and supported by rulings by the Internal Revenue Service, an athlete is like a piece of equipment, with a useful life like any piece of equipment. *USA Today* sportswriter Kevin Maney (1987) said in reference to the Boston Celtics that "the Celtics write off their players like a hot dog maker writes off packaging machines. The franchise took $3.1 million in depreciation last year"

(p. 11C). Professional athletes are typically depreciated over 4 to 5 years. So a player valued at $1 million, depreciated over 5 years, gives the team owners a tax writeoff of $200,000 for each of those years. Depreciation is, of course, subtracted from a team's gross income, so the owner pays less in taxes. Player depreciation is indeed a significant tax shelter for owners (Allen, 1987).

Annual Profits and Resale. Figures on annual profits of professional teams are extremely difficult to obtain because ownership is private (with the exception of the Green Bay Packers), and financial statements do not have to be opened to the public. Because professional sport is one of the most secretive industries in the country, very limited information is available about the actual annual profits or losses of the various franchises. The Packers, as a publicly owned corporation, are required by law to reveal their figures. Annual profits reported by Green Bay in the 1980s have exceeded $3 million. In 1987 the Boston Celtics began a public sale of their stock, and their financial statement revealed that they made $4.4 million in profit the previous year. In the fall of 1987, union officials claimed that the average profit for NFL teams the previous year was $3.6 million (Covitz, 1987). Civic leaders in the Charlotte, North Carolina, area estimated that the NBA's Charlotte Hornets made $8 million in their first year in the league. According to a report prepared by the office of the major league baseball commissioner, their 26 clubs posted a $100 million profit in 1988. All in all, then, claims from team owners about losing enormous amounts of money must be viewed with skepticism.

Investors in pro franchises do not buy for tax benefits and annual profits only. The history of sport franchises is unmistakably clear about one thing: the biggest financial benefit to a franchise owner accrues when the franchise is sold. According to an attorney whose law firm serves as counsel to one sport franchise owner, "When owners go into sports, they don't go in to make a lot of money; when they sell, they sell to make a lot of money" (Rosenblatt, 1988, p. 2). Table 7.1 provides ample proof of the appreciation of NFL franchises.

Promotion of Other Investments.   Sport team owners do not acquire their wealth through their investment in teams; one must be wealthy already to be able to buy a professional team. And an increasing pattern has been that beyond the direct financial rewards of sport ownership already described, such ownership opens up numerous promotional opportunities that can integrate sport with owners' diversified corporate interests. The most obvious investment link is found among sports owners with concomitant investments in the broadcasting industry. The symbiosis between sport and the mass media cannot be more complete than with common ownership in the two industries. This kind of organizational diversification is characteristic of corporate capitalism throughout American business, enabling a few giant firms to maintain their economic and political power.

Alternatives to Private Team Ownership

Private sport team ownership dominates professional sport so overwhelmingly that few people have ever considered that there might be alternatives. For the few who have, there is little understanding of how such alternatives might work. Matthew Goodman (1988), though, has described how public ownership of a professional team franchise might operate. He deserves to be quoted at length, if only to stimulate thinking about the issue of sport team ownership in light of the increasing mobility of franchises and the public demands for expansion of professional sports.

> Here's how a buy out might work: Fans within a community could set up a corporation and issue public stock. The corporation would then negotiate with the team's owners on purchase of the franchise, using the capital raised from the stock drive as a down payment. The host city might float general obligation bonds to back up the rest of the purchase price, or the corporation might buy special revenue bonds, using—to take just one example—a 10 percent tax on tickets as a revenue stream to guarantee long-term payments. . . . A few important principles would have to be maintained. . . . Stock ownership must be broadly dispersed; there must be no speculative profits available on shares; management must be delegated, so that the franchise can run on a day-to-day basis like any other club; the charter of incorporation must prohibit the team from moving. . . . The sports commissioners have already made clear their opposition to this type of ownership. Not only does it reek of socialism, more importantly it would require that the team open its books, and this has been anathema to owners and commissioners alike. . . . In the long run, professional sports might be rescued from the present system of ownership, in which city is pitted against city by men and women whose fortunes are often outstripped only by their own egos.[1]

In their frustration over losing a professional sport franchise or their inability to secure local ownership for an existing franchise, politicians and citizens groups in several cities have explored community ownership of professional teams. Little has come of their efforts. Two major

---

[1]From "The Home Team" ["Sports Today" section] by M. Goodman, January 1988, Z(eta) Magazine, 1(1), p. 65. Reprinted by permission. Z(eta) Magazine is located at 150 West Canton Street, Boston, MA 02118. A 1-year subscription costs $25. Z(eta) is a monthly political magazine.

obstacles confront them: First, convincing local taxpayers that an investment of this kind is a good use of their money would be an enormous task; second, the opposition of current team owners would be vigorous. The owners would view community ownership as a threat to the private enterprise structure of professional sport (the Green Bay exception notwithstanding).

Professional Athletes

Because of the immense popularity of professional sports and the incredible social prestige of the players, almost everyone who has ever hit a baseball, shot a basket, or caught a pass has imagined becoming a pro. But the enormous trivia disseminated about professional athletes contrasts markedly with the little knowledge the public has of them as a social group and in relationship to the power structure of the professional sport industry.

Every productive enterprise has a group of persons who are the actual producers of the good or service. In professional sport that group is the athletes. Without the athletes, there would be no sport event—no product—so the pro athlete is a commodity producer. Professional athletes are wage laborers who have acquired salable skills, and indeed that is what they do—sell their labor as an occupation and livelihood. As such, they also are a commodity themselves, a commodity that can be arbitrarily traded, sold, and moved according to the whims and impulses of team owners. In the summer of 1988, New York Yankee slugger Don Mattingly, one of major league baseball's superstars, said upon learning that the Yankees' owner was considering trading him, "I'm just an employee. If management wants to move me, I have no control over it" (Picking, 1988, p. 1C). A coach for the Dallas Cowboys succinctly described management's perception of one of their star running backs: "His job is no more and no less than to help the Dallas Cowboys win games. . . . If the guy is here, he's got to do the job" (Moore, 1988a, p. 20S). And, of course, both are absolutely right. These are accurate portrayals of the social relationship of production in professional sports.

Athletes' labor is crucial to professional sport as a commodity because it is their performances that attract the public and the mass media; their labor makes the economy of sport possible. In characterizing social relations of pro athletes as employees, Beamish (1982) said,

As a form of activity that is completely subsumed under capitalist relations, professional athletes . . . work under a historically specific set of production relations. Athletes do not own or control the means of producing their athletic labor-power. They have no access to professional leagues other than through the sale of their labor-power to existing franchise owners. (pp. 177-178)

Berry, Gould, and Staudohar (1986) have elaborated:

> The name of the game is show biz, and the players are the stars. . . .
> Players as actors are both the machinery and the product. . . . It is
> not just that athletes are part of the game: They are the game.
> (pp. 9-10)

Under the cartelized organization of professional team sport, leagues control athletes' contracts, mobility, and working conditions, and the cumulative effects enhance profits for the owners. Although the specific effects of cartel organization on athletes are difficult to delineate, the best example of their impact on salaries is vividly demonstrated whenever a rival league begins operating in a sport. Player salaries have consistently risen with the creation of new leagues and fallen with their demise. Basketball and hockey salaries almost doubled with the formation of the ABA and WHA. After the AFL-NFL merger, average salaries fell over 20%.

Salaries

As much as the public dotes on professional athletes, they often express resentment about the money athletes make. Why is there this resentment, aside from a probably natural envy of people with more money than we have? There are several reasons. In the first place, the average American has never really fully understood—or at least accepted—that professional sport is a business. Consequently, professional teams are commonly perceived as a sort of extension of one's high school athletic team and pro athletes as the lucky stiffs who get to go on having a great time playing games while everyone else has to earn a living. It is easy enough to understand why people feel this way about pro sports, given its similarities to youth and school sport teams: Game rules are basically the same, players wear the same type of uniforms, teams are led by coaches, and teams participate in similar rituals and use similar mascots. With this public mind-set, it is understandable that the average person has difficulty seeing pro sport as a business and athletes as independent entrepreneurs.

Much of this resentment would probably diminish if people more adequately understood the industry of professional sport. The celebrated salaries of athletes need to be seen in the light of factors like the scarcity of talent, the average length of pro sport careers, job-related injuries, comparison with other professions, and the profitability of franchises. For instance, most Americans subscribe to the talent principle of pay, that those who have rare talent should be paid for it—the good old supply-and-demand standard of capitalism. The athletic talent necessary to play a professional sport at the highest level is extremely rare; pro athletes are an exceptionally skilled group. There are only 725 major league baseball players, 1,400 NFL football players, 345 NBA basketball players, and 525 NHL hockey players; with a total under 3,000, each player represents 1 in 10,000 of the 22 million adult men in the U.S. between the ages of 20 and 30. Professional sports, then, provide a livelihood for very few. In fact, it is easier to become a brain surgeon than a professional athlete!

The acclaimed high salaries of professional sport workers need to be put in the context of a total career pattern. Most adults work in the same occupation until retirement; there may be job changes, to be sure, but they are usually within the same line of work. Professional team sport careers, by contrast, are very short; the average length is about 5 years! This average is for those who actually make a major team roster; it does not include players who sign a pro contract but are cut before the season begins. So the few who have the rare ability to become pros remain at that level of sport for only a brief time. Their high salaries end when they can no longer make the team.

A widely held scenario shows many attractive jobs waiting for professional athletes when their playing careers are over. This impression stems principally from the few former athletes who move into sport broadcasting and the filling of the professional coaching and managerial ranks with former pros. But these are the exceptions, the elite, of former players. Large-scale studies of former pro athletes are scarce, but the pattern seems to be that most move into occupations commensurate with their educational levels. Athletes with college degrees tend to wind up in occupations occupied by college graduates; those with only a high school education (many baseball and hockey players go right from high school into the pros) tend to enter jobs like those held by other high school graduates.

Athletes' work has become more difficult and dangerous in all professional team sports due mainly to longer seasons and higher and higher performance standards. Injuries are common, especially in football and hockey; they are considered part of the job. In fact, injuries are so numerous in the NFL that the league publishes a weekly list of injured players—a casualty list. Injuries have cut short the playing careers of many professional athletes, and for a few injury has brought permanent physical disability. In a survey of 440 former NFL football players, 78% said they suffer continuing football-related disabilities, 54% admitted to having psychological adjustment problems, and 66% said that they believe that playing has shortened their life expectancy ("Player Poll," 1988).

Stripped of the public adulation and media hype, professional athletes are entertainers. When the salaries of pro athletes are compared with others in the entertainment business, athletic salaries are not particularly impressive. The following list is the average 1989 salaries of athletes in the top four team sports.

National Basketball Association	$577,200
Major League Baseball	$490,000
National Football League	$212,000
National Hockey League	$156,000

The highest 1989 salaries in these sports are between $3 million and $3.5 million, and about four NBA players are in that range. About 20 major league baseball players had salaries between $2 million and $2.8 million, and top NFL and NHL players had salaries about $1 million below this.

These are unquestionably impressive salaries, and a few superstar athletes earn up to $5 million for endorsements and public appearance fees. But what about other entertainers? Each year *Forbes* magazine publishes the earnings of the top American entertainers. Its report for 1989 listed these figures:

Michael Jackson (pop singer)	$65 million
Bill Cosby (actor, comedian)	$60 million
Sylvester Stallone (actor)	$38 million
Jack Nicholson (actor)	$34 million
Eddie Murphy (actor)	$22 million

The top 40 entertainers all reportedly had earnings over $5 million. What is clear, then, is that as entertainers professional athletes' earnings are not exorbitant; in fact, one could argue that they are underpaid.

Professional athletes can also be viewed as workers who are tops in their field and their salaries can be compared to those of business executives considered the best in their field, chief executive officers of American corporations. *Forbes* also publishes an annual report of the total compensation of these CEOs. Some of the top earners in 1989 were these (Duggan, Fritz, Heuslein, & Scheer, 1989):

Michael D. Eisner (Walt Disney)	$39,318,000
Steven J. Ross (Warner Communications)	$11,947,000
Paul B. Fireman (Reebok)	$11,439,000
John Sculley (Apple Computer)	$9,492,000
Dean Buntrock (Waste Management)	$8,584,000

The median income of the top 100 Wall Street financial tycoons was $15 million in 1988 (Byrne, 1988). Again, what is indelibly clear is that professional athletes' salaries are not out of line with others who are at the top of particular professions.

Professional team owners always spend less on athlete salaries than they expect to earn in revenue. In occasional instances it is possible to demonstrate a rather direct relationship between the salary paid to hire an athlete and the income he generates. And invariably the business acumen of owners is proven sound. In 1985 the New York Knicks signed Patrick Ewing to a $1.5-million contract. Season ticket sales rose to nearly 11,000 from about 5,700 the year before, suggesting that Ewing's presence on the team increased revenues nearly $3 million. That same year, Chicago Bulls rookie Michael Jordan was paid $550,000. Between increased ticket sales and play-off revenue (the Bulls had not made the play-offs for years before Jordan arrived), Jordan brought the Chicago team $2 million.

In 1986 the Buffalo Bills invested some $1.5 million in quarterback Jim Kelly. The financial results of this investment were impressive:

- Average home attendance increased by 31,121 fans.
- At $25 per ticket, the increased revenue was $778,025 per game.
- $778,025 × 8 home games = $6,224,200 for the season.

In other words, for a $1.5-million investment, the Bills got better than a 400% return!

In the fall of 1988 the Los Angeles Kings of the NHL acquired purportedly the greatest hockey player of all time, Wayne Gretzky, from the Edmonton Oilers. Gretzky signed an 8-year, $20-million contract with the Kings, an annual salary of about $2.5 million. Season ticket sales to the Kings games skyrocketed, and the team grossed an extra $4.3 million with Gretzky in the lineup. But the "Gretzky effect" does not end there; Table 7.5 illustrates the estimated initial financial windfall for the Kings and the rest of the NHL (Fichtenbaum, 1988).

Table 7.5 The Estimated Initial Gretzky Effect

Type of effect	Revenue ($)
On the Los Angeles Kings	
Increased ticket revenue	4.4 million
Increased cable TV revenue	1 million
Increased concessions revenue	500,000
Rent kickbacks	250,000

(Cont.)

Table 7.5 (Continued)

Type of effect	Revenue ($)
On the Los Angeles Kings (continued)	
Increased licensing revenue	2 million
Increased TV advertising	800,000
Increased radio revenue	180,000
On the NHL	
Ticket and concession revenue increases	
St. Louis Blues	350,000
Vancouver Canucks	300,000
Washington Capitals	325,000
Minnesota North Stars	125,000
Buffalo Sabres	100,000
New Jersey Devils	100,000
Winnipeg Jets	200,000
Other teams, combined	600,000
Total team revenue increases	2.1 million
NHL licensing increases	1.5 million
Total initial effect	12.73 million

Note. From "The Gretzky Effect" by P. Fichtenbaum, 1988, *Sports inc.*, October 3, p. 21. Copyright 1988 by Times Mirror Magazines, Inc. Reprinted by permission.

Collusion by Owners. Evidence that owners pay professional athletes only what they believe they have to and that they will resort to illegal anti-competitive tactics is found in the recent rulings of two impartial arbitrators. The iron lock of the reserve system was broken in 1975 when professional baseball's arbitrator Peter Seitz ruled in favor of two players who had challenged the reserve system. His ruling modified the reserve system and created "free agency," which allows professional athletes to negotiate with owners of other teams under certain circumstances (the provisions of free agency vary from league to league and are too complex to examine here). Following the decision by Seitz a wave of spending on free agents swept major league baseball. Over the next 10 years a great disparity in spending arose, with teams like the New York Yankees and the California Angels spending lavishly while the Cincinnati Reds and Toronto Blue Jays spent little.

During these years great animosity developed among the owners; not only were the free agent player salaries escalating rapidly, and more and more players were becoming free agents each year, but those salaries were causing the overall salary structure of baseball to rise sharply. This open labor market was welcomed by the players but understandably despised by the owners. In 1985 free agents found that owners would not engage in legitimate bidding for those among them still coveted by their former teams. The same thing occurred in 1986. These actions were so patently obvious to the players and constituted such a flagrant violation of one of the contract provisions between the players' union and the owners ("Players shall not act in concert with other Players and Clubs shall not act in concert with other Clubs") that the players' union filed a grievance against the owners. After months of testimony, the arbitrator concluded that major league baseball owners were guilty of improperly engaging in "concerted conduct" to limit the market for free agent players in 1985; in other words, they colluded to illegally restrict player salaries. One year later a second arbitrator, evaluating the evidence for 1986, concluded that the owners conspired to rig the bidding for the 1986 free agents and that "there was no vestige of a free market" (Nicolau, 1988, p. 52); instead there was a clear pattern of collusion to hold down player salaries (Nicolau, 1988).

The Effects of Monopsony on Salaries.   For years the NFL Players Association (NFLPA) squabbled with owners over free agency, even striking over the issue on two occasions (1982 and 1988), but to no avail. The attitude of some owners was succinctly expressed in 1988 by the president of the Dallas Cowboys, Tex Schramm: "No free agency; not now, not ever." But in the spring of 1989, facing litigation from the NFLPA over restraints on player movement, the owners unilaterally established a free agency system. Under it, each team protected 37 players—presumably their best—from free agency while exposing the rest—619—to the open market. The result? Over 225 players were signed by other teams; their salaries rose 78% and signing bonuses averaged $40,000! Here was clear and unambiguous evidence of the adverse economic impact of monopsonistic practices on professional athletes (Weisman, 1989). It also dramatized the effects of movement restriction for those 37 players on each team who were not given free agency. If players considered expendable could increase their salaries over 75%, imagine what the best could do in an open market.

Players' Unions

To mitigate working conditions under capitalism, American workers have joined in unions designed to deal collectively, rather than individually, with management. Such organization began in the mid-19th century, originally to address the interests of workers for increased wages, shorter hours, safer and more humane working conditions, and benefits such as health plans. The union movement in the U.S. has had a checkered history spanning glorious successes and desperate failures. From 11.6% of all employees in 1930 to a high of 34.5% immediately after World War II, union membership has declined to only 17% of employed Americans in the late 1980s (U.S. Bureau of the Census, 1989). Unionization rates in the U.S. now rank near the bottom of all capitalist countries.

In a comprehensive analysis of the American working class, Vanneman and Cannon (1987) concluded that weaknesses in the union movement and in working class consciousness in general are not a product of working class indifference or of the generosity and good will of capital, but rather that throughout the history of American capitalism private capital has enjoyed "unchallenged control in almost every sector of the economy" (p. 7). They elaborate:

> There are good reasons to conclude that U.S. capital has had more power than the capitalist class of other Western democracies. In the face of this overwhelming power, the U.S. working class [has] had a more difficult time constructing political and class organizations to defend its interests. (p. 167)

Failures in the union movement largely represent, then, the successful application of political and economic repression by the dominant class.

The response of professional athletes to monopsony, abridgment of individual rights, and other job restrictions has been unionization, collective bargaining, and strikes. The first organizing effort of professional athletes was the founding of the National Brotherhood of Baseball Players in 1885, and the Brotherhood actually formed its own league in 1890. In that year, the Players' League successfully conducted a season of baseball but a poor financial base and intense attacks by powerful forces within the National League forced it to disband.

The modern era for collectivization of professional athletes began in 1954 with the Major League Baseball Players' Association, as major league ballplayers attempted to establish some power against the hegemony of the owners; it was not until the mid-1960s, however, that they emerged with real powers. The NBA Players' Association was established in 1952 but did not become an authentic force until 1963. In 1956 the NFL Players' Association was formed, but it had to wait over 12 years for full recognition by the league. Several attempts were made in the 1950s to organize NHL players, but it was not until 1967 that the National Hockey League Players' Association received formal recognition from team owners (Berry, Gould, & Staudohar, 1986; Freedman, 1987; Lowenfish & Lupien, 1980).

The organization of players' unions within professional sports needs to be seen in terms of the relations of production within a capitalist enterprise. As Giddens (1987) has noted,

> A distinctive feature of the capitalist labour contract . . . is that it is purely economic, a monetary relation. The worker is not accorded

any rights of participation in the policies which govern the nature of the labour task or other aspects of the work setting. The formation of unions, one major aspect of class conflict . . . represents an attempt of workers to gain a measure of control over the conditions of their labour. (p. 37)

Try as they might to gain some control of the productive relations in professional sports, the players' unions have never been particularly strong. There are several reasons for this.

- Because most pro athletes' careers are less than 5 years long and they have to compete intensely to maintain their jobs, many see no conspicuous advantages in joining and supporting unions. The result is that pro athletes usually lack the commitment to solidarity that is needed to challenge the power of the higher levels of the sport hierarchy.
- Pro athletes are isolated from the mainline working class and so cannot benefit from the experiences of organized labor nor draw support from it.
- The emphasis on individual achievement deeply embedded in the typical professional athlete militates against collective responses to the league system.
- The ethos of the sports world—a world most pro athletes have been part of since their youth—is extremely conservative and teaches obedience to superiors; thus many pro athletes have developed personal political philosophies that oppose (or at least are very lukewarm toward) unions.
- The awesome power of the league and its owners tends to foster antiunion sentiments among athletes. Building upon players' dim understanding of the economic oppressions they face (i.e., their underdeveloped class consciousness), owners have brought hegemonic ideology to bear through the various communications channels they control. Thus team owners not only control the productive process in order to accumulate wealth, they also dominate the belief system of professional athletes, thus reproducing its rule.

As a consequence of these weakening forces, pro players' unions have not functioned like trade or labor unions, and the scope of their interests has been extremely narrow, never really taking in broader economic, social, or political issues.

Despite the fact that the organization of professional players' unions has generally been rudimentary and inadequate, the unions have attempted to challenge the powerful interests that own and control the pro sport industry, and they have gradually gained some important concessions. Owner response to the players' union movement has been predictable: Annoyed and angered by unionization, they have fought it consistently. What Vanneman and Cannon (1987) said about labor unionization in society at large—that it has "aroused the unbridled wrath of American capital" (p. 30)—applies to pro owners as well. Players' unions are perceived not merely as an economic threat, but as an enemy to be destroyed. Team owners, like most members of the capitalist class, tend to view union activity as antithetical to their social and political orientations.

But beyond that is a more pervasive ideological view of sport, manifested in owners' not wanting their athletes to struggle against the paternalistic structure underlying professional sport. Brower (1976) refers to this as the neutrality of sport—that is, that sport is an isolated world unconcerned with external phenomena. Such a view of sport is not limited to team owners; it permeates society as well. The owners' consensus is to keep "inappropriate" matters, such as union organization (as well as issues of race, gender, politics, etc.), out of professional sport. The problem with this view is that it leaves no forum for confronting the "inappropriate" issues.

Clearly, the purpose of this hegemonic ideological perspective is to prevent any kind of reform. The message of the neutrality argument is that political, economic, and social reform has no place in professional sport (Brower, 1976). But such a strategy obscures the real social and material exploitation in professional sport.

The most overt example of the vulnerability of unionized players to coercion by owners is seen in the treatment of players who have served as representatives to their unions. Each players' union has a committee of player representatives, elected by their teammates, who make major decisions about union activities. Although these representatives are commonly among a team's better players, many of them get traded or are forced to retire. Such action is particularly conspicuous immediately after a strike or other acrimonious dispute between owners and the union.

Summary and Preview

Professional team sport is a significant component of the commercial sport industry. There are similarities to other capitalist industries—ownership of the means of production is privatized and workers, in this case athletes, produce the product (the sporting event)—but professional team sports have a number of unique characteristics.

Intercollegiate athletics, which began as student-sponsored and student-run physical recreation in American colleges and universities (and still is in most parts of the world) has become a commercialized sport industry. Under the guise of educational and amateur sport, major universities across the nation are engaged in a massive commercial entertainment enterprise. The peculiar aspects of intercollegiate athletics are examined in chapter 8.

CHAPTER 8

Power
and Ideology
in Intercollegiate
Sport

Nothing so symbolizes the moral bankruptcy of our colleges and universities as the shameless way they exploit the vulnerability and inexperience of their so-called "student-athletes."

Thomas Sowell, economist

We hear much about transformations in mass communication, transportation, medicine, and other fields, but little public attention has been given to the incredible changes in National Collegiate Athletic Association (NCAA) Division I football and basketball in recent decades, especially as manifested in the massive commodification and undisguised salience of the profit motive. As Don Canham, the former athletic director at the University of Michigan, once said, "This is a business, a big business. Anyone who hasn't figured that out by now is a damned fool" (Denlinger & Shapiro, 1975, p. 252). Indiana University's basketball coach Bobby Knight echoed that, saying major college athletic programs "are business programs, and they have to be run that way" (England, 1982, p. 159).

Consider these statistics (Allen, 1988; "Association Registers Surplus," 1988; Kellner, 1988; McCallum, 1986; Pilson, 1988; "Receipts Top $70 Million," 1989; Van Der Horst & Seely, 1988):

- Many major universities have athletic budgets exceeding $12 million.
- Football bowl games alone generate over $30 million for the competing teams.
- Total television money to the nation's colleges and universities will exceed $750 million between 1988 and 1992.
- A trip to basketball's Final Four is worth $1.37 million to participating teams.
- The NCAA has an annual budget in excess of $89 million, and it has reported annual profits of over $9 million in recent years.

Even corporate sponsorship of individual university athletic programs, basketball tournaments, and football bowl games has become a common feature of big-time college athletics.

The big-time collegiate sport industry organizes athletics not, as one might expect, to meet students' personal and social needs for physical recreation, but strictly on market principles (the pursuit of capital accumulation). College sports' nonprofit status does not mean that schools cannot make money but rather that any earnings—"excess revenues" in nonprofit accounting jargon—must be spent to further the purpose of the organization. The Internal Revenue Service generally allows a tax-exempt organization to avoid taxes on business income as long as the business is "substantially related" to the organization's founding purpose. In the case of intercollegiate sport, colleges keep team names the same as the institution's name and require student-athletes to be enrolled in course work, thereby claiming an educational linkage between the business of the sport teams and the universities. So regardless of the amount of their excess revenues, athletic departments find ways to spend them (higher staff salaries, new staff positions, facilities, equipment, recruiting, etc.) to avoid any appearance of profit. For example, it is common practice for universities participating in football bowl games and the Final Four basketball tournament to spend more than $100,000 treating guests (governors, state legislators, college administrators, big donors and the like) to free trips to the events out of bowl or tournament payouts. This money, of course, is "excess revenue" that would have to be declared as profit by any ordinary business.

Most people do not think of college sport as a commercial industry. The prevalent images of college athletics in the public's mind are of bright and bouncy cheerleaders urging their fellow classmates/athletes to victory over a rival, of alumni tailgate parties, of eager young athletes giving their all for their school, of universities upholding the ideals of good, clean, amateur athletics. But more accurately, college athletics on the NCAA Division I level (the focus of this chapter) are about capital accumulation and the bottom line. They are about economic exploitation, dominance, power, and control by one segment of the college sport industry and the powerlessness and subordination of another. They are also about employing ideological hegemony to sustain existing social arrangements.

Many people deny the possibility of any relationship between intercollegiate athletics and power, dominance, and exploitation. How could power wielding be possible in such a seemingly benign activity? Such an idea challenges the integrity of a practice that, for many people, exemplifies some of the most admired values and standards of American life and is the source of much exciting entertainment. Ironically, it is precisely this naive perspective that plays a compelling, albeit unintentional, role in perpetuating the relations of power and dominance in collegiate athletics. Although there is much potential good in college sport, the existing social arrangements in big-time collegiate football and basketball are inherently exploitative and unstable and harbor flagrant inequality.

Reams of literature and analyses are regularly published about intercollegiate athletics, but few examinations situate college sport in a structural context of power, dominance, and ideology, as must happen if we are to really understand this enormously popular cultural practice. This contextualization must begin by tracing the evolution of college athletics from a spontaneous student recreation to its present form.

From Student Games to Big-Time Sport

Intercollegiate athletics did not always have the look they have today. They began quietly enough—the year was 1852—when a group of Yale and Harvard rowers engaged in a boat race. It took place on a lake in New Hampshire, and this was America's first intercollegiate athletic contest. But the entire affair was regarded as a "jolly lark" by the crewmen. A writer for the *New York Tribune* commented that although the race was amusing and momentarily diverted the attention of participants and spectators from mundane matters, intercollegiate sport would "make little stir in the busy world" (Lewis, 1967, p. 639). Of course, subsequent events over more than a century certainly have proved this prophet wrong. College sports have made a very big stir in the busy worlds of higher education and commercial entertainment.

It did take 3 years for the second intercollegiate sporting event—another boat race between Harvard and Yale—to be staged. In 1859 baseball, popular among upper-class young men in that decade, became the second intercollegiate sport when Amherst and Williams Colleges organized a game (whose final score was 66-32!). After an interruption by the Civil War, most colleges in the late 1860s and early 1870s formed baseball teams, and the sport was quickly established as the most popular one on many campuses.

An 1869 game between Princeton and Rutgers is considered the first intercollegiate football contest, but there were no established rules like those found in baseball, and the team captains at the first game—and subsequent games for several years—spent considerable time haggling over the rules under which it would be played (Lucas & Smith, 1978). The last two decades of the 1800s witnessed growing numbers of sports being played on campuses throughout the country. By the turn of the century many had taken their place as intercollegiate sports, and college athletics were indeed making themselves known.

Student Initiative and Control

You may be surprised that collegiate sports were founded upon student initiative, unassisted and unsupported by faculties, administration, or alumni. As legendary Yale football coach Walter Camp put it, "Neither the faculties nor other critics assisted in building the structure of college athletics. . . . It is a structure which students unaided have built, and with pride they point to their labor, and love it more dearly for its difficulties" (Smith, 1983, p. 373). The original form of governance was modeled after the well-established sports in the private secondary schools of England. In the British model the sports were for the students, and as student recreations they were expected to be organized, administered, and coached through student initiative, not adult intervention. Much of 19th-century British school life in general featured student self-government—students supervising and governing each other. As British sport historian Peter McIntosh (1957) explained,

In no part of the school life was self-government so highly developed as in games and sports. The capacity to govern others and control themselves, the aptitude to combine freedom with order were practiced by the . . . [students] especially in their physical recreations. (p. 182)

This feature of sport persists today in British schools, colleges, and universities.

Just as with British school sports, early American intercollegiate sports were governed by the students themselves. Faculty refrained from interfering, viewing the games as a good expenditure of energy and adopting the British attitude that the games were valuable for the qualities of character that they brought out. It was believed that the best environment for nurturing good character traits was one in which students were in control. Accordingly, the elected captain of the team, usually an outstanding player with some leadership qualities, became the dominant team member. It was his job to organize practices, determine starting lineups, select team strategy, and set rules for the squad. He was in most respects the team's coach.

Management of the business end of intercollegiate programs was initially in the hands of students, organized as athletic associations. Most associations scheduled games, cared for fields, and handled other necessary transactions pertinent to the business; when hiring of professional coaches began, the associations did this too. The most pressing purpose of these associations was finding ways and means of financing their teams. Between 1870 and 1900 nearly every college formed a student athletic association to garner financial and student support for its teams.

The need for some form of collective governance arose as early as the second intercollegiate contest (the 1855 Harvard-Yale boat race), when the eligibility of a Harvard coxswain became an issue. It was from this impetus that the first intercollegiate governing body emerged at a meeting in New Haven, and the College Union Regatta was formed. Members agreed to hold an annual championship and award the winner a prize. A set of rules governing the race was agreed upon, and stipulations were made that the race would be between boats manned only by undergraduates, including members of the graduating class. Although the College Union Regatta soon folded into oblivion, interest in regulated competition remained, and athletic clubs from different campuses formed intercollegiate associations to govern their competition. The earliest governing associations, then, were initiated and run by students. An association's mission was generally threefold: to sponsor and conduct competition, outline playing rules, and determine eligibility criteria.

Decline of Student Control

A gradual transformation in governance began during the late 1870s; student control began to diminish and was eventually eliminated. The process began as university administrations, faculties, and alumni sought greater participation in the management of college athletics. All three groups agreed that the job was becoming too large for students to handle. Administrators and faculty thought that college students ought to be restrained from pursuing goals that appeared increasingly incongruent with higher education; they expressed alarm about growing professionalism, mismanagement of finances, lack of sportsmanship, glorification of athletics over academics, and other problems (Smith, 1988). Alumni, on the other hand, desired to bring greater competence to the pursuit of gate receipts and championships.

Concerns like these led to the formation of faculty athletic committees, which either worked closely with the student associations or took them over completely; they were the harbingers of faculty-controlled athletic conferences. Princeton in 1881 and Harvard a year later created the first college faculty athletic committees. Additional committees arose during the 1880s and 1890s, all with an eye toward placing athletics under systematic control. By 1900 nearly every college had an athletic committee that either gave the institution sole power to regulate athletics or divided the power with the students and alumni (Smith, 1988).

The expansion of collegiate athletics was so great after 1880 and the practices attending them were so varied that it became apparent that interinstitutional controlling agencies were needed for their regulation and supervision. Conferences of colleges were formed to standardize athletic procedures among schools in one geographic area and usually with similar enrollments, academic requirements, and financial standings. These conferences ordinarily set standards, made rules and regulations concerning athletic eligibility, provided a means of enforcing conference rules, and drew up playing schedules. As early as 1883 faculty representatives from eight colleges met in New York to discuss mutual resolutions to "the athletic problem." In 1895 the Intercollegiate Conference of Faculty Representatives (Big 10) was formed.

Not until 1905, however, did colleges join to formulate a collective national solution to the issue of interinstitutional governance. The impetus for this action was a crisis that developed in football. During the 1905 season there were 18 deaths and 149 serious injuries attributable to football. A public outcry about the brutality of the game led President Theodore Roosevelt to threaten to abolish it on college campuses unless rule changes were made. Within a few months colleges had banded together, modified the rules, and in the process formed the Intercollegiate Athletic Association of the United States. This name was changed in 1910 to the National Collegiate Athletic Association. From its inception, the NCAA stood for institutional control and order; the control has been sustained with little opposition, but the search for order has been elusive throughout the association's history (Hardy & Berryman, 1982; Smith, 1988).

Throughout these early years, students complained about the intrusions into their domain, but to no avail. By 1910 they had lost most of their authority to various governing groups and alumni. The students clearly were no longer masters of their own product. By the mid-1920s the structure of collegiate athletics as it exists today had been cemented. Its foundation was built on institutional control, with two main approaches to college sport. One views athletics as an integral part of student life and physical recreation; this is currently codified in NCAA Division III (smaller school) athletics. The second approach runs collegiate sport as an entertainment business and a training ground for professional and elite amateur athletes; this is currently codified in NCAA Division I (major university) athletics. Division II is a hybrid of the other two.

Governance of college athletics for women took quite a different course in its founding and early development. It was fully under faculty control from its beginnings because female students never established their own athletic networks. Instead, early women's sports were advised and directed by female faculty (Spears & Swanson, 1988). Sponsorship began with female physical educators and remained that way until the early 1970s. From this model, a course was charted to deliberately avoid the problems of the commercialized men's programs. Promotion of educational goals and philosophies were the guiding principles, but the success of this model came at the expense of not sponsoring high-level skill development.

Women's collegiate sport took a dramatic change of course in the early 1970s with the founding of the Association for Intercollegiate Athletics for Women (AIAW). The former purposes and philosophies were renounced because influential leaders in women's intercollegiate athletics were won over by the quest for high-level competition, records, championships, and public recognition. Women's athletics began to model the men's programs. The change became complete in 1981 when the NCAA began scheduling national championship events for women's collegiate sports. Within a year the AIAW was destroyed; women's athletics came under the jurisdiction of the NCAA and have come to mirror the men's system.

The Big Business of College Sport

Some commercialism was present in collegiate sport from its beginnings, but while control was in student hands its extent was minimal. But once institutional control was solidified, college presidents, alumni, and business interests forged a coalition and plunged wholeheartedly into the professionalization of intercollegiate athletics. In a quest to acquire increasing private and public financial support, college administrators envisioned the potential of their teams for advertising and for generating alumni interest and contributions. They also presumed that the achievements of the college's athletic teams and the attending publicity would help attract students, thus raising enrollments. For their part, the alumni and public viewed intercollegiate athletics as good entertainment. The result of these various interests was expanding commercialization. By the 1920s the course was set. A national mania had grown up around college football especially, "and its future would be linked with the development of mass entertainment in a growing industrial society" (Hart-Nibbrig & Cottingham, 1986, p. 22).

Although commercialized collegiate athletics was a growing industry before midcentury, financial domination of big-time collegiate football and basketball is a post–World War II phenomenon. Many factors have contributed: the growth of the mass media and especially the enormous television revenues, rapid and convenient air transportation making possible interregional rivalries, increased leisure time and discretionary income, and the advent of college sports information departments and their widely successful advertising efforts. All of these factors—and undoubtedly others—directly or indirectly increased interest in commodified forms of intercollegiate athletics.

The Fate of Amateurism

As almost all the earmarks of capitalist enterprise have come to characterize the *business* of big-time collegiate athletics, enormous inequalities and conflicts of interests have arisen, not the least of which is the social relationship of student-athletes to the commercial enterprise. As college sports have become imbued with commercial values and modes of operation, the commitment to amateurism has been jettisoned in the process. The single exception is that student-athletes, the major labor force in producing the product of the sport event, are still defined by the NCAA and its member universities as amateurs, and they are not paid wages or salaries based on market considerations. The collegiate sport industry gets away with this by an ingenious deployment of ideological hegemony.

The open acknowledgment by leading college athletic spokespersons about the business of major college athletics and the well-publicized facts about the vast sums of money driving big-time college football and basketball invite a social-structure analysis of the ways that the NCAA, by mystifying economic relations, manufactures support among the general public and student-athletes for this economic exploitation. Such an analysis requires examining patterns of social stratification in college sport.

Renowned philosopher Bertrand Russell (1938) said that "the fundamental concept in social science is Power, in the same sense in which Energy is the fundamental concept in physics" (p. 10). Indeed, social organizations tend to be stratified on the basis of power, with those holding the power gaining an unequal share of the benefits of that system. Power tends to get translated into a structure of dominance enabling the powerful to write their advantages into the system's very structure. Of course, the interests of a dominant group never appear pretentious; they are protected by laws, nurtured by the media, and fortified and elaborated by ideology. Ideology is the social lubricant of dominant groups—in this case, the NCAA and its member universities.

The enormously successful commercial entertainment business that has emerged from major college football and basketball is actually a popular cultural form of the same genre as theater, cinema, popular music, and, of course, professional sport. In each case, a group of persons talented and well trained in their specialty provide amusement and entertainment for audiences who pay to watch the performances. Although each of these forms of popular entertainment has a formal business organizational structure, they all, except for big-time college sports, operate throughout as commercial entities with an unambiguous labor market orientation; all employees are paid at least a minimum wage and they are free to negotiate for more money with employers in the industry. Even in the case of collegiate sport, many employees—athletic directors, coaches, athletic trainers, sports information directors, and sundry support staff—make a good living; indeed, some earn annual salaries in excess of $100,000, and with TV contracts, equipment endorsements, and speaking fees a few have incomes of over $400,000 (Jacobs, 1988; Somers, 1989; Sperber, 1988). Only the athlete is without a salary; indeed, the collegiate sport industry prevents universities from paying the athlete an outright salary and prohibits the athlete from accepting offers of salary or any other money under penalty of permanent banishment from collegiate sport participation. Instead, the athlete gets what is euphemistically called a scholarship, worth about $5,500 per year at a state university (in 1989) and said to be a free ride to a college education. A University of Kansas football player, Quinten Schonewise, articulately described the ''job'' of a collegiate football athlete in relation to the scholarship: ''My question is, after arriving early in August to three-a-day practices in 100-degree heat, and then into an 11-week season that takes a minimum of 60 hours a week in meetings, practice and travel, and then into a conditioning program until spring practice starts, who's the guy that called a football scholarship a free ride?'' (''Scorecard,'' 1984, p. 10).

This clever definition in the NCAA's terms projects an image of student-athletes as the beneficiaries of a generous philanthropy by institutions of higher education when in fact they are laborers subsidizing thousands of employees of the big-time intercollegiate athletic industry, the mass media, and corporations that advertise through college sports.

The managers of college sport are able to maintain this arrangement because almost no one really thinks of major college athletics as a commercial entertainment industry. The public accepts the premise that college athletes must remain untainted by money. Even the athletes do not view themselves as employees, and in the most recent court decisions—*Colemen v. Western Michigan University* (1983) and *Rensing v. Indiana State University Board* (1983)—the court held that the athletes were not employees under a labor contract. That is, of course, exactly the interpretation the sport establishment—NCAA executives, university administrators, and coaches—wants.

Amateur Ideology

It is normal for those dominant in an organization to interpret reality and create normative prescriptions so as to serve their interests, and the NCAA and its member universities have done this with the amateur ideology. These molders of American intercollegiate athletics have taken a 19th-century upper-class doctrine of amateur sport and welded it to a distorted idea of ancient Greek athletes competing for the love and excitement of the sporting experience. They have made their case so persuasively that alternative images have been made to seem unthinkable.

Analysts of social inequality and group consciousness view ideology as integral to relations of inequality because the dominant group typically uses it as a form of engineering of consent to promote its interests. Use of ideology to secure consent does not, it must be emphasized, necessarily require force or threats of force. Judiciously used, it molds, manipulates, and persuades potentially opposing factions. In fact, this is its genius (Williams, 1977). The ability of those in control of collegiate sport to justify existing conditions and power relationships hinges considerably on the promotion of an amateur ideology. This process of legitimation has been so successful that amateurism is widely accepted as a given, the natural and most just form of collegiate athletics. Thus, the institutionally powerful groups in collegiate sport have created an interpretation of reality that successfully serves their interests; they have made their advantage part of the very structure of their enterprise.

To fully understand amateurism, two points must be made. First, amateurism is one aspect of a 19th-century socially elitist approach to sport as a disinterested practice, which flourished first among the upper social classes in England. Social traditions and ideals among America's social elite were greatly affected by British customs and standards, and amateurism was introduced to the United States in the last two decades of the 19th century (McIntosh, 1963; Guttmann, 1978). Second, amateurism is founded upon a myth that ancient Greek athletes competed solely for fame and honor (Young, 1984).

Amateurism arose in Britain as an elitist mechanism designed to exclude the working class from competition, and it was an upper-class prejudice that disdained professional athletes, the product of a Victorian doctrine that work and play must be preserved as separate entities. This notion was readily congruent with the British history of class rule and traditions of deference.

As sport sociologist Allen Sack (1973) has explained,

In the English upper class, sport was a pastime of gentlemen and participation in the sporting life was to be clearly distinguished from sport as a profession. The former was a necessary part of a young gentleman's education and character development, the latter a preoccupation of those of humble origin [the working class]. (pp. 26-27)

In the latter 19th century, athletic clubs that limited their membership to upper-class gentlemen grew up, at first in England but soon after in the United States, explicitly separating their sport events from the working class. The words *gentleman* and *amateur* were synonymous, while *professional* meant working class. The question of social separation was clearly outlined in membership regulations for competition. The rules for the Henley Regatta, a popular British sporting event for the socially elite, stated, "No person shall be considered an amateur . . . who is or has been by trade or employment for wages a mechanic, artisan, or labourer, or engaged in any menial duty" (Whitney, 1895, p. 163). At first, then, amateurism was a question of social class; indeed, Guttmann (1978) claimed that the "amateur rule was an instrument of class warfare" (p. 31).

By the 1880s, amateurism was redefined, forbidding amateurs to accept money for their sport participation or achievements (Bailey, 1978). Though social distinctions were dropped, working-class persons were effectively excluded because they could not devote the time necessary to train and compete without remuneration. Thus social exclusivity was retained.

With the growth of American college sport from 1880 to 1900, prizes and cash awards were occasionally given, but objections surfaced immediately. Upper-class interests dominated American higher education during this period. Administrators and faculty, though not necessarily wealthy, were socially elite and held the values of that social stratum. Students, especially those at the prestigious colleges where sport was popular, were overwhelmingly from upper-class families (Sheldon, 1901). American universities, anxious to model themselves after the much-admired British universities, adopted many of the elitist trappings then fashionable, one of which was the amateur sport ideology.

Influential spokesmen for the view that American intercollegiate sport should remain strictly amateur solidified this doctrine for the public through their writings and speeches. Walter Camp, the Yale University football coach for many years and often called the father of American football, as well as one of the most respected representatives of college sport, counseled college men in his book *Walter Camp's Book of College Sports* (1893):

Be each, pray God, a gentleman! It is an easy word, and a pleasant one. I don't doubt but that you all pronounce it trippingly enough, and have each one his own high ideal of what a gentleman should be. Do you live up to it? Or are you letting it come down a little here and there; so little, perhaps, that you hardly notice it until you make comparison? A gentleman against a gentleman always plays to win. There is a tacit agreement between them that each shall do his best, and the best man shall win. A gentleman does not make his living, however, from his athletic prowess. He does not earn anything by his victories except glory and satisfaction. . . . A gentleman never competes for money, directly or indirectly. Make no mistake about this. No matter how winding the road may be that eventually brings the sovereign into the pocket, it is the price of what should be dearer to you than anything else—your honor. (pp. 1-2)

Such a statement makes explicit what is implicit in the amateur ideology.

Captain Palmer Pierce of the U.S. Military Academy, one of the leading forces in the organization of the NCAA, claimed in a speech to the 1907 NCAA convention that

this Association does not require acceptance of any particular set of eligibility rules. It does, however, bind its members to line up to the well-known principles of amateur sport. . . . In a word, this is a league of educated gentlemen who are trying to exercise a wise control over college athletics. (Falla, 1981, p. 33)

A final example: Casper Whitney, the powerful editor of *Outing*, one of the most popular sporting magazines of the late 19th and early 20th centuries, and an influential doctrineer of amateur sport and advocate of college athletics during this era, made emphatic the place of amateurism. He argued that it should be reserved for the upper classes: "The laboring classes are all right in their way; let them go their way in peace, and have their athletics in whatsoever manner suits their inclinations . . . [but] let us have our own sport among the refined elements" (Whitney, 1895, p. 166). It is quite clear, then, that the early molders of intercollegiate sport promoted an ideology-based doctrine of the adequacy and legitimacy of amateurism.

We now turn to the second force for the promotion of the amateur sport ideology in intercollegiate athletics. Formal organization of college athletics was achieved in the latter 19th and early 20th centuries, at the same time that the Olympic Games were revived. The Olympic movement adopted rules of amateurism largely for two reasons: First, its founder and early leaders were aristocrats who enthusiastically embraced the amateur doctrine (Lucas, 1980; MacAloon, 1981; Mandell, 1976). Second, influential historians had persuasively written that ancient Greek athletes were amateurs during Greece's Golden Age, competing only for fame and honor. Promoters of the modern Olympics, wishing to represent Greek athletics as a precedent for the Games they were establishing, adopted amateurism as a formal requirement for participation. But, it turns out, the Greek athlete-as-amateur is a historical hoax. David Young (1984), after a thorough study of these athletes, stated this:

> I can find no mention of amateurism in Greek sources, no reference to amateur athletes—no evidence that the concept "amateurism" was even known in antiquity. The truth is that "amateur" is one thing for which the ancient Greeks never even had a word. . . . With respect to money and the so-called "Ancient Greek amateurism," the results are hardly indecisive. . . . There is abundant proof, direct and indirect, in contemporary documents and later reports, to show that athletes could and did win large amounts of money. (pp. 7, 163)

The founders of the NCAA, many of whom were also leaders in the American Olympic Games movement or had close social contacts with those leaders, were adamant about maintaining college sport "on an ethical plane in keeping with the dignity and high purpose of education" (Falla, 1981). But events since the 1950s make quite clear that in big-time collegiate athletics amateur ideals have been replaced by marketplace priorities driven by a prominent and undisguised profit motive. As Hart-Nibbrig (1984) noted in an insightful analysis of collegiate sports, modern intercollegiate athletics are "more akin to the values of the modern corporation or professional sports than to the basic values and purposes of the university" (p. 12).

The Beneficiaries of Amateur Ideology

In light of the fact that major college football and basketball have been commodified, the present-day amateur ideology is obviously not founded on any interest in amateurism per se. Valorization of amateurism is merely a subterfuge to avoid paying the athletes a legitimate wage. Human capital is a combination of skills and knowledge that can be used to "purchase" employment and social status. The major-college sport establishment has used a highly valued source of human capital—a college education (which, ironically, can be obtained at a relatively low cost)—as the sole compensation for athletes. In reality, the scholarship is nothing but a work contract. What colleges are really doing is hiring entertainers. The deceit of claiming that educational purposes preclude salaried compensation for athletic performance is testimony to the extensive attempts of the collegiate sport establishment to avoid its financial responsibilities. Athletic scholarships are actually a form of economic exploitation, the establishment of a wage below poverty level for student-athlete–entertainers who directly produce millions of dollars for athletic departments.

Stripped of the rhetoric used to convince athletes and the public that athletic scholarships are philanthropic free rides to college educations, the NCAA scholarship is first and foremost a conspiracy to hold down athletes' "wages." College athletes are caught in the clutches of the NCAA. They cannot sell their skills on the open market to the highest bidder because of the wage limit that all universities must observe. Some collegiate athletes generate 10 to 20 (and a few as high as 100!) times the amount of their scholarship in income for their schools. And consider the situation with bowl games: Payouts to the college football teams who play in bowl games approximate $40 million a year, and it is customary for a coach to receive a "bonus" of several thousand dollars when a team qualifies for a bowl. Teams get to bowl games through the hard work of both coaches and athletes, but athletes earn no bonuses for bowl appearances. Similarly, participating institutions in the NCAA Division I men's basketball tournament make about $35 million! Coaches whose teams qualify for the tournament typically receive healthy boosts in their new contracts as a reward, but athletes on those same teams make no more than the NCAA scholarship allows (Somers, 1989).

The benefits of this wage-fixing for the NCAA and the universities are quite evident: the lower the wages, the greater the profits. In effect, then, intercollegiate athletics makes the labor of many into the wealth of a few. At a congressional hearing, attorney Lana Tyree charged that

> the NCAA can market products and use the athletes' images to do so. By restricting the amount of scholarships . . . and by restraining the athlete, they have cornered the market. . . . Why should the athlete generating a financial empire be singled out for restraint. (Good, 1979a, p. 38)

Paying as little as possible to operate a business is called keeping overhead low; it's what every business owner strives to do. The NCAA and major universities have mastered this principle. No other American business operates so pretentiously, making huge sums of money but insisting the enterprise be viewed as an educational service. Even though athletes, the only students who generate money for a university, are the key to the financial success of college sports through their indispensability in the sport production process, they do not receive compensation commensurate with their contributions (Yasser, 1984).

One of the foundations of capitalism is that market forces will determine wages. There seems to be no inherent reason that college athletes should not be subject to market forces like all other laborers and free to realize their actual market value. If big-time collegiate athletics must be granted its commercial orientation, then it should be held accountable to those whose labor creates the product, for without them there would be no sport event. Continuing to define athletes as amateurs can legitimately be viewed as an evasion of a responsibility to either treat athletes as equal members of a commercial enterprise or to withdraw from commodified sport and return to promoting an educational model of college sports, using sport as a medium for the individual development of the participants.

The athletic scholarship is only one of the many NCAA regulations designed to restrain athletes and boost profits for NCAA members. An athlete who enrolls and participates in sport at one NCAA institution and then subsequently transfers to another is ineligible for competition at the second school for a full year. Such a requirement seriously reduces the interorganizational mobility of collegiate athletes, thus stabilizing the labor market and saving the management untold dollars that might otherwise be spent in competitive bidding for the best players.

Here again, the major beneficiaries of this restriction on college athletes' mobility are obvious. On the one hand the NCAA promotes and sells competition through sport, but it severely restricts competition for wage labor within its own industry with the complex rules and practices it has adopted. Athletic directors and coaches are fond of expounding on the virtues of competition, but they have formulated nationwide regulations to avoid competing for those who actually produce their product.

But it is only the athletes whose mobility is restricted. The NCAA does not apply such limitations to others involved in athletic production (athletic directors, coaches, athletic trainers, etc.). Indeed, "jumping" contracts is so common among college coaches that it has almost become an annual ritual in the college sports business (Reilly, 1989). As Paul Good (1979b) noted in examining the betrayal athletes feel when a coach resigns after recruiting them,

> Student-athletes are exhorted to demonstrate loyalty to their schools and are penalized by losing a year's eligibility if they transfer to another school. But if the Astro-Turf looks greener on the other side to the coach, he's gone without penalty. (p. 62)

In addition to the policies limiting athletes' wages and mobility potential are other rules that benefit management. The "letter of intent" regulation prevents an athlete from investigating other programs after signing a letter. Once having accepted a scholarship offer, the athlete may not negotiate with any other university for his or her athletic labor; a year of ineligibility is the punishment for this offense. There is also a scholarship limitation policy that prescribes the number of scholarships a university may grant. The effect of these rules and numerous others is to restrain competition and reduce costs among NCAA members, to the disadvantage of collegiate athletes. Taken together, the NCAA's policies constitute a formidable assault on athletes. When one analyzes the NCAA rules and regulations for athletes from the standpoint of who benefits, the pattern is clear: The prime beneficiaries are the NCAA and its member universities.

It seems rather obvious, then, that although the official ideology of the NCAA proclaims a promotion of amateur sport, its operative goals involve maximizing power and oppression over student-athletes. As a structure of domination, the NCAA is organized to achieve the commands of those who control it. Student-athletes are expected to comply with the formally rational expectations of their roles. At the same time, they are excluded from participation in substantive decisions and are not even privy to information about them.

Scandals and Reform in Big-Time College Sport

Probably few people are unaware that numerous scandals have beset major university football and basketball programs during the past few years (Golenbock, 1989; Kirshenbaum, 1989; Looney, 1985a, 1985b; Marx, 1988; Nack, 1986; NCAA Committee on Infractions, 1987a, 1987b; Neff, 1989; Smith, 1988; Sullivan & Neff, 1987). There has been a steady stream of horror stories about violations of NCAA rules, reports of how few athletes at State U. graduate, and disclosures of athletes receiving illegal money from boosters. One ignominious tale is followed by another of greater proportions. Hardly a week goes by without new violations of NCAA rules being reported. Each revelation is followed by righteous promises from university authorities and the NCAA that change is on the way, that collegiate athletics are going to be cleaned up. But, as Padilla & Weistart (1986) noted, "Scandals develop with a frequency that is astonishing even to the most cynical of observers, and the major regulatory body, the NCAA, seems unable to stop them or the conditions from which they breed" (p. 6C). And Cramer (1986) contended after a thorough study of the NCAA and major college athletics that "a glimpse at the workings of college sports programs and at the efforts of the NCAA to reform them is not exactly a pretty sight" (p. 6). Comments by the NCAA president, John Davis, at the 1987 NCAA annual convention graphically illustrate Cramer's perceptiveness: "I don't think we are going to do anything that will impair quality of major intercollegiate sports" (p. 1).

The most recent NCAA attempt to address the endemic problems of major college sports has been the creation of a university Presidents Commission, which has promised to reform and redirect the directions of intercollegiate athletics. But it, too, has floundered; in summarizing its 1986 meeting Sullivan (1986a) reported that the Commission "gave no firm evidence of any commitment to reform" (p. 17). Results of a survey of presidents and chancellors of NCAA Division I member schools regarding issues to be considered at the 1987 special NCAA convention painted a vivid picture of how little the university CEOs are really committed to substantive reform. Their responses can best be characterized as a little tinkering with the system, while leaving intact the existing distribution of powers ("Complete Results," 1987; also see Sullivan, 1989). The chairman of the Presidents Commission has echoed their sentiments: "It will be more a matter of fine-tuning and adjusting than making major changes" (Allen & Wieberg, 1988).

For all of the chest pounding about reform by the NCAA, university athletic departments, and the Presidents Commission, an analysis of changes that have been made or proposed over the past few years shows that most are cost containment measures directed primarily at athletes (reducing scholarships, dropping sports, making promises to hold athletes to tougher academic standards). Any attempt to reorganize existing structural relations is conspicuously absent from reform in intercollegiate athletics. The *structure* of big-time, commercial college athletics—a structure that is largely responsible for the pervasive corruption and abuses—has been left intact, with no substantive changes. Hope for meaningful reform by the NCAA so that it would better serve the interests and needs of all college athletes seems nowhere to be found.

By the structure of college athletic programs I mean the rigidly authoritarian system in which rules and policies affecting student-athletes are enacted and imposed without any input from the largest group in college sports—the student-athletes themselves. I am also referring to the now-common practice of keeping athletes involved in one way or another with their sport during the season for 40 to 60 hours per week—practicing, watching films, traveling to games, and being away from campus and missing classes.

I'm referring to weight training programs, film analysis, and "informal" practice sessions in the "off-season"; indeed, athletes are expected to remain in training year-round. I'm referring to the pressures brought to bear by mass media attention and the expectations of alumni and boosters who demand championship teams. I'm referring to universities who use athletes as public relations. This is the essential structure of major university football and basketball programs.

Analyses of the time the average major college football player devotes to his sport suggest that it is near 2,200 hours per year, or 275 eight-hour days, and it has been estimated that college football players devote about 55 hours per week and basketball players 50 hours per week during their respective seasons. Time devoted to the sport does not end with the last game; football and basketball college athletes report devoting up to 18 hours per week during the off-season (Edwards, 1984; Eitzen & Purdy, 1986; Looney, 1988). A study by Sack & Thiel (1979) found that 68% of the Notre Dame football players who later played NFL football reported that playing at Notre Dame was as physically and psychologically demanding as professional football.

Blaming the Victim

Instead of addressing structural issues that perpetuate scandals, the NCAA has labeled student-athletes as the major cause of the continuing problems suffered by collegiate sports, and various forms of legislation have been passed that are designed to convince the public that the NCAA is right. Fostering individualism (the student athlete, in this case) as the source of the problem is a tactic frequently used by dominant groups seeking to divert attention from group grievances, thus undercutting their legitimacy.

Through the rules they have enacted to further control and restrict student-athletes, the NCAA and university authorities claim to be attempting to solve the problems of college sport. What they have done instead is to blame the student-athlete for their own failure to address the real causes of corruption, cheating, and unethical behavior that are now well-documented. They have engaged, clearly and directly, in a classic display of blaming the victim. They have fashioned an ostensible legitimacy for their actions so persistently that alternative images have become unthinkable. In doing this, athletic authorities have sought to co-opt, undermine, and marginalize any alternatives for addressing the deep-seated problems of big-time college sport.

In his insightful volume *Blaming the Victim*, William Ryan (1976) described a scene in a popular play. A southern Senator is investigating why the American military was unprepared for the Japanese attack on December 7, 1941; wanting to find a way to exonerate the military, he booms out, "And what was Pearl Harbor *doing* in the Pacific?" We laugh at the obviously convoluted reasoning that leads to such a question, but the same sort of convoluted reasoning is being touted by the NCAA and its member universities in their responses to the many outcries for reform. Blaming the victim is an ideological process, meaning it is a more or less integrated set of ideas and practices promulgated by a dominant social group about how things should and do work. Ryan (1976) said that "victim blaming is cloaked in kindness and concern, and . . . it is obscured by a perfumed haze of humanitarianism" (p. 6). Rather than addressing the inherent structural problems that plague big-time collegiate sports, the college sport establishment disguises the fundamental issues by repeatedly blaming the victim, in this case student-athletes.

An Academic Scapegoat. The NCAA's Proposition 48 (Bylaw 5-1-[j]) is a good example of focusing the blame for problems in college sport on student-athletes. By requiring that student-athletes achieve certain minimum high school grades and standardized test scores to be eligible for participation, the NCAA can appear to legitimize its supposed insistence upon having qualified students as college athletes; of course, no rational person can really quarrel with holding athletes to academic standards. Even many black leaders who recognized the unequal and adverse effects that this legislation would have on black athletes supported the passage of Proposition 48 because to have opposed it would imply that they did not favor academic standards. (There is a large body of literature on the ramifications of Proposition 48; see, for example, Sack [1985] and Edwards [1984].)

Focusing on athletes' academic achievement—something around which everyone can rally—and seemingly showing how athletes are being held to standards deflects attention from the exploitative commercialized structure of major college athletic programs. It also serves to suggest to the public that some social pathology within the athletes is the reason for the recurring scandals in collegiate athletics, not the social structure of which they are a part. Thus, exhortations for a national effort toward improving athletes' academic performances, even when they come from respected and well-meaning persons, ignore the more endemic problems (Brady, 1988; Reed, 1988). They actually constitute a classic case of intensification of the labor process through what is called in the workplace a speedup (a demand for increased output without increased pay). Focusing on the athletes and ignoring the system of power, privilege, and revenue is a little like blaming the corpse for the murder (Parenti, 1978).

The only reason for an academic standards problem in big-time college sport is that coaches and other university officials have admitted—indeed, have recruited—academically unqualified students, and through various ingenious methods have been able to keep them eligible for one purpose: to help the university athletic teams maintain competitive success in the world of commercialized sport. Moreover, for athletes who are academically qualified and genuinely interested in pursuing college degrees, the intensity and structure of major college sport forces many of them to choose between academic performance and athletic performance (Adler & Adler, 1985).

Double Standards. Another example of blaming athletes for collegiate sport ills is the punishment of football athletes for improper distribution of complimentary tickets (Copeland, 1986; Latimer, 1986; Looney, 1986). NCAA rules forbid athletes from giving their complimentary tickets to anyone except family members, relatives, and fellow students designated by the student-athlete. Student-athletes who have sold their complimentary tickets have been characterized as ungrateful liars for violating NCAA rules. The athletes were defined as the problem, and measures were taken to punish them. What is astonishing is that it is common practice for coaches to receive a liberal allotment of complimentary game tickets—for example, one football coach receives 20 season tickets and one basketball coach 200 (valued at $24,000!)—with no restrictions on their distribution (Becker, 1986b; Jacobs, 1988; Mayfield, 1986; Sperber, 1987; Wieberg, 1986a).

There is a related and larger issue here. Collegiate athletes cannot endorse products or engage in any commercialization of their athletic talent or name recognition. Meanwhile, coaches can engage in an incredible variety of commercial activities to supplement their salaries. Some of the perks common for major college coaches are television and radio shows (worth up to $80,000), free use of a car, university housing, and use of university facilities for summer camps. A few coaches also have lucrative sporting equipment endorsement contracts. For some coaches the perks and benefits push their annual income above $300,000 (Jacobs, 1988; Kirkpatrick, 1988; Sperber, 1987; Wieberg, 1986b, 1986c).

Universities have capitalized on the popularity of college athletics to license and sell a wide variety of sport equipment and souvenirs. Universities with the biggest licensing programs earn $450,000 to $650,000 a year (Krupa, 1988b). A market of this kind exists primarily because of the interest in collegiate sports generated by talented and skilled student-athletes. But the athletes themselves get no money from the profits derived in this market.

So while the NCAA preaches the virtues of amateurism and a Spartan existence to student-athletes, it winks at the lavish lifestyles of coaches and athletic directors and condones the university licensing market in equipment and souvenirs. Inconsistencies like these in the NCAA rules brought this comment from economist Thomas Sowell (1989):

> If General Motors or Exxon formed a cartel to treat their workers even half as badly as college athletes are treated, there would be antitrust suits across the country and whole armies of executives would be led away in handcuffs. (p. 31)

The most prominent strategies of the NCAA and universities—the powerful and dominant interests in the current crisis—have involved reaction and retrenchment within existing forms, and a rather arrogant attitude of impunity from any serious challenge to their policies. Enacting legislation that focuses on the control, restrictions, monitoring, and punishment of student-athletes is a brilliant strategy for diverting attention from the real sources of the fundamental problems and for justifying a perverse system of social action. Meanwhile, the exploitation and victimization of collegiate athletes continues unabated. Far from desiring to change the basic commercial and exploitative structure of major college sports, the NCAA and member universities seem to be striving for a change in social conditions by means of which existing patterns will be made as tolerable and comfortable as possible while meaningful reform remains largely a false promise. (Some point to the "death penalty" imposed on SMU by the NCAA as an example that serious reform is on the way, but they overlook several important facts. First, this action does not address in any way the endemic structural problems of big-time collegiate athletics. Second, it was done only after SMU quite literally forced such a course of action by continued flagrant violation of NCAA rules. And third, it is probably a one-shot effort to scare other universities into temporary compliance with NCAA policies.)

A question may be raised about the lack of protest from intercollegiate athletes about the prevailing conditions under which they labor. In one way it can be expected that the athletes would not find anything to question; they have been thoroughly conditioned by many years of organized sport involvement to obey athletic authorities. Indeed, most college athletes are faithful servants and spokespersons for the system of college sport. They tend to take the existing order for granted, not questioning the status quo because they are preoccupied with their own jobs of making the team and perhaps gaining national recognition. As a group, athletes tend to be politically passive and apathetic, resigned to domination from above because, at least partly, the institutional structure of athletics is essentially hostile to independence of mind. Hence, athletes are willing victims whose self-worth and self-esteem have largely become synonymous with their athletic prowess. Their main impulse is to mind their own business while striving to be successful as athletes. In the work world, this is referred to as *pragmatic role acceptance*.

Awareness, Opposition, and Potential Reform

Although real opposition to the present collegiate sport order has been minimal and sporadic, some foundations in the way of opposition and raised consciousness suggest a sustained critique of the current situation and give hope for bringing about social and economic justice. Hardly a week goes by without some public figure in politics, business, law, education, or the media expressing dismay with the current system of big-time college sport. Five years ago there was no support in any sector of public life for paying college athletes salaries. In 1988 45% of callers to a *USA Today: The Television Show* survey supported payment to college athletes. Several college coaches have recently called for outright payment to athletes, and politician Ernie Chambers has submitted bills to the Nebraska legislature calling for the same.

Effecting change will undoubtedly require continued efforts to interpret the social reality of big-time college athletics accurately. Although the reality is that dominant economic interests make major university athletics virtually impenetrable, it is not necessary to concede that inequities in the distribution of money, violations of basic human rights, and victimization of athletes are legitimate. Indeed, the absence of critical commentary is a precondition to all forms of domination. Ignoring or retreating from criticism of the NCAA not only renders its current forms of domination natural and acceptable, it also hinders meaningful reform to alleviate conditions of those who are victimized by that system. There is nothing about the current system that is natural or universal. All social arrangements are human creations. Built and sustained by humans, they can also be changed by humans.

Summary and Preview

Big-time intercollegiate athletics has become another part of the massive commodified sport industry, a part that plays a significant role in the overall entertainment business. As collegiate athletics has grown from student-sponsored, student-run campus recreation, it has taken on most of the trappings of conventional capitalist entertainment enterprises. The major exception to the typical business model is that the workers who produce the product—the sport event—are paid no wages or salaries. Universities avoid direct payments by proclaiming collegiate sport as an integral component of the educational mission of the university and by applying the ideology of amateurism to college sport.

Chapter 9 moves one level lower in the sport hierarchy to high school and youth sports. It is in these programs that most people first become involved in organized sport, and they are the forms of organized sport with the greatest active participation.

"Building character" is frequently cited as a major purpose and achievement of high school and youth sport programs. In chapter 9 I analyze the ideological meanings of this seemingly innocent goal and examine the growing commodification and its consequences in these forms of sports.

CHAPTER 9

Building Character Through Sport

I haven't given any thought to what I would be if I weren't a speed skater. It's taken up so much of my life I haven't had time to think about anything else.

Nathaniel Mills, 15-year-old member
of the U.S. national outdoor
speed skating team

People participate in sport more during childhood and adolescence than during any other time in their lives. The informal sandlot games of yesteryear—though they are still played occasionally today—have given way to highly organized youth sports, which have become one of the most popular cultural practices in American life. Some 30 million boys and girls are involved in community-sponsored youth sport programs each year, and another 5.2 million adolescents participate on high school athletic teams annually. Little League baseball is the largest of the youth sport organizations, with about 1.5 million American youngsters playing. In addition, more than 3,000 YMCAs provide some 2 million boys and girls the opportunity to play organized sports, and the Junior Olympics Sports Program sponsors over 2,000 local, state, regional, and national events in 21 different sports. Emily Greenspan (1983) has written on the subject of child sports stars:

> For almost every parental ambition there is a well-organized outlet. Parents who want to get a jump on the competition can enroll their children in age-group swimming programs at three years, ice hockey at four, and football, baseball, or soccer at six. (p. 136)

It is not an exaggeration, then, to say that sport plays a central role in the lives of millions of young participants.

Although the popular impression of sport for children and adolescents is that it provides an opportunity for young people to learn and enjoy organized games—which is true—there is another firmly held belief that sport experiences help youngsters learn valuable social skills and values that are useful in other spheres of life. It is on this belief that I focus in this chapter. As with the other aspects of sport we have examined thus far, an accurate analysis requires historically situating and culturally locating community-based youth sport and interscholastic athletics.

From Informal Play to Organized Sport

A new industrial era emerged in America after the Civil War. The years from 1875 to 1910 saw the most rapid expansion of capital and industry of any period in our history. As industrial jobs boomed, many people left their farms and small towns and converged on the growing industrial cities. These migrations, along with an influx of millions of immigrants, flooded the cities and formed a growing urban industrial work force. In the first 10 years of this century, 8.8 million immigrants came to America, representing more than half of our population increase. In 1909, 58% of the industrial workers in manufacturing were foreign; of the immigrant male heads of households from non-English-speaking countries living in cities, only 45% could speak English (Szymanski, 1983).

The rapid transformation from rural to urban lifestyles and from agricultural to industrial occupational roles created a host of social problems; one of the major ones was raising and educating children. The traditional context for doing so within the family became unsuitable in an industrialized society, where one or both parents worked outside the home and children were away from home more often (either in the streets or working). In addition, immigrant children needed a way to learn the English language and American values and customs. So traditional, informal education was gradually taken over by public schools, churches, and other social organizations, and in these settings children learned about living as citizens, workers, and consumers in America.

As with many spheres of modern society, the state has taken an increasingly larger role in education, and the growth of public education during the past 100 years illustrates the expansion of the state into the former role of the family. In 1890 about half of the children ages 5 to 17 were in some type of public school; by 1930 this had grown to 81% and by 1985 to about 90%. In 1890 about 7 million children attended public schools; by the late 1980s there were some 59 million students. Between 1890 and 1930 the percentage of 17-year-olds in high school grew from 4% to 29%; now it is more than 80%. These figures give impressive testimony to the public school's expanding responsibility for socializing American youth, and they signify that passage through the school system has become an important initiation rite for becoming an adult member of the American community.

Public school growth went hand in hand with industrial capitalism. At the end of the Civil War the industrial output of the United States was small compared with that of Great Britain. But by 1900 the U.S. had surpassed Britain in the quantity and value of its manufactured products and had become the world's foremost industrial nation. Corporate capitalism was a stalwart supporter of public education, regarding it as important for providing both support for capitalist enterprise and skilled workers for increasingly specialized jobs.

Public schools have been organized in ways consistent with the needs of dominant political and economic interests, shaping students' attitudes and values to conform to the demands of hierarchical models of authority and producing graduates fitted for their places in corporate and state bureaucracies. The reigning hegemonic ideology has stressed the importance of the schools for teaching discipline, obedience, orderly work habits, respect for authority, and an uncompromising admiration for the social, political, and economic order. Its voice has consistently won out over proponents of more progressive educational ideas. Thus, schools are a fundamental part of the hegemonic power framework, structurally and ideologically dedicated to the political and economic forces that nourish them. By serving as an agent of legitimation, public education, then, has become central in the reproduction of the labor power as well as the class, gender, and race structures of American society. (I don't mean to say that schools are *merely* institutions of reproduction; this would be much too simplistic. For an extended discussion, see chapter 1 in Apple [1982].)

Social control is also at the heart of ideas about public education. Controlling and channeling students is crucial to training them in the skills and discipline to hold jobs in modern capitalism and also to infusing them with broader values of morality, patriotism, and loyalty. An educated citizenry willing to comply with the established laws and customs is considered essential to making a political democracy work.

Interscholastic Athletics

As public education expanded and modified its curriculum to meet changing social and student needs at the turn of the century, various extracurricular activities, such as debate teams and student government, began to grow. One of the activities that quickly gained a commanding popularity among high school students was athletics. Colleges had begun playing intercollegiate sports shortly before the Civil War, and by the beginning of the 20th century the games had achieved a prominent place in college life. In the meantime, high school students had begun to organize their own athletic contests.

Writing about the growth of school sports in Boston, Hardy (1982) said that by 1888 several area high schools were fielding football teams and had formed an Interscholastic Football Association. Furthermore,

within two decades, baseball, track, basketball, and ice hockey leagues operated among the city's secondary schools. . . . By the turn of the century, interscholastic sports had become a fixture. The daily newspapers carried not only regular coverage of the competition, but also feature articles on the prominent schoolboy stars and the prospects of each team for the upcoming season. (pp. 112, 115)

In New York City a Public Schools Athletic League was started in 1903, and by 1910 over 17 other cities had developed similar leagues (Jable, 1979). Surveys about secondary school athletics in 1905 and 1907 showed that most high schools fielded teams in at least one sport. The 1905 survey found that football was played in 78% of the schools; the figures for baseball and basketball were 65% and 58%, respectively. The 1907 survey indicated that all of the 225 responding public high schools had some form of interscholastic competition (Lowman, 1907; McCurdy, 1905).

At first school faculty and administrators either discouraged or ignored these student-organized and student-controlled activities, but eventually they began to see potential in them for serving some of the schools' purposes. Seeking to capitalize on the popularity of sports, authorities gradually and inevitably wrested control of school athletics from the students. Hardy (1982) explained that educators had come to accept "the notion that schools should convey to students the specific skills, behavior, and values necessary to a productive life in the new industrial order" and in athletics they presumed that "the lessons of teamwork, self-sacrifice, and discipline were . . . transferable from the playing field to the business world or the factory" (p. 121). Even more significant, according to Hardy, it was believed that the qualities thought to be developed by school sport—loyalty, social morality, and social conscience—were those "upon which rested the greatness of America's cities and corporations" (p. 123). By the 1920s, high school athletics was firmly under the control of school authorities, with teams supervised by coaches hired as full-time faculty. There has been little change in the basic purposes or structural arrangements of high school athletics since that time.

Public Parks and Playgrounds

In conjunction with the expansion of the public school system, nonschool social activities concerned with the personal and social development of youth experienced enormous growth. Goodman (1979) has asserted that "by 1905 almost everyone concerned with social reform was concerned with play and almost every reform organization was involved in assisting the rise of organized play in one form or another" (p. 61). Like schools, parks and playgrounds were regarded as resources for replacing the socializing influence of family life, which was seemingly being suppressed with the growth of urban America. Beginning with private, uncoordinated, voluntary efforts that gradually gave way to various public agencies, play opportunities were increasingly provided for youngsters. From 1890 to 1910 city and state governments nationwide organized recreation programs, built parks, formed playgrounds, and hired leaders to direct programs and maintain facilities. Even private business groups began to sponsor organized play opportunities for youngsters.

The play movement was a product of the desire among social reformers, educators, and concerned business interests to protect children from the harmful effects of city life and to supply a mechanism for controlling the process of socialization. In addition to providing recreation and physical activity, organized play was regarded as a forum for teaching good habits, such as group loyalty, common ideals, and subordination of self. Another major goal was a desire to reduce juvenile crime (Cavallo, 1981). Recounting the drive for community support for playgrounds in Massachusetts, Hardy (1982) wrote this description:

When the Massachusetts Civic League barnstormed the state to drum up support for a referendum on playgrounds, they found a ready audience among businessmen who agreed that organized play promoted qualities that were fundamental to the successful worker. Among them were the capacity for teamwork, good health, enthusiasm . . . honesty, clean play, temperance, and imagination. (p. 104)

Social reformer Jacob Riis (1903) envisioned an even broader purpose. He said, "The problem of the children is the problem of the State. As we mould the children of the toiling masses in our cities, so we shape the destiny of the State" (p. 1).

Community-Sponsored Youth Sports

High school athletic programs were enthusiastically endorsed by educators and community leaders and the same was true of the park and playground movement, but neither provided organized sport opportunities for preadolescent youth. In fact, both groups discouraged such activity. Sport historian Jack Berryman (1975) has explained: "The policy statements of professional physical education and recreation groups as well as other leading educators . . . illustrated their discouragement of highly competitive sports for children" (p. 117). But preadolescent youngsters (mostly boys) and their parents clamored more and more for organized sport opportunities, and some community leaders advocated the value of sport experiences for the same reasons that high schools had adopted them. Finally, "the idea that what was thought to be good for the teenagers and adults would also be good for the children in a scaled-down version led to attempts at providing organized sport competition for the younger members of society" (p. 114). Accordingly, community business leaders and service organizations, and some municipal recreation departments as well, stepped forward and began to provide opportunities for preadolescents in organized sport competition. From its beginnings, this form of organized sport has been popular, and it has continued to grow unabated.

As part of this movement in our public high schools and community youth agencies to pursue a broad commitment to preparing youth for their places in a rapidly expanding industrial society, community and school authorities began to envision that well-organized sport programs could also promote social and moral attributes and thus contribute to the goal of a particular interpretation of good citizenship. In both the schools and the community-based programs, structured physical activity was linked to moral development. Community youth sport programs and high school athletics were gradually colonized as ideological instruments for socializing American youth to the formation of a common consciousness, to a sense of common allegiance, and for different positions in the social, economic, and occupational hierarchy. Organized sport for young people began to receive recognition as an educational medium for transmitting advanced capitalist ideology in the name of building character (O'Hanlon, 1980; Spring, 1974). Formal sport programs, then, were not solely organized to provide an outlet for human expression and self-fulfillment. According to one educational historian:

> Educational administrators and leading physical educators saw athletics as a valuable means of developing those characteristics associated with efficient citizenship in a modern industrial society. Through organized sport they sought to inculcate a conception of citizenship with a high degree of corporate consciousness. . . . Citizenship in twentieth century America required a strong sense of cooperation, institutional national loyalty, and a willingness to subordinate personal interests to those of the group. (O'Hanlon, 1980, p. 89)

Thus, athletics was praised as an important medium for instilling young participants with common ideals, common modes of thought, cooperation, and social cohesion in the service of the instrumental culture of capitalism (Miracle, 1985). In short, sport was used as a mechanism to produce a social consciousness willing to accept, and even embrace, conditions of structural social inequality. Community youth and school sport, then, became an agent in the maintenance and reproduction of the reigning politically and economically powerful and dominant groups in American society. The norms, values, and dispositions of the sport subculture provided legitimation for their ideology.

A slogan emerged that became a powerful image of the supposed purpose of sport for children and adolescents: *Sport builds character*. This assertion was, and still is, frequently made by community leaders, school officials, parents, and even average citizens when a discussion turns to the purpose of organized sport for children and adolescents. Sport, it is argued, provides a social environment for acquiring culturally valued personal and social attitudes, values, and behaviors; moreover, it has always been implied that what is learned in the sport setting transfers to other spheres of life. So this creed canonizes a widespread faith in sport as an agent of social development and a medium for the formation of a particular ideological consciousness.

Until the early 1970s high school and youth sport programs were overwhelmingly for boys only, and the character traits usually identified as expected outcomes of organized sport experiences were those typically valued as masculine. Thus, school and nonschool sports reinforced traditional gender role differentiation. Excluding females from these programs kept them from being socialized into the traits presumed to bring success in American public life.

Ideological Dimensions of Sport as a Character Builder

A major task in any society facing dominant groups who wish to maintain their status and power is to mold a common consciousness among the people, animate it with the appropriate ethics, and use it to shape attitudes, habits, and lifestyles. But, as I have repeatedly stressed, dominant groups cannot usually exercise hegemony in direct, overt ways. Instead the methods are diffuse, circumspect, and suffused by a complex of ideological apparatuses that permeate the social institutions and practices of society, including cultural and leisure activities. Thought of in this way, hegemonic ideology is like a protective wrapping around the structures and processes of domination and exploitation; it legitimates and encourages patterns of activity that ensure that a particular set of social relations is sustained and reproduced. Ideological work in this context preserves the dominant group practices and visions of the world as universal.

Dominant groups use political, economic, and cultural resources to extend their influence. Their interests are legitimated by compatible ideologies disseminated by schools, mass media, and various agencies of social control. As I have repeatedly shown, modern sport forms are a part of the terrain upon which the dominant ideology is built and sustained. Here, as in other spheres, systems of symbols, such as mottoes, slogans, and clichés, are used to shape and manipulate attitudes and to engineer consent in the service of dominant interests. The motto *Sport builds character* must be seen in light of its ideological intent. It is not an empirical statement of fact, nor neutral commentary. Like other slogans and mottoes, it expresses much more than its intrinsic content, and it embodies and represents wider patterns of meaning, expressing and sustaining valued patterns of activity and beliefs. It is a servant of ideology.

Social Origins

How did the notion that sport builds character develop? To understand its ideological dimensions we must understand its origins and evolution. The idea of positive social outcomes through sport participation grew slowly in the U.S. during the 19th century. Sport historian Donald Mrozek (1983) contends that "at the beginning of the 19th century, there was no obvious merit in sport—certainly no clear social value to it and no sense that it contributed to the improvement of the individual's character" (p. xiii).

But in England a tradition arose in the mid-1800s that was to profoundly influence sporting practice across the Atlantic. With the emergence of student sport teams in British private secondary boarding schools, school sports won recognition as a medium for socialization, acculturation, and social control and they became imbued with a moralistic ideology that came to be known as *athleticism* (Mangan, 1981, 1986).

Although school authorities first disdained as frivolous the sports played by the students, sports gradually came to be valued by the headmasters, more for the qualities of social character they were presumed to develop than for the physical exercise they provided. In a description of British boarding school sports, sociologist Christopher Armstrong (1984) observed that they were considered an excellent way to develop "moral authority and exemplary character in England's evolving ruling class. . . . Here the ideal was intended to allow boys to prove themselves as potential leaders on the playing fields through moral courage, devoted team work, and group spirit" (p. 315). British sport historian Peter McIntosh (1957) stated emphatically that character training was the real justification for the support of school sport. In 1864 the Royal Commission on Schools succinctly identified the purpose of sports:

> The cricket and football fields . . . are not merely places of exercise or amusement; they help to form some of the most valuable social qualities and manly virtues, and they hold, like the classroom and the boarding house, a distinct and important place in . . . school education. (p. 178)

These school sports, British historian J.A. Mangan (1986) emphasized, "were the wheel around which moral values turned. They were the pre-eminent instrument for the training of a boy's character" (p. 18).

An unstated social logic and ideological underpinning to athleticism also supported the British attitude that sport taught valuable social traits. Sports were pragmatically related to the expansion of the British Empire, which required "the production of self-confident, hardy soldiers, administrators and . . . [majestic] missionaries . . . capable of withstanding the physical and psychological rigours of imperial duty" (Mangan, 1975, pp. 148-149). Graduates of the British private boarding schools became leaders in many spheres of life—government, the military, the domestic industry, commerce—throughout the British Empire. These young men were destined to govern and control. So a tradition of self-government was foundational in these schools because the British believed that experiences in controlling self and governing others was good training for future leadership. The school sports were almost totally governed by the students themselves. Games were lively and competition was spirited, but there was an emphasis on fellowship, sacrifice, cooperation, sportsmanship, and a willingness to accept defeat gracefully. How one played the game was more important than the outcome of the contest; indeed, there was a sense that how one played was an indicator of how one would later behave, and that is why team sports were valued so highly (Mangan, 1981).

Although no one ever empirically verified the social-development effects of school sport, belief that sport did build character was unshakable. A popular saying that "the Battle of Waterloo was won on the playing fields of Eton" (a private boarding school) suggested that Arthur Wellington, the victorious British general at the Battle of Waterloo, had acquired skills and values while playing sports at Eton that prepared him to defeat Napoleon. (In fact, though, there is compelling evidence that as an adolescent attending Eton Lord Wellington did not play sports. There were no compulsory, organized games at Eton while he was there, and even the most casual cricket or boating contest did not attract his participation [Langford, 1969, pp. 15-17].)

Exporting the Theme

Like so many ideas and practices of the British upper-class, athleticism and its accompanying character-building theme were imported to America with little thought of the profound differences in cultural conditions and circumstances. Consequently, character development has been proclaimed as a goal and an outcome for organized school and preadolescent sports in the U.S. for a century, even though the cultural milieu and social meanings that prevailed in British private schools did not and do not underlie American sport programs. Whereas British schools were preparing an elite group of young men for leadership positions in government, business, and the military, American organized sports were popularized in the first half of the 20th century, when educational programs were increasingly directed at lower- and middle-class youth (except in private boarding schools). This was a time of great social transformation. Vast numbers of immigrants and their children needed to be educated; rapid urbanization stretched community housing, sanitation, health care, and employment resources; city crime became a major social problem; and the growth of monopoly corporate enterprise revolutionized the labor market and working conditions. The kind of character formation needed in America was quite different than that considered indispensable for the leaders of the British Empire. Social conformity, obedience, and respect for authority seemed more congruent with future roles in America than did leadership, initiative, and self-discipline.

Youth and School Sport

Formal and objective aspects of sport and the mottoes and slogans popularized by the sport world capture only a fragment of the day-today social relationships of the sporting experience. Beyond that, sports have immense power to manipulate the consciousness, values, and beliefs of athletes and to pass on selected aspects of the dominant culture. Indeed, the distinctiveness of the sporting process is to be found not in learning skills or in teamwork but in the *social relations* of the sporting encounter—the relationships between coaches and athletes, athletes and athletes, and athletes and their sport tasks. When viewed from this perspective, we can see that the structure of American organized sport tends to integrate participants into American culture through a congruence between its social relations and those of contemporary American society.

The structure of social relations in organized sport programs not only introduces the hierarchy and authoritarianism of the larger society to participants, it also nurtures social characteristics, self-images, and class identifications that are important for complaisant transition to adult roles. According to sociologist Charles Page (1973), this is exemplified in

> rules and routine, the ascendancy of work over play, and the rise of the coach's authority within and beyond the athletic realm. . . . [This structure has] penetrated deeply into collegiate and high school sports and even into the adult-controlled, highly organized "little leagues" in baseball and football. (p. 33)

Alan Ingham and Stephen Hardy (1984) have suggested that sport for young athletes has become a form of "anticipatory productive labor." By this they mean that sport helps prepare young athletes to accept authoritarian leadership and the norms of specialization and rationalization in the workplace. Athletic programs are designed to socialize players by supplying both a model and an actual system whereby persons slated for specialized roles of varying prestige and importance learn to cooperate for the good of the organization. Individual athletes are expected to do what is thought best for the team. From the little leagues through high school, aspiring athletes learn to please their coaches; if they wish to play organized sports, they must play the social acquiescence game properly.

Coaches are the autocratic center of the athlete's world; they set the standards of excellence and prescribe methods for attaining them. This is justified as necessary to achieve the team's objectives. This total authority is vividly evident in popular locker room slogans: "My way or the highway"; "There is no I in team"; "A player doesn't make the team, the team makes the player." Whitson (1986) contends that in structure and ethos youth and school sport tends to prepare

> young men [and women] to take for granted the norms of the capitalist workplace; and central among these is that every aspect of the process is necessarily geared to the "natural" goal of increasing productivity. Never can player (or worker) satisfaction, let alone the

possibility of restructuring the "relations of production" so as to afford opportunities for personal growth, take precedence over the imperative of building a winner. (p. 101)

Thus a collective consciousness is fostered, strengthened by myths and slogans and infused with the virtues of conformity, obedience, respect for external rewards, and unquestioned loyalty. These are the character traits that are labeled desirable. Hegemony, it can be seen, is maintained and reproduced not only through the diffusion of ideas but also in the routines and rituals of sport involvement and in its system of rewards and punishments. The tightly managed organizational arrangement of the world of youth and school sport will be encountered again in the occupational world (O'Hanlon, 1980). Presumably those who have been athletes will be well trained for it because hierarchical structures that stress relations of control, obedience, and conformity give rise to a distinct socialization that tends to reproduce itself (Ellis, Lee, & Patersen, 1978; Kohn, 1981).

In effect, then, the social relationships typical in organized sport replicate the traditional hierarchical division of labor and social values, in part through a correspondence between their internal social relationships and those of the larger society. The real achievement of organized sport programs is training participants to accept the prevailing social structure and their fate as future workers in advanced capitalist enterprise. After 3 years of direct observation of the role of adults—coaches, umpires, parents—in structuring Little League baseball, sociologist Gary Fine (1987) concluded this:

There are components of the playing of Little League baseball that can usefully be seen as "work," at least in a moral sense. Coaches and many players expect the participants to adhere to a Puritan work ethic, preparing themselves for adult life. When they don't, moral disparagement is seen as warranted and is judiciously applied. (p. 51)

Increasingly, youth and school sport has taken on many of the trappings of the commodified sport industry, seen in meritocracy, the endorsement of the performance principle, overemphasis on winning, assault on records, and the intensifying use of child athletes as public entertainers. In a series on high school athletics published in *The New York Times*, one of the writers noted the following:

High school athletics have become the latest entree on the American sports menu, served up to help satisfy the voracious appetite of the fan. As a result, scholastic athletes are on the verge of becoming as important to the billion-dollar sports industry as their college brothers and sisters—and just as vulnerable to big-time exploitation. . . . The fans' interest is more than equaled by that of three other forces: college and pro coaches hungry to see potential recruits, television companies craving more sports programming, and advertisers seeking new ways to reach the teen-age market. (Eskenazi, 1989, p. 1)

John Albinson (1976) nicely summed up the situation by saying that to expect organized sports for young athletes to encourage "personal growth, honor, generosity, tolerance, or just plain fun, may simply be to overlook the degree to which the logic of our adult world structures [youth sport]" (p. 390). This is not to suggest that sport participants never experience fun or excitement; indeed, these very real experienced emotions are effective tools for legitimizing the nature and features of youth sport while at the same time inculcating the dominant ideology.

Patriarchy and Character Development.   A final ideological aspect of youth and school sport needs to be addressed—namely, its contributions to patriarchy, the set of social relations between men and women through which women are dominated by men. A prime reason that patriarchy continues is that so many of our cultural institutions and practices are based on relations between men and women, sport of course being one of the most prominent. In the ideology of athleticism fashioned in Great Britain in the 19th century, manliness was an intricate link in the presumed character development achieved by athletic competition. According to Bundgaard (1985), "The playing of such team sports as rugby and cricket became closely associated with moral training; the game field provided the laboratory for the outward display and the reinforcement of manly traits" (p. 29). He goes on to describe the incorporation of this ideology in the United States: "In America, too, manliness, character building, and moral education became the key concepts justifying athletics" (p. 29).

Central to youth and school sport programs have been their patriarchal features and the roles they play in supporting male dominance. These activities continue to be in large part an arena for the inculcation of "manliness" while actively and contemptuously excluding females, celebrating "masculinity," and reinforcing patriarchy. Consider how vigorously and persistently male-dominated sport organizations have fought female inroads into sport over the past 20 years.

Sport is a social institution constituted primarily among men only and through which men support and reproduce the ideology of patriarchy. Part of the ideological content in the idea that sport builds character conceals a subtle message that reinforces, through intention and innuendo, male power and superiority. It fosters gender inequality by promoting the building of character traits traditionally associated with men.

Evidence for Sport as a Character Builder

In presenting the origins and evolution of the American belief that sport builds character, I have begged the obvious: Does it? Let me address this question.

Although many Americans take this motto for granted, there have been few well-conceived and implemented empirical research studies on the effects of organized sport involvement on social development. There are several reasons for this. First, the word *character* is vague; it can have many meanings, and when left unspecified there is no way of knowing which meaning is intended. The definition must be anchored to a set of attitudes, values, and behaviors, and there are differing cultural ideas about which of those are considered valuable. So the exhibition of a particular behavior or trait in a specific situation might be considered a demonstration of good character in one culture but bad character in another. *Character*, then, is a socially constructed concept amenable to a variety of interpretations.

And even if one clearly defines what one means by character in a given setting, it is extremely difficult to empirically verify the character-building effects of sport involvement. Traditional experimental designs are impractical because it is almost impossible to arrange the necessary controlled conditions for collecting data. Cross-sectional research designs, which provide data about relationships, are worthless to substantiate causal effects. Certain studies have attempted to analyze the effects of sport involvement on a single discrete variable, such as courage or loyalty, but at the expense of almost trivializing the symbolic interactions that occur in a complex social setting like sport. So such an approach is too simple to yield anything meaningful.

Because we cannot statistically verify that sport builds character, we are left to relating anecdotes about how particular athletes displayed courage, perseverance, or self-discipline in the course of a game or how a team showed dedication and teamwork. But a perusal of the nation's newspapers on any given day will reveal stories of courage, loyalty, perseverance, and so on, by people who have never participated in sport. So character qualities often attributed to athletes are neither confined to nor peculiar to them. Another common form of anecdotal evidence is the ode to "what sport did for me." Such testimonials are often made by former athletes who attribute their postplaying achievements to their sport experiences. Regardless of the form, of course, anecdotal evidence is unacceptable as scientific proof.

To these problems of verification I would add questions of whether the "character" displayed by athletes or former athletes was present before they joined sport or whether their particular character predispositions may have led them to take up sport in the first place. Several scholars in sport studies have suggested such possibilities.

I hope that my comments about the problems of empirically supporting claims that sport builds character will not be misunderstood. I am not asserting that sport experiences have no effect on the personal-social development of participants. Indeed, there is convincing, empirically grounded knowledge that salient social experiences are powerful socializers. Sport involvement is an exciting form of human expression; many people find sports a source of great fun, joy, and self-satisfaction, and young athletes' values and beliefs are undoubtedly shaped by their experiences. But the exact effects of sport on attitudes, values, and behaviors depend greatly on the social contextual conditions of a sporting experience. Moreover, perhaps the sport setting is merely a particularly good setting for enabling persons to exhibit preexisting character traits; that some athletes or former athletes display culturally valued personal and social characteristics cannot be wholly attributed to their sport experiences without an enormous leap of faith (Coakley, 1987; Sage, 1986).

Any cultural practice has the potential to tutor its participants about values and actions, and, as I have emphasized earlier in this chapter, that is the deliberate objective of our organized community and school sports. But though it seems evident that social experiences do affect attitudes, values, and behaviors, there tends to be a blind, cultish assumption that sport transmits only universally admired ethical and moral attributes.

Just what do young athletes learn from the sport culture? What is the ethos of the programs? Many do learn lessons about fair play, self-discipline, cooperation, and respect for human rights and dignity. But many also learn—and are taught—to break the rules. Indeed, in some sports rule-breaking has actually become part of the strategy of the game. Moreover, by observing coaches, parents, and older athletes, many young athletes learn to cheat and violate basic codes of moral conduct in big and little ways.

It is understandable that participants may interpret some of what they learn in sport to mean that anything goes as long as you don't get caught. If one accepts the notion that youth can learn culturally valued beliefs and behaviors from sport, and if one agrees that rule-breaking is widespread in sport, it becomes clear that sport experiences may be providing patterned reinforcement of attitudes, values, and behaviors that are antithetical to the character-building ideals of fair play and the morality of justice (Arnold, 1984). Certainly young athletes learn more from youth and school sport than how to cheat and to disrespect moral codes. But I do suggest that there is a growing element in these sport programs that is detrimental to the development of higher order ethical and moral attributes. Sociologist T.R. Young (1986) has expressed serious misgivings about the moral and social lessons often promulgated in organized sport for youth:

> As far as moral character in . . . competitive sports in general, one must wonder whether that particular character is, indeed, an ideal to be adopted. The widespread cheating by coaches and players, the envy, disappointment, cynicism and hypocrisy entailed in commercialized competitive sports, as well as the abusive and profane behavior of the fans leave one in doubt about the psychological benefits accruing from and calling for such social investments. (p. 7)

Transformative Potential

I am not suggesting that youth and school sport is merely an ideological mirror of the dominant interests in our society nor that all of the talk about sport building character is a conscious hegemonic conspiracy. Furthermore, no assemblage of ideological practices and meanings and no set of social and institutional arrangements can totally eliminate countervailing tendencies and oppositional practices. Athletes can and do resist in subtle and overt ways; they often contradict and partly transform modes of control into opportunities for resistance, and they maintain their own informal norms that guide the sport process (Fine, 1987). Gruneau (1982b) has argued that "critics of youth sport underestimate the capacities of young people to act creatively and define spaces of autonomous expression and resistance even in the most repressive of sport settings" (p. 50). Some correspondence between sport and the social conditions in which participants live is unmistakable, but the social context of sport does not warrant linking it inextricably to the larger social world in which participants live.

Organized sport can be transformative as well as reproductive. A genuine, widespread public interest in truly promoting youth and school sport as a medium for personal enrichment and development, enabling participants to acquire and practice the universal moral qualities for which sport has been valorized, would certainly promote their transformative potential. But for this to happen, large-scale public discussion and debate would have to take place with a vision of substantially transforming the current purposes and forms of sport for the younger generation. Where is such activity going on today? Who is challenging the present assumptions and practices about sport? Critical commentary is almost nonexistent. Judging from prevalent trends, the attitudes, values, and behaviors with the greatest currency in sport have more to do with socialization into the larger social system and internalization of advanced capitalist ideology than with universal morality.

Although sport for young athletes does have many problems, there are few viable alternatives for filling the substantial free time of young people. Pleas for a return to the good old days "seem increasingly utopian—more like intermittent cries of anguish in protest" over the professionalization of youth and school sport (Ingham & Hardy, 1984, p. 97). Parents and other adults have come to accept organized sport as a feeder system that is anchored in an atmosphere of capital and labor. Moreover, they see no alternative models to the dominant sport forms that are now popular.

Summary and Preview

I have focused in this chapter on the connections between school and youth sport and other sectors of American life in terms of production and cultural reproduction and on the contradictions that exist in this system of sport. It is a rare youngster who is not touched in some way by school and youth sport in passing through childhood and adolescence, and these programs are a powerful means for inculcating social norms, values, and beliefs. As a cultural practice, organized youth sport is closely connected to other sectors of American society, and the forms and functions of youth sport are grounded in and contoured by dominant political, economic, and cultural interests of the wider community.

The next and final chapter turns to examining the broad issues of the oppositional and transformative potential in contemporary sport. Sport is analyzed as a terrain in which different means and ends are contested, as a site for struggle and resistance against dominant definitions and meanings, and as an arena for human emancipation and freedom.

CHAPTER 10

Resistance and Transformation in Sport

America would gain far more than she would lose through the initiation of . . . an alternative sport structure . . . in which the younger generation can be socialized with values stressing cooperation rather than antagonism, participation and self-actualization rather than confrontation and domination.

Harry Edwards, sociologist

I have sought in this book to introduce you to some new perspectives on the typical analysis of American sport. In doing this I have taken the theoretical perspective of hegemony—an approach relying on insights about the historical construction of dominance and the roles of political, economic, and cultural institutions in society. According to this approach, privileged, elite social groups that control the critically important economic and political institutions of a society also have principal access to the fundamental ideological institutions. Privileged access to the ideological institutions allows these groups to write society's rules in the form of norms, values, and beliefs, and the rules they write enable them to continue to write the rules, reinforcing and reproducing their structural advantages (Lieberson, 1985).

I have used selected aspects of the theory of hegemony to sensitize you to the role of the state, the economic system, mass media, and education in American sporting practices and to the role of institutionalized sport in promoting conformity to the dominant cultural consensus. I have explored power, domination, and ideology and their ties to social class, gender, and race as they are related to sport. My overall purpose has been to reach beyond the clichés, myths, and slogans disseminated through hegemonic ideology to examine sporting practices in American culture.

One of the most fundamental insights of applying a hegemonic image is to see sport as an important platform upon which dominant ideology is advanced. In fact, one of the most compelling roles of institutional sport is to promote activities that help fashion the tools of economic, political, and cultural hegemony of the dominant class. Sport's social importance, then, is rooted in its power to structure and promote social relations in accordance with the requirements of the dominant interests who control or own it. As a type of cultural practice and as a direct reflection of dominant group interests, sport can be seen as promoting and supporting various forms of social inequality in American society.

Issues relevant to analyzing sport from a hegemonic perspective address how sport is associated with social class, race, and gender and with the control, production, and distribution of economic and cultural power. Because the social practices and relations of sport are structured by the culture in which it exists, any adequate account must be rooted in an understanding of its social, economic, political, and cultural context. As Gruneau (1979) has argued,

> The *dramatizations* of social life that are provided by games and sports are far from innocent individual and collective experiences; rather they represent a powerful affirmation of the legitimacy of existing social conditions and thereby tend to reinforce these conditions. (p. 2)

The key to understanding sport as a cultural phenomenon, then, is found in the nature of its relationship to broader societal forces of which it is a part.

A major trend of sporting practice during the past century has been its transformation from a spontaneous, informal form of play to a commodified productive enterprise. There are many opportunities for dominant groups to associate themselves with sport and use it to further their own interests: Commercialized sport is mediated by the mass media, the government intervenes in it, and it plays an important role in the educational system. Meanwhile, spontaneously initiated, informal, and creative sport and leisure have steadily diminished. Every effort to nurture informal, anonymous, unorganized sport is quickly incorporated into the marketplace by the drive for capital.

The characteristics of commodified sports and their widespread popularity make it easy for them to penetrate everyday life and to represent and reproduce the dominant ideology. This does not mean, however, that there is only passive compliance with hegemonic domination in sport or any arena; resistance to, evasion of, challenges to the oppressive measures of hegemony are constantly taking place.

In summary, sport is one of various cultural settings in which the hegemonic structure of power and privilege in capitalist society is continually fortified. Learning to see sport through a perspective of hegemony enables one to be more aware of the role of sport in producing and reproducing relationships of power and dominance. One becomes skeptical of assertions about the naturalness of contemporary sport practices and events and more open to alternatives that would elevate personal development and social justice. This inevitably raises questions about alternatives to the present sport system.

Hegemony Challenged

Despite the enormous power and resources of dominant groups, hegemony always has elements of uncertainty and changing balance. Ideological contradictions render it vulnerable to oppositional tendencies and to cultural change in general. As Williams (1977) has persuasively argued, hegemony "does not just passively exist as a form of dominance. It has continually to be renewed, recreated, defended, and modified. It is also continually resisted, limited, altered, challenged by pressures not at all its own" (p. 112). Dominant groups must work hard to sustain their power through an active process of accommodation and compromise (Kellner, 1978). Well-established traditions of popular evasion of and resistance to programs and policies of dominant groups on the part of subordinate groups show that hegemony and compliance can never be assured. No set of social institutional arrangements and no collection of hegemonic practices and meanings can completely eliminate counterhegemonic initiatives.

Cultural practices are often on the forefront of opposition and resistance to hegemony. Historical traditions of the theater, the arts, and literature show them to be common springboards for such actions, and that pattern remains alive today. Many athletes and others connected with sport have resisted hegemonic patterns in subtle and not-so-subtle ways. In so doing, they have modified, contradicted, and sometimes transformed definitions and modes of control into opportunities for nurturing their own informal norms and values in sport.

So sport practices, like any other cultural activities, are a domain for the expression of various forms of resistance. They are sites of contest and conflict between dominant social groups and various factions of subordinate groups. Bourdieu (1978) has observed that even

the *social definition of sport* is an object of struggles. . . . The field of sporting practices is the site of struggles in which what is at stake . . . is the monopolistic capacity to impose the legitimate definition of sporting practice and of the legitimate function of sporting activity. (p. 826)

I cannot adequately examine here the many resistance and transformational movements that have occurred in American sports. But by describing selected examples I hope to illustrate several areas of sporting practices in which cultural struggles have taken place. If my discussion evokes interest in more extended discussions, you will find them in Donnelly (1988) and Eichberg (1984).

Class and Political Resistance

As part of a larger system of social control, dominant groups have historically attempted to define appropriate sporting practices. One strategy has been to outlaw certain sports. For example, pit sports such as cockfighting and dogfighting, traditionally popular with the working class, have been illegal since colonial times. They have been labeled as violent, inhumane, and cruel to animals and as sports that promote drinking and gambling. Despite the overwhelming sanctions against them, these sports have thrived among a rural subculture of farmers, ranchers, and migrant workers and an urban working-class following. Contests are held in such diverse spots as barnyards, abandoned sawmills, forest clearings, and abandoned buildings—wherever a pit can be constructed. It is impossible to accurately estimate the extent of cock- and dogfighting in the United States, but for cockfighting alone there are three nationally distributed monthly publications. Both sports continue to be popular, in resistance to dominant definitions and models of sport practices.

The capitalist workplace has always had a contested terrain; indeed, worker struggles against the power of those who own the means of production are endemic to capitalist production. I have already described the long history of professional athletes' struggles against team owners to protect their basic rights as well as their material interests. All professional team sports have eventually established players' unions, always against the wishes of the owners and league commissioners. The growing strength and militancy of the unions have enabled them to wrest many concessions from the owners, with perhaps the most significant breakthrough being their successful challenge to the reserve clause.

In recent years individual athletes and activist groups have used the sporting venue to demonstrate against hegemonic public policies and practices. Students at various colleges have used sport events to stage protests against war, racism, nuclear proliferation, and environmental pollution. Literature distribution, speeches, or placard displays typically are done outside the playing facility, but demonstrations have also occurred inside during pregame or half-time ceremonies.

In spite of American government and corporate support for South Africa, its apartheid policies have led various sport groups to successfully protest the participation of South African athletes in sporting events in the U.S. Over the past 15 years almost every event scheduled to include South African competitors has been met with resistance (Krotee, 1988). In fact, sport has been the leading American social institution in condemning South African apartheid.

Some sport events have had transformative as well as resistive potential. They have been planned to confront certain social attitudes, practices, and even laws in an effort to raise public consciousness and effect legal change. Historically, there has been little toleration for homosexuality in America, and despite substantially improved attitudes over the past decade, gays and lesbians still suffer various forms of structured social stigma and inequality. In an effort to call public attention to discrimination against homosexuals and to improve public attitudes about them, national leaders of the homosexual community planned to hold a Gay Olympic Games in 1982. The event was quickly crushed by a lawsuit from the United States Olympic Committee claiming that the use of the word *Olympics* violated a trademark the USOC was granted under the Amateur Sports Act of 1978. The USOC's suit was upheld by the Supreme Court (*San Francisco Arts & Athletics v. United States Olympic Committee*, 1987).

Gender and Race Resistance

Although much resistance to sport has revolved around political policies and class relations, issues of gender and race have also given rise to opposition and transformation. Many black athletes have been outspoken about racism in American society, and they have challenged the powerful sport establishment over racism in sport in a variety of ways. In 1968,

American black athletes threatened to boycott the Mexico Olympic Games to protest racism in the U.S. I described in chapter 3 how black athletes Tommie Smith and John Carlos raised gloved, clenched fists during the awards ceremony as a symbol of protest. Heavyweight boxing champion Muhammad Ali refused to serve in the military and participate in the Vietnam War, saying that he didn't have anything against the North Vietnamese.

Over the past 20 years, black and white athletes and coaches have boycotted several sport events because of racist policies or practices of the sponsors. Blacks have expressed pride in their race through hairstyles and handshakes and other rituals carried out in connection with sport events. Most recently, black and white athletes and coaches have stepped up the pressure on the sport establishment for greater black representation in coaching and managing. Even though black resistance has been episodic and transient, organized sport has become a medium for demonstrating black pride and dignity, a means of affirming black capabilities and challenging the subordination imposed by politically and socially powerful groups.

Some feminists contend that societal structures and values are defined in male-relevant terms, subjecting women to live in a world that celebrates and rewards male values. They argue that dominant sport images are defined and shaped by men's values and men's understandings of the world, tending to alienate women from their sport experiences; for these women, the male-dominated sport world results in little self-fulfillment for females. As a result, initiatives have emerged among women in sport aimed at transforming it from a male-dominated domain to one in which women can express themselves on their own terms and satisfy their own needs.

Certain feminists believe that true liberation for women requires constructing countercultural practices and institutions, and there is a movement in sport aimed at reshaping the emphasis from achieving equality with men to exploring ways and means of establishing female autonomy. Birrell and Richter (1987) assert that the male sport model, imbued with patriarchal ideology emphasizing winning, elitism, and rigid hierarchy of authority, is an alienating model for women. They describe "how women who define themselves as feminists actively construct and maintain alternatives to the male preserve of sport" (p. 395). They report that this alternative form of sport "is process oriented, collective, inclusive, supportive, and infused with an ethic of care" (p. 395). The result is that sport is transformed from a vehicle for bearing male values to a celebration of alternatives for women. Such an alternative sport model displays resistance to masculine hegemony and dominant, male definitions of sport and illustrates that deliberate transformations—collective constructions of different ways of playing sports—are possible.

Countercultural Transformation

During the past two decades there has been a growing disillusionment with the extreme competitiveness that characterizes organized sport programs and cultivates the ethos of winning as supreme. Initiatives to transform the dominant sport culture have arisen in various "counterculture" groups. Those struggling to create alternatives to the dominant model believe it generates feelings of conditional self-worth, perception of self as a means, role-specific relationships, and excellence based on competitive merit, all concepts they oppose as counterproductive to personal and social development. Individuals and groups active in trying to reconstruct the social order of sport have devised play activities and games in which competition is muted or entirely removed. Fun and the expressive character of these activities are emphasized precisely because the dominant sport forms lack these qualities and seem "overly rationalized, technological, and bureaucratized" (Donnelly, 1988, p. 74).

The best-known of these approaches, New Games, is fostered and communicated by the New Games Foundation, whose goal is to change the way people play by replacing competitive games with cooperative, no-win pastimes. By using simple homemade equipment or none at all and avoiding activities that require unusual physical prowess or specific sport skills, leaders attempt to create an atmosphere of fun and relaxed voluntary participation. The foundation conducts weekend workshops throughout the country for recreation specialists, educators, and health-care professionals.

There is additional and growing support from others for games that emphasize cooperation rather than competition, games that promote intrinsic rather than extrinsic rewards, and activities that move people away from the role of spectators and toward active sport involvement. It is argued that if we value cooperation, then what people learn in sport activities should be less competitive and aggressive.

Books like *Changing Kids' Games* (Morris & Stiehl, 1989), *The Second Cooperative Sports and Games Book* (Orlick, 1982), and *More New Games* (Fluegelman, 1981) describe many physical activities that focus on cooperation and sociability rather than competition. In his book *No Contest: The Case Against Competition*, Alfie Kohn (1986) has argued that competition is inherently destructive. He urges Americans to develop a more critical consciousness of the effects of competition and suggests that embracing a spirit of cooperation in all human affairs, including sport, has powerful potential for enhancing human relations and social justice.

Other forms of resistance and evasion of the dominant, highly competitive organized sport forms can be found in such diverse activities as the martial arts and outdoor and wilderness sports. Several Oriental martial arts have witnessed an enormous growth in popularity. In some, competition is not important for mastery of the skills; indeed, in aikido competition is forbidden. Outdoor activities such as hiking, orienteering, rock climbing, rafting, hang gliding, skydiving, and scuba diving, where the process (i.e., participation) has priority, have boomed among a clientele who have turned away from the organized, commercial, and corporate forms of American sport. Participation, rather than spectating, is made the focal point.

Social Change or Incorporation?

Although resistance and transformative actions of the type just described are a continuing part of American sport, I must emphasize that they are not usually coordinated into social expressions of direct challenge to the structure of the larger political economy and cultural hegemony of American society, nor even to the dominant sport culture. It is difficult in any area to coordinate resistance into alternatives to dominant structures and practices (Gruneau, 1988). The very existence of hegemony greatly restricts the ability of subordinate social groups to create and sustain counter-hegemonic initiatives. Thus, although oppositional efforts often win a hearing among society for a group or movement, significant impact on the existing social structure is often minimal.

Furthermore, as Donnelly (1988) noted, "Whatever oppositional content might be found in popular 'alternative' practices can be quickly lost through incorporation" (p. 74). It is ironic that activities that began as true alternatives to institutionalized sport have often become commodified spectator sports. Jogging, frisbee, and aerobic exercise are three examples; others, such as three-on-three playground basketball and beach volleyball—once the epitome of informal, player-controlled sports—have recently become commodified with corporate sponsorship, national and international tournaments, and prize money for winning teams (Moore, 1989a).

Although dynamic forces within the sport culture ensure that some social change will always be occurring, the difficulty in successfully achieving meaningful structural change in sport—or any other sector of American society—is that those who control the state apparatus and the means of production have power over those without such control (Piven & Cloward, 1977). They are not about to give up their privileged places without a fight. As Michael Parenti (1989) said, "History provides no examples of a dominant class voluntarily relinquishing its social position so to better the lot of the downtrodden" (p. 100).

Effecting structural change of any kind, then, requires overcoming enormous resources vested in powerful social groups. Struggles against the dominant models and meanings of contemporary sport are met by a variety of tactics. One of the most common, as well as effective, involves working to make oppositional groups appear disruptive and counterproductive to the desired social order of sport. When this is achieved, their efforts are diffused.

Initiatives for resistance and transformation in sport are not always denounced or rejected by dominant forces. Various forms of institutional accommodation and compromise are sometimes enacted to restore quiescence without conceding major changes. For example, over the past 20 years numerous concessions and compromises have been made to minorities and women without changing the basic power and ideological structure of American sport.

But in spite of the overwhelming odds, we can expect everyday forms of resistance to continue. At the individual, personal level is the impulse to play, to enjoy, to experience the rich exhilaration and sheer pleasure that comes with the sporting experience. As Gruneau (1979) has articulately argued, people continue to seek this despite the hegemony of capitalist life:

> An appreciation of the essential drama of the contest and the attempt to realize the promise of play in our private lives helps individuals cope with the injustices of a society that correlates dignity and personal worth with abstract notions of skill acquisition, efficiency and productive capacity. That such "coping" generally fails to challenge the sources of domination in social life (it is accommodative rather than transformational) is tragic but not hopeless. Hope remains in the fact that . . . hegemony is far from complete and far from immune to the possibilities of change. (p. 48)

Those who continue to strive to win cultural and societal space represent a major obstacle to the vision and program that hegemony imposes on us all. But real alternatives to the present sport culture will have to be linked to the forces and movements that have been successful in overcoming the entrenched hegemony of society.

A Vision for Sport

I have no detailed agenda for changing contemporary sport practices, but like many people I have a vision of the kind of system I would like to see. I imagine it something like this:

A good society guarantees conditions in which all citizens can develop their potentials and control their lives. The values of a decent, progressive sport system will center on equality rather than hierarchy in social relations, and power and control will be both democratized and humanized. This does not mean that all positions of authority in sport will be forsaken, but coaches and other sport leaders will abandon authoritarian roles that deny athletes subjectivity and control to create and explore their own meanings and visions. All sport leaders will manage without authoritarian structures and will carry out their tasks in the context of shared trust and respect.

My egalitarian sport system will provide adequate facilities and equipment for everyone, regardless of means. A truly caring society takes seriously the health of its citizens because it knows good health to be the most precious human resource. Because sport and physical recreation nurture health, a public commitment will exist to provide all citizens the wherewithal to stay healthy through sport and to enjoy the deep satisfactions of physical efforts.

Maximizing participation will be a major goal for sport. Although gifted athletes will be provided reasonable resources to allow them to test their skills against other top athletes, resource allocation will be emphasized to cultivate widespread sport experiences.

In a society committed to egalitarianism, in which active participation is encouraged and adequate resources are universally available, the vicarious stimulation provided by commodified sport will lose much of its appeal. Sport will be linked to a larger effort to make performers out of spectators. Meeting social needs, rather than maximizing private profits, will be the overarching societal theme.

Arbitrary distinctions of sex, race, and age will cease to function as forms of oppression or criteria for limiting sport opportunities. Only out of such a moral stance will a humane as well as a sensible sporting culture be achieved.

Is such a sport system possible? Of course. Because all social organization and patterns are socially constructed, social change of almost any kind is possible. Esteemed sociologist Anthony Giddens (1987) has eloquently described why we might look forward optimistically to a more humane and egalitarian sport system: "As critical theory, sociology does not take the social world as a given, but poses the questions: what types of social change are feasible and desirable, and how should we strive to achieve them?" (p. 157).

Summary

I began this chapter with a summary of the preceding ones. Although the hegemony of capitalist life is pervasive and powerful, people are the creators of their destiny; hegemony does not preclude changes in social structure nor does it totally dominate social relations. Space for resistance, even transformation, is available. Though the odds are overwhelmingly against those who strive for social change in the pursuit of greater freedom and social justice, change can and does occur. As for sporting practices, the presence of hegemony cannot completely stifle the human urge to play nor prevent the immediate, pleasurable satisfaction that many obtain from their sport experiences.

References

Acosta, V., & Carpenter, L.J. (1988). *Women in intercollegiate sport: A longitudinal study—Eleven year update 1987-1988*. Unpublished manuscript, Brooklyn College, Department of Physical Education, New York.

Adelman, M.L. (1986). *A sporting time*. Champaign: University of Illinois Press.

Adler, P., & Adler, P.A. (1985). From idealism to pragmatic detachment: The academic performance of college athletes. *Sociology of Education*, **58**, 241-250.

Adorno, T.W. (1975). Culture industry reconsidered. *New German Critique*, **6**(6), 12-19.

Albinson, J.G. (1976). The "professional orientation" of the amateur hockey coach. In R. Gruneau & J.G. Albinson (Eds.), *Canadian sport: Sociological perspectives* (pp. 377-392). Don Mills, ON: Addison-Wesley.

Allen, K. (1988, April 1). Million-dollar franchise cost the NCAA $2,500. *USA Today*, p. 4E.

Allen, K., & Wieberg, S. (1988, November 30). Academic, financial pressures dictate minor changes. *USA Today*, p. 8C.

Allen, M.P. (1987). *The founding fortunes: A new anatomy of the super-rich families*. New York: E.P. Dutton.

Alt, J. (1976). Beyond class: The decline of industrial labor leisure. *Telos*, **28**, 55-80.

Alternatives for American growth: A conversation with Ralph Nader and Herman Kahn. (1979, August/September). *Public Opinion*, pp. 10-15, 58-59.

Altheide, D.L., & Snow, R.P. (1979). *Media logic*. Beverly Hills, CA: Sage.

Anderson, D.F., & Gill, K.S. (1983). Occupational socialization patterns of men's and women's interscholastic basketball coaches. *Journal of Sport Behavior*, **6**(3), 105-116.

Anderson, P. (1976-1977). The antinomies of Antonio Gramsci. *New Left Review*, **100**, 5-80.

Apple, M.W. (1982). *Education and power*. Boston: Routledge & Kegan Paul.

Armstrong, C.F. (1984). The lessons of sports: Class socialization in British and American boarding schools. *Sociology of Sport Journal*, 1, 314-331.

Arnold, P.J. (1984). Sport, moral education and the development of character. *Journal of Philosophy of Education*, 18, 275-281.

Aronowitz, S. (1973). *False promises: The shaping of American working class consciousness*. New York: McGraw-Hill.

Association registers surplus. (1988, January 6). *The NCAA News*, pp. 8, 18.

Baade, R.A., & Dye, R.F. (1988). Sports stadiums and area development: A critical view. *Economic Development Quarterly*, 2, 265-275.

Bagdikian, B.H. (1987). *The media monopoly* (2nd ed.). Boston: Beacon Press.

Bailey, C.I., & Sage, G.H. (1988). Values communicated by a sports event: The case of the Super Bowl. *Journal of Sport Behavior*, 11(3), 126-143.

Bailey, P. (1978). *Leisure and class in Victorian England: Rational recreation and the contest for control, 1830-1885*. London: Routledge & Kegan Paul.

Baka, R.S. (1986). Australian government involvement in sport: A delayed eclectic approach. In G. Redmond (Ed.), *Sport and politics* (pp. 27-32). Champaign, IL: Human Kinetics.

Barrett, N. (1987). Women and the economy. In S.E. Rix (Ed.), *American woman, 1987-88* (pp. 100-149). New York: Norton.

Barsamian, D. (1989). Interviewing Michael Parenti. *Zeta Magazine*, 2(1), 100-104.

Bates, T.R. (1975). Gramsci and the theory of hegemony. *Journal of the History of Ideas*, 36, 351-366.

Beamish, R. (1982). Sport and the logic of capitalism. In H. Cantelon and R. Gruneau (Eds.), *Sport, culture and the modern state* (pp. 141-197). Toronto: University of Toronto Press.

Beaud, M. (1983). *A history of capitalism, 1500-1980*. New York: Monthly Review Press.

Becker, D. (1986a, September 16). Title IX has lost its clout on campuses. *USA Today*, p. 2C.

Becker, D. (1986b, December 10). All not created equal. *USA Today*, pp. 1-2A, 10C.

Berg, I., & Zald, M. (1978). Business and society. *Annual Review of Sociology*, 4, 115-143.

Berger, P.L. (1963). *Invitation to sociology: A humanistic perspective*. Garden City, NY: Doubleday Anchor Books.

Berry, R.C., Gould, W.B., & Staudohar, P.D. (1986). *Labor relations in professional sports*. Dover, MA: Auburn House.

Berryman, J.W. (1975). From the cradle to the playing field: America's emphasis on highly organized competitive sports for preadolescent boys. *Journal of Sport History*, 2, 112-131.

Betts, J.R. (1974). *America's sporting heritage: 1850-1950*. Reading, MA: Addison-Wesley.

Bielby, D.D., & Bielby, W.T. (1988). She works hard for the money: Household responsibilities and the allocation of work effort. *American Journal of Sociology*, **93**, 1031-1059.

Birrell, S. (1988). Discourses on gender/sport relationship: From women in sport to gender relations. In K.B. Pandolf (Ed.), *Exercise and Sport Sciences Review* (Vol. 16, pp. 459-502). New York: Macmillan.

Birrell, S., & Richter, D.M. (1987). Is a diamond forever? Feminist transformations of sport. *Women's Studies International Forum*, **10**, 395-409.

Blumberg, P. (1980). *Inequality in an age of decline*. New York: Oxford University Press.

Boring, E.G. (1963). *History, psychology, and science*. New York: Wiley.

Boston, T.D. (1988). *Race, class, and conservatism*. Boston: Unwin Hyman.

Bourdieu, P. (1978). Sport and social class. *Social Science Information*, **17**, 819-840.

Brady, E. (1988, April 6). For athletes, it's one for the books. *USA Today*, pp. 1C-2C.

Braverman, H. (1974). *Labor and monopoly capital*. New York: Monthly Review Press.

Brohm, J. (1978). *Sport: A prison of measured time* (I. Fraser, Trans.). London: Ink Links.

Brower, J. (1976). Professional sports team ownership: Fun, profit, and ideology of the power elite. *Journal of Sport and Social Issues*, **1**, 16-51.

Brown, B. (1988, October 24). New order of business in the NFL? *USA Today*, pp. 1C-2C.

Bundgaard, A. (1985, April). Tom Brown abroad: Athletics in selected New England public schools, 1850-1910. *Research Quarterly for Exercise and Sport* Centennial issue, 28-37.

Buying low, selling high. (1988, July 25). *Sports inc.*, pp. 20-21.

Byrne, J.A. (1988, October 21). Putting a price on CEOs. *Business Week*, pp. 34-36.

Camp, W. (1893). *Walter Camp's book of college sports*. New York: Century.

Carnoy, M., & Shearer, D. (1980). *Economic democracy*. New York: M.E. Sharpe.

Carroll, J. (1986). Sport: Virtue and grace. *Theory, Culture, & Society*, **3**, 91-98.

Castells, M. (1980). *The economic crisis and American society*. Princeton, NJ: Princeton University Press.

Caulk, S. (1989, June 18). The villain. *Rocky Mountain News*, pp. 1S, 16S-17S.

Cavallo, D. (1981). *Muscles and morals*. Philadelphia: University of Pennsylvania Press.

Chafetz, J.S. (1984). *Sex and advantage*. Totowa, NJ: Rowman & Allanheld.

Chomsky, N. (1987). *On power and ideology*. Boston: South End Press.

Citizens for Tax Justice. (1988). *The corporate tax comeback: Corporate income taxes after reform.* Washington, DC: Author.

Clarke, A., & Clarke, J. (1982). Highlights and action replays—Ideology, sport and the media. In J. Hargreaves (Ed.), *Sport, culture, and ideology* (pp. 62-87). Boston: Routledge & Kegan Paul.

Clement, A. (1987). Professional female athletes: Financial opportunities. *Journal of Physical Education, Recreation, and Dance, 58*(3), 37-40.

Closius, P.J. (1985). Professional sports and antitrust law: The ground rules of immunity, exemption, and liability. In A.T. Johnson & J.H. Frey (Eds.), *Government and sport: The public policy issues* (pp. 140-161). Totowa, NJ: Rowman & Allanheld.

Coakley, J.J. (1987). Children and the sport socialization process. In D. Gould and M.R. Weiss (Eds.), *Advances in Pediatric Sport Sciences: Vol. 2. Behavioral Issues* (pp. 43-60). Champaign, IL: Human Kinetics.

Colemen v. Western Michigan University, 336 N.W. 2d. 224 (1983).

Comisky, P., Bryant, J., & Zillmann, D. (1977). Commentary as a substitute for action. *Journal of Communication, 27*(3), 150-153.

Complete results of survey of Division I CEOs. (1987, April 8). *The NCAA News*, pp. 8-9.

Comte, E., Girard, L., & Starensier, A. (1989, January 2). Embracing stars, ignoring players. *Sports inc.*, pp. 41-43.

Connell, R.W. (1987). *Gender and power: Society, the person, and sexual politics.* Palo Alto: Stanford University Press.

Copeland, J.L. (1986, December 23). NCAA drug-testing program functioning according to plan. *The NCAA News*, p. 1.

The corporate elite: Chief executives of the Business Week top 1000. (1988, October 21). *Business Week* [Special bonus issue].

Covitz, R. (1987, December 27). Best-paid teams showing losses on investment. *Rocky Mountain News*, p. 2S.

Cramer, J. (1986). Winning or learning? Athletics and academics in America: Kappan Special Report. *Phi Delta Kappan, 67*, 1-8.

Cravens, J. (Ed.) (1988). *U.S. Olympic team media guide: 1988 games of the XXIVth Olympiad.* Colorado Springs: U.S. Olympic Committee.

Crompton, R., & Mann, M. (1986). *Gender and stratification.* New York: Basil Blackwell.

Dahl, R. (1961). *Who governs?* New Haven: Yale University Press.

Davis, J.P. (1966). The Negro in American sports. In J.P. Davis (Ed.), *The American Negro reference books: Vol. 2* (pp. 747-795). Englewood Cliffs, NJ: Prentice-Hall.

Deford, F. (1988, August 15). An old dragon limbers up. *Sports Illustrated*, pp. 36-43.

Dempsey will meet only white boxers. (1919, July 6). *The New York Times*, p. 17.

Denlinger, K., & Shapiro, L. (1975). *Athletes for sale.* New York: Thomas Y. Crowell.

Dewart, J. (Ed.) (1989). *The state of black America 1989.* New York: National Urban League.

Domhoff, G.W. (1978). *The powers that be: Processes of ruling class domination in America.* New York: Vintage Books.

Domhoff, G.W. (1983). *Who rules America now?* Englewood Cliffs, NJ: Prentice-Hall.

Donnelly, P. (1988). Sport as a site for "popular" resistance. In R. Gruneau (Ed.), *Popular cultures and political practice* (pp. 69-82). Toronto: Garamond Press.

Duggan, P., Fritz, M., Heuslein, W., & Scheer, L. (1989, May 29). People at the top in their own words. *Forbes,* pp. 162-188.

Duncan, M.C., & Hasbrook, C.A. (1988). Denial of power in televised women's sports. *Sociology of Sport Journal,* **5,** 1-21.

Dworkin, J.B. (1985). Balancing the rights of professional athletes and team owners: The proper role of government. In A.T. Johnson and J.H. Frey (Eds.), *Government and sport: The public policy issues* (pp. 21-40). Totowa, NJ: Rowman & Allanheld.

Dye, T.R. (1986). *Who's running America?* (4th ed.). Englewood Cliffs, NJ: Prentice-Hall.

Eder, D., & Parker, S. (1987). The cultural production and reproduction of gender: The effect of extracurricular activities on peer-group culture. *Sociology of Education,* **60,** 200-213.

Edsforth, R. (1987). *Class conflict and cultural consensus.* New Brunswick, NJ: Rutgers University Press.

Edwards: Only the ink is black. (1988, January 21). *USA Today,* p. 2C.

Edwards, H. (1984). The collegiate athletic arms race: Origins and implications of the "Rule 48" controversy. *Journal of Sport and Social Issues,* **8**(1), 4-22.

Edwards, R.C. (1979). *Contested terrain: The transformation of the workplace in the twentieth century.* New York: Basic Books.

Ehrenreich, B. (1989). The silenced majority. *Zeta Magazine,* **2**(9), 22-23.

Ehrenreich, B., & Ehrenreich, J. (1979). The professional-managerial class. In P. Walker (Ed.), *Between labor and capital* (pp. 5-45). Boston: South End Press.

Eichberg, H. (1984). Olympic sport—Neocolonization and alternatives. *International Review for the Sociology of Sport,* **19,** 97-105.

Eisenstein, Z.R. (1979). Developing a theory of capitalist patriarchy and socialist feminism. In Z.R. Eisenstein (Ed.), *Capitalist patriarchy and the case for socialist feminism* (pp. 5-40). New York: Monthly Review Press.

Eitzen, D.S., & Purdy, D.A. (1986). The academic preparation and achievement of black and white collegiate athletes. *Journal of Sport and Social Issues,* **10**(1), 15-27.

Eitzen, D.S., & Sage, G.H. (1986). *Sociology of North American sport* (3rd ed.). Dubuque, IA: Wm. C. Brown.

Eitzen, D.S., & Sage, G.H. (1989). *Sociology of North American sport* (4th ed.). Dubuque, IA: Wm. C. Brown.

Ellis, G.J., Lee, G.R., & Petersen, L.R. (1978). Supervision and conformity: A cross cultural analysis of parental socialization values. *American Journal of Sociology, 84,* 386-403.

England, D.A. (1982). Athletes, academics, and ethics: An interview with Bob Knight. *Phi Delta Kappan, 64,* 159-163.

Epstein, C.F. (1988). *Deceptive distinctions: Sex, gender, and the social order.* New York: Yale University and Russell Sage Foundation.

Eskenazi, G. (1989, March 5). Arena of big-time athletics is showcasing a younger act. *The New York Times,* pp. 1, 18.

Espy, R. (1981). *The politics of the Olympic Games.* Berkeley: University of California Press.

Falla, J. (1981). *NCAA: The voice of college sports.* Mission, KS: National Collegiate Athletic Association.

Fave, L.R.D. (1980). The meek shall not inherit the earth: Self-evaluation and the legitimacy of stratification. *American Sociological Review, 45,* 955-971.

Feagin, J.R. (1984). The social costs of private enterprise. In M. Lewis & J.L. Miller (Eds.), *Research in Social Problems and Public Policy, Vol. 3* (pp. 115-150). Greenwich, CT: JAI Press.

Femia, J. (1975). Hegemony and consciousness in the thought of Antonio Gramsci. *Political Studies, 23,* 29-48.

Femia, J. (1987). *Gramsci's political thought.* New York: Oxford University Press.

Ferguson, M. (1983). *Forever feminine.* London: Heinemann.

Fichtenbaum, P. (1988, October 3). The Gretzky effect. *Sports inc.,* pp. 14-21.

Final Report of the President's Commission on Olympic Sports 1975-1977. (1977). Washington, DC: U.S. Government Printing Office.

Fine, G.A. (1987). *With the boys: Little League baseball and preadolescent culture.* Chicago: University of Chicago Press.

Fishman, J. (1978). Crime waves as ideology. *Social Problems, 25,* 531-543.

Flint, W.C., & Eitzen, D.S. (1987). Professional sports team ownership and entrepreneurial capitalism. *Sociology of Sport Journal, 4,* 17-27.

Fluegelman, A. (1981). *More new games!—Playful ideas from the New Games Foundation.* Garden City, NY: Dolphin Books.

Foner, P.S. (1950). *The life and writings of Frederick Douglass* (Vol. 2). New York: International.

Ford, G., & Underwood, J. (1974, July 8). In defense of the competitive urge. *Sports Illustrated,* pp. 16-23.

Frankfurt Institute for Social Research. (1972). *Aspects of sociology.* Boston: Bacon Press.

Freedman, W. (1987). *Professional sports and antitrust*. New York: Quorum Books.

Fussell, P. (1983). *Class*. New York: Ballantine.

Gamble, A. (1981). *An introduction to modern social and political thought*. New York: St. Martin's Press.

Gerbner, G. (1964). Ideological perspectives and political tendencies in news reporting. *Journalism Quarterly*, **41**, 495-508, 516.

Gerbner, G. (1973). Cultural indicators—The third voice. In G. Gerbner, L. Gross, & W. Melody (Eds.), *Communications technology and social polity* (pp. 553-573). New York: Wiley.

Gerbner, G., & Gross, L. (1976). Living with television: The violence profile. *Journal of Communication*, **26**, 173-199.

Gerbner, G., Gross, L., Signorelli, N., & Morgan, M. (1980). Aging with television: Images on television drama and conceptions of social reality. *Journal of Communication*, **30**, 37-47.

Giddens, A. (1987). *Sociology: A brief but critical introduction* (2nd ed.). New York: Harcourt Brace Jovanovich.

Gieber, W., & Johnson, W. (1961). The city hall beat: A study of reporter and source roles. *Journalism Quarterly*, **38**, 289-297.

Gitlin, T. (1982). Television's screens: Hegemony in transition. In M.W. Apple (Ed.), *Cultural and economic reproduction in education* (pp. 202-246). Boston: Routledge & Kegan Paul.

Gitlin, T. (1987). Television's screens: Hegemony in transition. In D. Lazere (Ed.), *American media and mass culture: Left perspectives* (pp. 240-258). Berkeley: University of California Press.

Glasgow Media Group. (1976). *Bad news. Vol. 1*. Boston: Routledge & Kegan Paul.

Gloede, B., & McManus, J. (1988, August 8). The power of positive cash flow. *Sports inc.*, pp. 14-21.

Goldsen, R.K. (1977). *The show and tell machine*. New York: Dial Press.

Golenbock, P. (1989). *Personal fouls*. New York: Carroll and Graf.

Good, P. (1979a). The shocking inequities of the NCAA. *Sport*, **68**(1), 35-38.

Good, P. (1979b). I feel betrayed. *Sport*, **68**(6), 62-68.

Goodman, C. (1979). *Choosing sides: Playground and street life on the lower east side*. New York: Schocken.

Goodman, M. (1988). The home team ["Sports Today" section]. *Zeta Magazine*, **1**(1), 62-65.

Gordon, D.M., Edwards, R., & Reich, M. (1982). *Segmented work, divided workers*. Cambridge, England: Cambridge University Press.

Gramsci, A. (1971). *Selections from the prison notebooks* (Q. Hoare & G.N. Smith, Eds.). New York: International Publishers.

Grant, C.H.B. (1989). Recapturing the vision. *Journal of Physical Education, Recreation and Dance*, **60**(3), 44-48.

Green, M. (1986, October 28). Stamping out corruption. *The New York Times*, p. A35.

Greenspan, E. (1983). *Little winners: Inside the world of the child sports star.* Boston: Little, Brown.

Grove City College v. Bell, 465 U.S. 555 (1984).

Gruneau, R. (1979). Power and play in Canadian social development. In *Working papers in the sociological study of sports and leisure*, 2(1). (Published as part of the Sports Studies Research Group, Queens University, Kingston, Ontario)

Gruneau, R. (1982a). Sport and the debate of the state. In H. Cantelon & R. Gruneau (Eds.), *Sport, culture and the modern state* (pp. 1-38). Toronto: University of Toronto Press.

Gruneau, R. (1982b). Considerations on the politics of play and youth sport. In A.G. Ingham and E.F. Broom (Eds.), *Career patterns and career contingencies in sport* (pp. 48-79). Vancouver: University of British Columbia, Department of Physical Education.

Gruneau, R. (1988). Modernization or hegemony: Two views on sport and social development. In J. Harvey & H. Cantelon (Eds.), *Not just a game* (pp. 9-32). Ottawa, ON: University of Ottawa Press.

Guttmann, A. (1978). *From ritual to record.* New York: Columbia University Press.

Hall, M.A. (1985). Knowledge and gender: Epistemological questions in the social analysis of sport. *Sociology of Sport Journal*, **2**, 25-42.

Hall, M.A. (1988). The discourse of gender and sport: From femininity to feminism. *Sociology of Sport Journal*, **5**, 330-340.

Hall, S., Crutcher, C., Jefferson, T., Clarke, J., & Roberts, B. (1978). *Policing the crisis: Mugging, the state, and law and order.* New York: Macmillan.

Hallin, D.C. (1985). The American media: A critical theory perspective. In H. Forester (Ed.), *Critical theory and political life* (pp. 121-146). Cambridge, MA: MIT.

Hardy, S. (1982). *How Boston played.* Boston: Northeastern University Press.

Hardy, S.H., & Berryman, J.W. (1982). A historical view of the governance issue. In J.H. Frey (Ed.), *The governance of intercollegiate athletics* (pp. 15-28). Champaign, IL: Leisure Press.

Hargreaves, J. (1982). Sport and hegemony: Some theoretical problems. In H. Cantelon & R. Gruneau (Eds.), *Sport, culture, and the modern state* (pp. 103-135). Toronto: University of Toronto Press.

Hargreaves, J. (1986). *Sport, power and culture.* New York: St. Martin's Press.

Hartman, H.I. (1981). The family as the locus of gender, class, and political struggle: The example of housework. *Signs: Journal of Women in Culture and Society*, **6**, 366-394.

Hart-Nibbrig, N. (1984). Corporate athleticism: An inquiry into the political economy of college sports. In N. Struna (Ed.), *Proceedings of the National Association for Physical Education in Higher Education, Vol. V* (pp. 11-20). Champaign, IL: Human Kinetics.

Hart-Nibbrig, N., & Cottingham, C. (1986). *The political economy of college sports*. Lexington, MA: Lexington Books.

Herman, E.S., & Chomsky, N. (1988). *Manufacturing consent: The political economy of the mass media*. New York: Pantheon.

Hilliard, D.C. (1984). Media images of male and female professional athletes: An interpretative analysis of magazine articles. *Sociology of Sport Journal, 1*, 251-262.

Himmelstein, H. (1984). *The television myth and the American mind*. New York: Praeger.

Hoberman, J.M. (1987a, April). *The future of scientific sport*. Paper presented at the annual meeting of the American Alliance for Health, Physical Education, Recreation and Dance, Las Vegas, NV.

Hoberman, J.M. (1987b). Sport and the technological image of man. In W.J. Morgan & K.V. Meier (Eds.), *Philosophic inquiry in sport* (pp. 319-327). Champaign, IL: Human Kinetics.

Hoffman, J. (1984). *The Gramscian challenge*. New York: Basil Blackwell.

Holt, P. (1984, September 25). Today's patriotism borders on chauvinism. *Rocky Mountain News*, p. 33.

Hughes, R., & Coakley, J. (1984). Mass society and the commercialization of sport. *Sociology of Sport Journal, 1*, 57-63.

Ingham, A.G., & Hardy, S. (1984). Sport, structuration and hegemony. *Theory, Culture, and Society, 2*, 85-103.

Ingham, A.G., Howell, J.W., & Schilperoort, T.S. (1987). Professional sports and community: A review and exegesis. In K.B. Pandolf (Ed.), *Exercise and Sport Sciences Review* (Vol. 15, pp. 427-465). New York: Macmillan.

Isaacs, N.D. (1977). *Checking back: A history of the National Hockey League*. New York: Norton.

Jable, J.T. (1979). The Public Schools Athletic League of New York City: Organized athletics for city school children, 1903-1914. In W.M. Ladd and A. Lumpkin (Eds.), *Sport in American education: History and perspective* (pp. 1-18). Washington, DC: American Alliance for Health, Physical Education, Recreation and Dance.

Jacobs, B. (1988, February 8). Coaching for dollars. *Sports inc.*, pp. 42-43.

Jacobs, D. (1988). Corporate economic power and the state: A longitudinal assessment of two explanations. *American Journal of Sociology, 93*, 852-881.

Johnson, A.T., & Frey, J.H. (Eds.) (1985). *Government and sport: The public policy issues*. Totowa, NJ: Rowman & Allanheld.

Johnson, H. (1988, May 10). Racism still smolders on campus. *USA Today*, p. 1D.

Johnson, W.O. (1988, August 15). The image has altered. *Sports Illustrated*, pp. 86-88.

Jolidon, L. (1988, September 27). Canadians in Seoul are angry. *USA Today*, p. 7E.

Jones, V.N., & Crewell, C. (1987, May 31). Training becomes science. *Rocky Mountain News*, pp. 13M-16M.

Kane, M.J. (1988). Media coverage of the female athlete before, during, and after Title IX: *Sports Illustrated* revisited. *Journal of Sport Management*, **2**, 87-99.

Kellner, D. (1978). Ideology, Marxism, and advanced capitalism. *Socialist Review*, **8**(6), 37-65.

Kellner, J. (1988, January 18). Making the most of no. 1. *Sports inc.*, pp. 50-51.

Kidd, B. (1987). Sports and masculinity. In M. Kaufman (Ed.), *Beyond patriarchy: Essays by men on pleasure, power, and change* (pp. 250-265). New York: Oxford University Press.

Kimmel, M.S. (1987). The cult of masculinity: American social character and the legacy of the cowboy. In M. Kaufman (Ed.), *Beyond patriarchy: Essays by men on pleasure, power, and change* (pp. 235-249). New York: Oxford University Press.

Kirkpatrick, C. (1988). The old soft shoe. *Sports Illustrated: Special college basketball 1988-89 issue*, pp. 98-105.

Kirshenbaum, J. (1989, February 27). An American disgrace. *Sports Illustrated*, pp. 16-19.

Klatell, D.A., & Marcus, N. (1988). *Sports for sale: Television, money, and the fans*. New York: Oxford University.

Kliever, L.D. (1988). God and games in modern culture. *The World and I*, **3**, 561-571.

Kohn, A. (1986). *No contest: The case against competition*. Boston: Houghton Mifflin.

Kohn, M.L. (1981). Personality, occupation, and social stratification: A frame of reference. In D.J. Treiman & R.V. Robinson (Eds.), *Research in social stratification and mobility, Vol. 1* (pp. 267-297). Greenwich, CT: JAI Press.

Kowet, D. (1977). *The rich who own sports*. New York: Random House.

Kraus, R.G. (1988). Changing views of tomorrow's leisure. *Journal of Physical Education, Recreation, and Dance*, **59**(6), 82-87.

Krotee, M.L. (1988). Apartheid and sport: South Africa revisited. *Sociology of Sport Journal*, **5**, 125-133.

Krupa, G. (1988a, October 24). Giving new life to Title IX. *Sports inc.*, pp. 26-27.

Krupa, G. (1988b, December 5). Big bucks on campus. *Sports inc.*, pp. 24-25.

Lamm, R. (1988, April 25). The uncompetitive society. *U.S. News & World Report*, p. 9.

Langford, E. (1969). *Wellington—The years of the sword*. New York: Harper & Row.

Lapchick, R.E. (1988). Discovering fool's gold on the golden horizon. *The World and I, 3*, 603-611.

Lasch, C. (1977). The corruption of sports. *New York Review of Books, 24*, 24-30.

Latimer, C. (1986, September 26). CU reports 21 misuse tickets. *Rocky Mountain News*, p. 113.

Leach, B., & Conners, B. (1984). Pygmalion on the gridiron: The black student-athlete in a white university. *New Directions for Student Services, 28*, 31-49.

Lebowitz, M.A. (1988, May). Social justice against capitalism. *Monthly Review, 40*(1), 28-37.

Lehr, C.A., & Washington, M.A. (1987). Beyond women's collegiate athletics: Opportunities to play for pay. *Journal of Physical Education, Recreation, and Dance, 58*(3), 28-32.

Lenskyj, H. (1986). *Out of bounds: Women, sport, and sexuality*. Toronto: Women's Press.

Lewis, G.M. (1967). America's first intercollegiate sport: The regattas from 1852 to 1875. *Research Quarterly, 38*, 637-648.

Lieberson, S. (1985). *Making it count*. Berkeley: University of California Press.

Lipman-Blumen, J. (1984). *Gender roles and power*. Englewood Cliffs, NJ: Prentice-Hall.

Lipsitz, G. (1984). Sports stadia and urban development: A tale of three cities. *Journal of Sport and Social Issues, 8*(2), 1-18.

Looney, D.S. (1985a, April 8). Big trouble at Tulane. *Sports Illustrated*, pp. 34-39.

Looney, D.S. (1985b, June 24). Troubled times at Memphis State. *Sports Illustrated*, pp. 36-41.

Looney, D.S. (1986, September 15). Tickets, please. *Sports Illustrated*, p. 65.

Looney, D.S. (1988, September 5). Gee, it's great to be a Badger. *Sports Illustrated*, pp. 74-81.

Lowenfish, L., & Lupien, T. (1980). *The imperfect diamond*. New York: Stein and Day.

Lowman, G.S. (1907). The regulation and control of sports in secondary schools of the United States. *American Physical Education Review, 12*, 307-323.

Lucas, J. (1980). *The modern Olympic Games*. South Brunswick, NJ: A.S. Barnes.

Lucas, J., & Smith, R.A. (1978). *Saga of American sport*. Philadelphia: Lea & Febiger.

MacAloon, J.J. (1981). *This great symbol: Pierre de Coubertin and the origins of the modern Olympic Games*. Chicago: University of Chicago Press.

MacAloon, J.J. (1987). An observer's view of sport sociology. *Sociology of Sport Journal*, **4**, 103-115.

Macaulay, S. (1987). Images of law in everyday life: The lessons of school, entertainment, and spectator sports. *Law and Society Review*, **21**, 185-218.

MacIntosh, D., Bedecki, T., & Franks, C.E.S. (1987). *Sport and politics in Canada*. Montreal: McGill-Queens University Press.

Maitland, I. (1983). House divided: Business lobbying and the 1981 budget. *Research in Corporate Social Performance and Policy*, **5**, 1-25.

Mandell, R. (1971). *The Nazi Olympics*. New York: Macmillan.

Mandell, R.D. (1976). *The first modern Olympics*. Berkeley: University of California Press.

Maney, K. (1987, March 23). Celtics could make foes green with envy. *USA Today*, p. 11C.

Mangan, J.A. (1975). Athleticism: A case study of the evaluation of an educational ideology. In B. Simon & I. Bradley (Eds.), *The Victorian public school* (pp. 147-167). London: Gill & Macmillan.

Mangan, J.A. (1981). *Athleticism in the Victorian and Edwardian public school*. London: Cambridge University Press.

Mangan, J.A. (1986). *The games ethic and imperialism*. New York: Viking Penguin.

Mangan, J.A., & Walvin, J. (Eds.) (1987). *Manliness and morality: Middle-class masculinity in Britain and America 1800-1940*. New York: St. Martin's Press.

Mannheim, K. (1936). *Ideology and utopia*. New York: Harcourt Brace and World.

Many who work still in poverty. (1988, September 27). *Tribune*, p. 1.

Martzke, R. (1987a, December 28). Sierens, under scrutiny, makes debut a success. *USA Today*, p. 3C.

Martzke, R. (1987b, December 29). Anchor job not big news to Gardner. *USA Today*, p. 1C.

Marx, J. (1988, November 14). A champion takes a fall. *Sports Illustrated*, pp. 40-42.

Mayfield, M. (1986, September 25). College football: Rolling in dough. *USA Today*, pp. 1C-2C, 8C.

McCallum, J. (1986, October 6). In the kingdom of the solitary man. *Sports Illustrated*, pp. 64-78.

McCurdy, J.H. (1905). Study of the characteristics of physical training in public schools of the U.S. *American Physical Education Review*, **10**, 202-213.

McIntosh, P.C. (1957). Games and gymnastics for two nations in one. In J.G. Dixon, P.C. McIntosh, A.D. Munrow, and R.F. Willetts (Eds.), *Landmarks in the history of physical education* (pp. 177-208). London: Routledge & Kegan Paul.

McIntosh, P.C. (1963). *Sport in society*. London: C.A. Watts.

McManus, J. (1988, October 31). Roger Werner: ESPN's boy wonder. *Sports inc.*, pp. 28-31.

Meadow, J.B. (1988, April 11). Can all-sports radio work? *Sports inc.*, pp. 40-41.

Messner, M.A. (1988). Sports and male domination: The female athlete as contested ideological terrain. *Sociology of Sport Journal, 5*, 197-211.

Meyrowitz, J. (1985). *No sense of place: The impact of electronic media on social behavior*. New York: Oxford University Press.

Miliband, R. (1969). *The state in capitalist society*. New York: Basic Books.

Miliband, R. (1977). *Marxism and politics*. Oxford: Oxford University Press.

Miller Lite Report on American Attitudes Toward Sports. (1983). Milwaukee, WI: Miller Brewing Company.

Mills, C.W. (1959). *The sociological imagination*. New York: Oxford University Press.

Mills, C.W. (1962). *The Marxists*. New York: Dell.

Min, G. (1987). Over-commercialization of the Olympics 1988: The role of the U.S. television networks. *International Review of the Sociology of Sport, 22*, 137-142.

Mintz, B., & Schwartz, M. (1985). *The structure of power of American business*. Chicago: University of Chicago Press.

Miracle, A.W. (1985, November). *Corporate economy, social ritual and the rise of high school sports*. Paper presented at the annual meeting of the North American Society for Sport Sociology, Boston, MA.

Mitchell, S. (1977). Women's participation in the Olympic Games, 1900-1926. *Journal of Sport History, 4*, 208-228.

Moore, D. (1988a, January 3). Dallas coach expresses no sympathy for Dorsett. *Rocky Mountain News*, p. 20S.

Moore, D.L. (1988b, December 6). Overseas overtures only choice. *USA Today*, pp. 1C-2C.

Moore, D.L. (1989a, March 15). Basketball junkies off to Ireland. *USA Today*, pp. 1C-2C.

Moore, D.L. (1989b, March 31). The perfect sporting event. *USA Today*, pp. 1A-2A.

Morris, G.D., & Stiehl, J. (1989). *Changing kids' games*. Champaign, IL: Human Kinetics.

Mouffe, C. (1979). Hegemony and ideology in Gramsci. In C. Mouffe (Ed.), *Gramsci and Marxist theory* (pp. 168-204). Boston: Routledge & Kegan Paul.

Mrozek, D.J. (1983). *Sport and American mentality, 1880-1910*. Knoxville: University of Tennessee Press.

Murphy, B. (1988, October 24). A tailor-made sport. *Sports inc.*, pp. 38-39.

Nack, W. (1986, February 24). This case was one for the books. *Sports Illustrated*, pp. 34-42.

NCAA Committee on Infractions. (1987a, March 4). South Carolina men's basketball placed on probation. *The NCAA News*, pp. 12, 16.

NCAA Committee on Infractions. (1987b, March 4). Texas Tech placed on probation for NCAA rules violations. *The NCAA News*, p. 12.

Neff, C. (1988, March 21). Equality at last, part II. *Sports Illustrated*, pp. 70-71.

Neff, C. (1989, January 16). A grand slam. *Sports Illustrated*, p. 9.

Neustadtl, A., & Clawson, D. (1988). Corporate political groupings: Does ideology unify business political behavior? *American Sociological Review*, **53**, 172-190.

New York Times first woman sports editor. (1978, November 20). *Newsweek*, p. 133.

Nicolau, G. (1988, September 12). A pattern of collusion. *Sports inc.*, p. 52.

Noll, R.G. (1974). The U.S. team sports industry: An introduction. In R.G. Noll (Ed.), *Government and the sports business* (pp. 2-32). Washington, DC: Brookings Institution.

Oates, B. (1979, June 8). The great American tease: Sport as a way out of the ghetto. *The New York Times*, p. 32A.

Ogbu, J.U. (1988). Class stratification, racial stratification, and schooling. In L. Weis (Ed.), *Class, race, and gender in American education* (pp. 163-182). Albany: State University of New York Press.

O'Hanlon, T. (1980). Interscholastic athletics, 1900-1940: Shaping citizens for unequal roles in the modern industrial state. *Educational Theory*, **30**, 89-103.

Okner, B.A. (1974). Subsidies of stadiums and arenas. In R.G. Noll (Ed.), *Government and the sports business* (pp. 325-347). Washington, DC: Brookings Institution.

Orlick, T. (1982). *The second cooperative sports and game book*. New York: Pantheon.

Padilla, A., & Weistart, J.C. (1986, July 6). National commission needed to improve college athletics. *The Washington Post*, p. C6.

Page, C.H. (1973). Pervasive sociological themes in the study of sport. In J.T. Talamini and C.H. Page (Eds.), *Sport and society* (pp. 14-39). Boston: Little, Brown.

Parenti, M. (1978). *Power and the powerless*. New York: St. Martin's Press.

Parenti, M. (1988). *Democracy for the few* (5th ed.). New York: St. Martin's Press.

Parenti, M. (1989). *The sword and the dollar*. New York: St. Martin's Press.

Picking, K. (1988, August 29). Mattingly: Steinbrenner to trade him. *USA Today*, p. 1C.

Pilson, N.H. (1988, January 20). Forum. *The NCAA News*, p. 10.

Piven, F.F., & Cloward, R.A. (1977). *Poor people's movements: Why they succeed, how they fail.* New York: Pantheon.

Player poll. (1988, June 27). *USA Today,* p. 1C.

Poll: Minorities remain society's unequal partners. (1988, August 8). *USA Today,* p. 5A.

Poulantzas, N. (1978). *State, power, socialism* (P. Camiller, trans.). London: NLB.

Purdy, D.A., Eitzen, D.S., & Hufnagel, R. (1982). Are athletes also students? The educational attainment of college students. *Social Problems, 29,* 439-448.

Rader, B.G. (1977). The quest for subcommunities and the rise of American sport. *American Quarterly, 29,* 355-369.

Rader, B.G. (1983). *American sports: From the age of folk games to the age of spectators.* Englewood Cliffs, NJ: Prentice-Hall.

Receipts top $70 million for men's tournament. (1989, July 19). *The NCAA News,* p. 1.

Redmond, G. (Ed.) (1986). *Sport and politics.* Champaign, IL: Human Kinetics.

Reed, W. (1988, April 4). Learn from the athletes. *Sports inc.,* p. 56.

Reilly, R. (1989, March 27). Here today, gone today. *Sports Illustrated,* p. 102.

Reiss, C. (1988, July 25). Editor's letter. *Sports inc.,* p. 9.

Rensing v. Indiana State University Board, 444 N.E.2d. 1170 (1983).

Reston, J. (1971, November 26). Sports and politics. *The New York Times,* p. 37.

Rigauer, B. (1981). *Sport and work.* New York: Columbia University Press.

Riis, J. (1903). *Children of the tenements.* New York: Macmillan.

Rintala, J., & Birrell, S. (1984). Fair treatment for the active female: A content analysis of *Young Athlete* magazine. *Sociology of Sport Journal, 1,* 231-250.

Riordan, J. (1977). *Sport in Soviet society.* New York: Cambridge University Press.

Riordan, J. (1987). Soviet muscular socialism: A Durkheimian analysis. *Sociology of Sport Journal, 4,* 376-393.

Rix, S.E. (Ed.) (1987). *The American Woman, 1987-88.* New York: Norton.

Roberts, H. (1953). *The story of pro football.* New York: Rand McNally.

Rogers, B. (1980). *The domestication of women.* New York: St. Martin's Press.

Rogoznica, J. (1988, May 16). Survival of the fittest. *Sports Illustrated,* pp. 84-86.

Rojek, C. (1985). *Capitalism and leisure theory.* New York: Tavistock Publications.

Rosaldo, M.Z. (1974). Women, culture, and society: A theoretical overview. In M.Z. Rosaldo & L. Lamphere (Eds.), *Women, culture, and society* (pp. 17-42). Stanford, CA: Stanford University Press.

Rosenblatt, R. (1988, June 6). Flurry of team sales continues. *Sports inc.*, p. 2.

Rosentraub, M.S., & Nunn, S.R. (1978). Suburban city investment in professional sports. *American Behavioral Scientist, 21*, 393-414.

Rosner, D. (1988, September 5). USOC sells multi-sport event. *Sports inc.*, p. 50.

Rozelle, P. (1964, June 4). Antitrust law and professional sports. *Virginia Law Weekly*, pp. 94-97.

Russell, B. (1938). *Power: A new social analysis*. London: Allen and Unwin.

Ryan, W. (1976). *Blaming the victim*. (rev. ed.). New York: Vintage Books.

Sack, A. (1984, Winter/Spring). Proposition 48: A masterpiece in public relations. *Journal of Sport and Social Issues, 8*(1), 1-3.

Sack, A.L. (1973, Winter). Yale 29-Harvard 4: The professionalization of college football. *Quest, 19*, 24-34.

Sack, A.L., & Thiel, R. (1979). College football and social mobility: A case study of Notre Dame football players. *Sociology of Education, 52*, 60-66.

Sage, G.H. (1980). Parental influence and socialization into sport for male and female intercollegiate athletes. *Journal of Sport and Social Issues, 4*(2), 1-13.

Sage, G.H. (1984). Sports in American society: Its pervasiveness and its study. In D.S. Eitzen (Ed.), *Sport in contemporary society* (pp. 1-20). New York: St. Martin's Press.

Sage, G.H. (1985). American values and sport: Formation of a bureaucratic personality. In D. Chu, J.O. Segrave, & B.J. Becker (Eds.), *Sport and higher education* (pp. 275-282). Champaign, IL: Human Kinetics.

Sage, G.H. (1986). Social development. In V. Seefeldt (Ed.), *Physical activity and well-being* (pp. 343-371). Reston, VA: American Alliance for Health, Physical Education, Recreation and Dance.

Sallach, D.L. (1974). Class domination and ideological hegemony. *The Sociological Quarterly, 15*, 38-50.

Sandomir, R. (1988, November 14). The $50-billion sports industry. *Sports inc.*, pp. 14-23.

San Francisco Arts & Athletics v. United States Olympic Committee, 483 U.S. 522 (1987).

Scorecard. (1984, September 3). *Sports Illustrated*, p. 10.

Seelmeyer, J. (1988, September 22). Market competition is pocketbook issue. *Tribune*, p. 3A.

Seymour, H. (1960). *Baseball: The early years*. New York: Oxford University Press.

Shaikin, B. (1988). *Sports and politics: The Olympics and the Los Angeles Games*. New York: Praeger.

Shakeshaft, C. (1986). A gender at risk. *Phi Delta Kappan, 67*, 499-503.

Sharing the best: Women sportswriters in locker rooms. (1979, April 9). *New Yorker*, pp. 46-53.

Sheldon, H.D. (1901). *Student life and customs*. New York: Appleton.

Shuster, R. (1987, June 26). Big league baseball's few minorities in the media. *USA Today*, p. 8C.

Shuster, R. (1988, February 3). Networks now focusing on black sports-casters, *USA Today*, p. 3C.

Siedentop, D. (1987). The theory and practice of sport education. In G.T. Barrette, R.S. Feingold, & C.R. Rees (Eds.), *Myths, models, and methods in sport pedagogy* (pp. 79-85). Champaign, IL: Human Kinetics.

Simon, R. (1977, March). Gramsci's concept of hegemony. *Marxism Today*, **22**, 78-86.

Smith, D. (1988, December 20). Sanctions don't sit well in Oklahoma. *USA Today*, p. 9C.

Smith, R.A. (1983). Preludes to the NCAA: Early failures of faculty inter-collegiate athletic control. *Research Quarterly for Exercise and Sport*, **54**, 372-382.

Smith, R.A. (1988). *Sport & Freedom*. New York: Oxford University Press.

Snow, R.P. (1983). *Creating media culture*. Beverly Hills, CA: Sage.

Somers, C. (1989, April 13). Olson remaining at Arizona. *USA Today*, p. 1C.

Sowell, T. (1989, January 9). Colleges don't play fair with their athletes. *Rocky Mountain News*, p. 31.

Spears, B., & Swanson, R.A. (1988). *History of sport and physical education in the United States* (3rd ed.). Dubuque, IA: Wm. C. Brown.

Sperber, M.A. (1987). The college coach as entrepreneur. *Academe*, **73**, 30-33.

Spring, J. (1974). Mass culture and school sports. *History of Education Quarterly*, **14**, 483-498.

Stanton, M. (1987). Playing for a living: The dream comes true for very few. *Occupational Outlook Quarterly*, **31**(1), 1-15.

Staples, R. (1986). *The urban plantation: Racism and colonialism in the past civil rights era*. San Francisco: Black Scholar Press.

Stein, R. (1972). *Media power*. Boston: Houghton Mifflin.

Steinberg, R. (1982). *Wages and hours: Labor and reform in twentieth century America*. New Brunswick, NJ: Rutgers University Press.

Strober, M.H. (1984). Toward a general theory of occupational sex segre-gation: The case of public school teaching. In B.F. Reskin (Ed.), *Sex segregation in the workplace: Trends, explanations, remedies* (pp. 144-156). Washington, DC: National Academy Press.

Sullivan, E.V. (1987). Critical pedagogy and television. In D.W. Living-stone (Ed.), *Critical pedagogy and cultural power* (pp. 57-75). South Hadley, MA: Bergin & Garvey.

Sullivan, R. (1986, October 13). Barely touching the platter. *Sports Illus-trated*, p. 17.

Sullivan, R. (1989, June 19). A study in frustration. *Sports Illustrated*, p. 94.

Sullivan, R., & Neff, C. (1987, March 9). Shame on you, SMU. *Sports Illustrated*, pp. 18-23.

Szymanski, A. (1983). *Class structure: A critical perspective*. New York: Praeger.

Theberge, N. (1985). Toward a feminist alternative to sport as a male preserve. *Quest, 37*, 193-202.

Theberge, N., & Cronk, A. (1986). Work routines in newspaper sports departments and the coverage of women's sports. *Sociology of Sport Journal, 3*, 195-203.

Tuchman, G. (1978). The symbolic annihilation of women. In G. Tuchman, A.K. Daniels, & J. Benet (Eds.), *Hearth and home* (pp. 3-29). New York: Oxford University Press.

Turner, J.H. (1982). *The structure of sociological theory* (3rd ed.). Homewood, IL: Dorsey.

Twin, S.L. (1979). *Out of the bleachers: Writings on women and sport*. New York: McGraw-Hill.

Tygiel, J. (1983). *Baseball's great experiment: Jackie Robinson and his legacy*. New York: Oxford University Press.

U.S. Bureau of the Census. (1989). *Statistical Abstracts of the United States: 1989*. Washington, DC: U.S. Government Printing Office.

Useem, M. (1984). *The inner circle*. New York: Oxford University Press.

Van Der Horst, R., & Seely, H. (1988, March 21). Bushels of oranges. *Sports inc.*, pp. 26-28.

Vanfossen, B.E. (1979). *The structure of social inequality*. Boston: Little, Brown.

Vanneman, R., & Cannon, L.W. (1987). *The American perception of class*. Philadelphia: Temple University Press.

Veblen, T. (1899). *Theory of the leisure class*. New York: Macmillan.

Vincent, T. (1981). *Mudville's revenge: The rise and fall of American sport*. New York: Seaview Books.

Wallerstein, I. (1974). *The modern world-system*. New York: Academic Press.

Walton, J. (1986). *Sociology and critical inquiry*. Chicago: Dorsey Press.

Watson, G.L. (1987). *Dilemmas and contradictions in social theory*. New York: University Press of America.

Weber, M. (1938). *The rules of sociological method* (8th ed.). Chicago: University of Chicago Press.

Weber, M. (1978). *Economy and society, Vol. 2*. Berkeley: University of California Press. (Original work published 1922)

Weisman, L. (1989, March 31). New system boosts salaries of players allowed to move. *USA Today*, p. 4C.

Wendel, T. (1988, October 10). The value of major league baseball. *Sports inc.*, pp. 26-27.

We're watching more TV. (1988, December 13). *USA Today*, p. 1D.

Whitford, D. (1988, April 4). Bottom line baseball. *Sports inc.*, pp. 19-21.

Whitney, C. (1895). *A sporting pilgrimage*. New York: Harper.

Whitson, D. (1984). Sport and hegemony: On the construction of the dominant culture. *Sociology of Sport Journal*, **1**, 64-78.

Whitson, D. (1986). Structure, agency and the sociology of sport debates. *Theory, Culture, and Society*, **3**, 99-107.

Wieberg, S. (1986a, September 24). Money and college athletics: Coaches, administrators cashing in on perks. *USA Today*, pp. 1C-2C, 8C-9C.

Wieberg, S. (1986b, December 9). Paying coach, going first class. *USA Today*, pp. 1C-2C, 10C-11C.

Wieberg, S. (1986c, December 11). Getting a foot in the door. *USA Today*, p. 9C.

Wiggins, D.K. (1977). Good times on the old plantation: Popular recreations of the black slave in Antebellum south, 1810-1860. *Journal of Sport History*, **4**, 260-284.

Wiggins, D.K. (1980a). The play of slave children in the plantation communities of the old south, 1820-1860. *Journal of Sport History*, **7**(2), 21-39.

Wiggins, D.K. (1980b). Sport and popular pastimes: Shadow of the slave-quarters. *Canadian Journal of History of Sport and Physical Education*, **11**(1), 61-88.

Williams, B. (1987). *Black workers in an industrial suburb: The struggle against discrimination*. New Brunswick, NJ: Rutgers University Press.

Williams, G.A. (1960). The concept of "egemonia" in the thought of Antonio Gramsci: Some notes on interpretation. *Journal of the History of Ideas*, **21**, 586-599.

Williams, R. (1977). *Marxism and literature*. Oxford: University of Oxford Press.

Willis, P. (1982). Women in sport in ideology. In J. Hargreaves (Ed.), *Sport, culture and ideology* (pp. 117-135). Boston: Routledge & Kegan Paul.

Wilson, W.J. (1987). *The truly disadvantaged: The inner city, the underclass, and public policy*. Chicago: University of Chicago Press.

Woodward, S. (1988, August 22). Our athletes are woefully funded. *USA Today*, pp. 1C-2C.

Yasser, R. (1984). Are scholarship athletes at big time programs really university employees? You bet they are! *Black Law Journal*, **9**, 65-78.

Yergin, M.L. (1986). Who goes to the game? *American Demographics*, **8**(7), 42-43.

Young, D. (1984). *The Olympic myth of Greek amateur athletes*. Chicago: Ares.

Young, T.R. (1986). The sociology of sport: Structural Marxist and cultural Marxist approaches. *Sociological Perspectives*, **29**, 3-28.

Zeitlin, I.M. (1973). *Rethinking sociology: A critique of contemporary theory*. Englewood Cliffs, NJ: Prentice-Hall.

Zinn, M.B., & Eitzen, D.S. (1987). *Diversity in American families*. New York: Harper & Row.

Index

P. 197, 198.
Mangan pus reference
& beginning